WILDFLOWER HIKES

Washington

D1009975

WILDFLOWER HIKES
Washington

Art Kruckeberg

Art Kruckeberg
with **Karen Sykes**
& **Craig Romano**
Photos by Ira Spring

THE MOUNTAINEERS BOOKS

The Mountaineers Books
is the nonprofit publishing arm of The Mountaineers Club,
an organization founded in 1906 and dedicated to the exploration,
preservation, and enjoyment of outdoor and wilderness areas.

1001 SW Klickitat Way, Suite 201, Seattle, WA 98134

First edition, 2004

Published simultaneously in Great Britain by Cordee, 3a DeMontfort Street, Leicester, England, LE1 7HD

Manufactured in China

Editor: Christine Clifton-Thornton
Cover: The Mountaineers Books
Book design: Mayumi Thompson and Marge Mueller, Gray Mouse Graphics
Layout: Marge Mueller, Gray Mouse Graphics
Cartographer: Marge Mueller, Gray Mouse Graphics
Cover photograph: *Seed pod of the western pasque flower growing near Mount Baker*
Frontispiece: *Lupine, Sitka valerian, and false hellebore along the Canyon Ridge trail near Yellow Aster Butte (Hike 6)*

Library of Congress Cataloging-in-Publication Data
Kruckeberg, Arthur R.
  Best wildflower hikes Washington / Art Kruckeberg with Karen Sykes & Craig Romano ; photos by Ira Spring.
    p. cm.
  Includes bibliographical references and index.
  ISBN 0-89886-964-1 (pbk. : alk. paper)
1. Hiking—Washington (State)—Guidebooks. 2. Wild flowers—Washington (State)—Guidebooks. 3. Washington (State)—Guidebooks. I. Sykes, Karen, 1943- II. Romano, Craig. III. Title.
  GV199.42.W2K78 2004
  917.97--dc22
                                    2004002053
                                    CIP

 Printed on recycled paper

CONTENTS

KEY TO THIS MAP

- **00** Hike number
- ■ Town
- ■ City
- National park
- National recreation area
- Freeway
- Major road
- Secondary road

WASH

OLYMPIC
NATIONAL
PARK

PACIFIC
OCEAN

MAPLE FALLS   **6**
7
Mount
Baker   **8**

BELLINGHAM

NORTH
CASCADES
NATIONAL
PARK

12
11   MAZAM

5

20

MOUNT VERNON

9

NORTH
CASCADES
NATIONAL
PARK   **10**

WINTHROP
Rainy
Pass

DARRINGTON

530

17

Glacier Peak

OLYMPIC
NATIONAL
PARK

PORT
ANGELES

FORKS

101

LaPUSH   **1**

2   Mount
Olympus

3

4

OLYMPIC
NATIONAL
PARK   **5**

101

PORT
TOWNSEND

GRANITE
FALLS

VERLOT

20
18   **19**

EVERETT   Mountain
Loop
Highway

23

2   **21**   **22**   **24**
Stevens   **25**
Pass   LEAVEN-
WORTH

SEATTLE

90   **26**   **27**
28
Snoqualmie
Pass

30   **32**
31
29   WENATCHEE
97

2

HOODSPORT

101

ABERDEEN   12

OLYMPIA

TACOMA

410   CLE ELUM

90

ELLENSBURG

34   **33**
82

5

7   MOUNT
RAINIER
NATIONAL
PARK   Mount
Rainier   **40**
41   410
43   **42**
44   123
48

SELAH

YAKIMA

12

CHEHALIS

12

RANDLE   **47**

45   **46**

MOUNT
ST. HELENS
NATIONAL
MONUMENT   25

49   26
Mount
St. Helens   **48**   Mount
Adams

KELSO

4

503

TROUT
LAKE

141

50

97

GOLDENDALE

VANCOUVER   14   Columbia River

NGTON

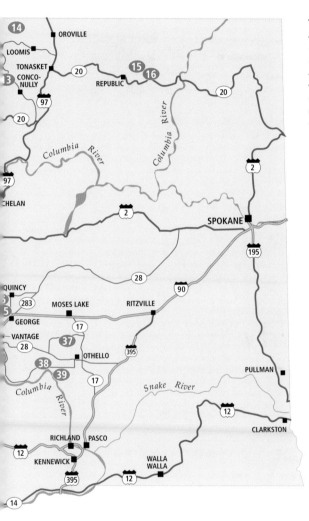

KEY TO HIKE MAPS

	divided highway
	paved road
	improved road (coarse gravel or dirt)
	primitive (jeep) road
	gated road
	described trail
	other trail
	cross-country route
	park boundary
	railroad
	ski lift
	power line
90	interstate highway
97	U.S. highway
14	state route
26	county route
2107	described national forest road
2107	other national forest road
611	described trail number
611	other trail number
	building
	ranger station
	parking
T	trail start
	toilet
A	campground
	backcountry shelter
	wilderness campsite
	lookout
	mine
][	bridge
)(	pass
▲	summit
	glacier
	river or stream
	waterfall
	lake
	marsh
	flowers

TRAIL FINDER

The recommended time of year for hiking a particular trail is when the trail is generally free of snow. From year to year the hiking and flower finding season varies by a week or more; for a few weeks after the recommended time, snow patches can be expected on the trail. Above 5000 feet snowstorms occur quite frequently until mid-July and after late Aug and occasionally in between. However, midsummer snow usually melts in a few hours or a day.

Easy (E): 2–3 miles each way, not more than 500 feet elevation change, trail generally well maintained

Moderate (M): 4–10 miles each way, not more than 1500 feet elevation change, trail generally well maintained

Strenuous (S): Indicates considerable mileage, elevation gain, and/or poor trail conditions

HIKE	DIFFICULTY	BEST FLOWERS	HIKABLE
1. Rialto Beach	E	Summer	Year-round
2. Hoh River Nature Trails and Happy Four Camp	E to M	May through Aug	Year-round
3. Hurricane Hill	M	July through Aug	Late June through Oct
4. Marmot Pass via Big Quilcene Trail	S	Late June through Aug	Late June through Oct
5. Camp Pleasant	M	Late April through Aug	May through Nov
5. Staircase Loop	E	Late April through Aug	May through Nov
5. Home Sweet Home	S	Late April through Aug	July through Oct
6. Yellow Aster Butte	S	July through Aug	July through Oct
7. Chain Lakes Loop	M	July through Aug	Late July through Oct
8. Railroad Grade via Park Butte Trail	M	July through Aug	Mid-July through Oct
9. Sauk Mtn	M	Late June through Sept	Mid-June through Oct
10. Maple Pass	M	Mid-July to mid Aug	Mid-July to mid-Oct
11. Slate Peak	E	July through Aug	July to mid-Oct
12. Windy Pass via PCT	M	July through Aug	July to mid-Oct

HIKE	DIFFICULTY	BEST FLOWERS	HIKABLE
13. Tiffany Mtn	M	July through early Aug	Late June to mid-Oct
14. Disappointment Peak	M	Mid-May to mid-July	May through Oct
15. Copper Butte	M	Late May through July	Mid-May through Oct
16. Wapaloosie Mtn	M	May to mid-July	May through Oct
17. Green Mtn	S	July through Aug	Late June through Oct
18. Walt Bailey Trail	M	July through Aug	July through Nov
19. Big Four Ice Caves Trail	E	June through Aug	May through Nov
20. Mount Dickerman Trail	S	July through Aug	Late June through Oct
21. Scorpion Mtn via Johnson Ridge	S	Late June through Sept	June through Oct
22. Josephine Lake via PCT	M	July through Sept	Late June through Oct
23. Round Mtn Trail to Nason Ridge	S	July through Sept	June through Oct
24. Chiwaukum Creek	M	Late May through July	June through Oct
25. Tumwater Pipeline Trail	E	May through July	April through Oct
26. Ira Spring Memorial Trail	M	June through Aug	Late May through Oct
27. Kendall Garden Katwalk	M	Mid-July to mid-Aug	Mid-July to early Oct
28. Lodge Lake	E	June through Aug	Late June through Oct
29. Esmerelda Basin	M	June to Aug	Mid-June to mid-Nov
30. Navaho Pass	M	Late June to mid-July	Mid-June to Nov
31. Kruckeberg Country	M	July to late Aug	July to Nov
32. Tronsen Ridge	M	June	Late May through Oct
33. Umtanum Ridge	S	April through June	April through Oct
34. Black Canyon	M	April through June	Late April through Oct
35. Dusty Lake	E	May through June	Year-round
36. Ancient Lakes	E	April through June	Year-round
37. Blythe Lake and Coulee	E to M	May	April through Oct

HIKE	DIFFICULTY	BEST FLOWERS	HIKABLE
38. Saddle Mtns	E	April through June	Year-round
39. White Bluffs	E	April through June	Year-round
40. Rainier View Trail	E	June through Sept	Late June through Oct
41. Sheep Lake and Sourdough Gap	M	July through Aug	July through Oct
42. Naches Peak Loop	E	July through Aug	Mid-July through Oct
43. Burroughs Mtn Loop	M	July through Aug	Late June through Oct
44. Paradise Flower Trails	E to M	July through Aug	July through Oct
45. McCoy Creek Flower Walks	M	Early July to mid-Aug	July through Oct
46. Sunrise Peak and Jumbo's Shoulder	M	Early July to mid-Aug	July through Oct
47. Conrad Meadows	M	May to early July	Mid-July to mid-Oct
48. Adams Creek Meadow	M	Mid-July through Aug	Mid July to mid-Oct
49. Norway Pass	E	July through Sept	July through Sept
49. Mount Margaret	M	Aug through Sept	July through Sept
50. Dog Mtn	S	April through June	March to Jan

NOTE: There are no absolute rules on the formation of common flower names—therefore, versions of the names differ from one field guide to the next. Your autocratic botanist has been the final arbiter on the form of common names found in this book. Thus, multiple-word names may be separated, joined without hyphens, or hyphenated: biscuit root and bead lily; western redcedar and wax-myrtle. Except at the start of a sentence or in a heading, common names are mostly decapitalized, except if they include a person's name (Flett's violet) or a place name (Oregon grape). For the most part we have followed Pojar and MacKinnon or Hitchcock and Cronquist for preferred variants of common names.

Art Kruckeberg
Botanist

Harebells

FOREWORD

As we prepare to send the final book files for *Best Wildflower Hikes in Washington* to the printer, I note on the calendar that it has been seven months since Ira Spring passed away. I find this somewhat hard to believe, because my dialogs with Ira have continued inside my head, guiding this project to the very end. This is Ira's last guidebook—his last words on more than forty years of hiking and photographing for twenty-five guidebooks for Washington State. Ira acted as ambassador of the lessons and pleasures of the great outdoors to three generations of recreationists and conservationists. Through "green-bonding," a term Ira coined, it was his fervent dream to encourage hikers to become environmental activists—by introducing them to the experience of what was precious, and what was at stake.

Ira was passionate about wildflowers. The visual delights of the flower fields were rich, photographic canvases that stirred him. When Ira and I decided to do this wildflower hiking guide more than three years ago, he energetically began to recapture his portfolio of black-and-white imagery in color. Guidebooks of the past required that photos be shot in black and white; here was his chance to work in full color, and he relished the exercise. My days were equally enriched by his weekly phone calls and conferences. I

Ira Spring, 1986

was treated to details of what flowers were blooming when and his stories of natural history that spanned a lifetime of more than eighty years of exploring Washington.

Ira came from a line of long-lived relatives—his father passed away only recently at the age of 104. I believed we had many productive years ahead of us and experienced the same denial Ira must have felt when, a year ago, his doctors told him the cancer he had been fighting would soon take his life. The completion of this guidebook became a central focus of his remaining days—an activity that was, I'm sure, a welcome diversion from darker thoughts.

This book would not have been possible without the dedication of many individuals who came together to make sure this book would be completed.

Partnering with the amazing Art Kruckeberg, professor of Botany at the University of Washington, was an honor for us all. Art's wealth of information on the flora of Washington is unsurpassed. Art's firsthand hiking experiences and encompassing enthusiasm for wildflowers is an equal match to Ira's imagery.

As editor, project manager, and Ira's assistant during the final stages of his work, Christine Clifton-Thornton's expertise, diplomacy, and flexibility was the glue that held the project together, resulting in this book.

When it was clear that Ira would not be able to finish the hikes he intended for the book, Karen Sykes literally put her life on hold and did the fieldwork required to provide accurate and up-to-date hiking information. She was assisted by Craig Romano, who equally and without hesitation put his projects aside to complete five of the hikes east of the Cascades. They both mentioned many times how honored they were to collaborate on this final book "with" Ira. Without their time and enthusiasm, this book would not have been possible.

Art director and book designer Marge Mueller collaborated with Ira for more than forty years as mapmaker, book designer, and even photographic model when the first *100 Hikes in*™ books were published. We are fortunate she was able to work on this final project and make it his most beautiful guidebook ever.

Ira's family—his wife Pat, son John, daughter Vicky, and son-in-law Tom—were all helpful and accommodating during this time. We appreciate that they made themselves available to help bring this project to completion during incredibly stressful personal times while Ira's health declined.

This spring, I will navigate to one of the special places Ira mentions in this book. There I will seek out the flowers he particularly favored and pay homage to him, expressing my gratitude for the richness he brought to me as his publisher, and as his friend.

Helen Cherullo
Publisher
January 2004

INTRODUCTION

In Washington State, the word "hike" might bring to mind the generous wealth of natural beauty with which our state is blessed. However you get there, often the treasure at the end of the trail is a spectacular, one-of-a-kind Washington view, punctuated by miniviews along the way.

There's no denying the pleasures of a breathtaking view, but as in most journeys, there is more to hiking than just reaching the destination. In *Best Wildflower Hikes in Washington,* we'll not only guide you to scenic locations—we'll also tell you where to stop and smell the flowers along the way.

In this new volume of the *Best* series, the views range dramatically, from the rugged seascapes found at Rialto Beach to the temperate rain forest of the Hoh on the Olympic Peninsula; from the high mountain meadows of Paradise at Mount Rainier to glistening Josephine Lake near Stevens Pass; from the sagebrush grasslands of Wapaloosie Mountain to the wide-open spaces of Wahluke Slope's White Bluffs—and everything in between.

And the intimate focus is everything wildflowers. The book begins with Dr. Art Kruckeberg, esteemed professor emeritus of Botany at the University of Washington and cofounder of the Washington Native Plant Society, as he takes you exploring across Washington in "Wildflower Habitats: Their Ecologies and Natural Histories." Then brush up on your understanding of plant names in "The Naming of Plants." Following is a section detailing the nuts and bolts of using this guidebook, including useful information on maps and other helpful hints. In the hiking section, you'll find the fifty best trails to wildflowers across the state, each paired with delightful tidbits by Dr. Kruckeberg in "Art's Notes." "Wildflower Portraits" is a selected guide to thirty-nine stunning color photographs are found throughout, illustrating flower descriptions and hikes.

For flower watchers, finding the flowers is only half the delight: *Best Wildflower Hikes in Washington* includes wildflower details and personal anecdotes from the most highly regarded botanist in the Northwest. And for the dedicated hiker, *Best Wildflower Hikes in Washington* offers an unforgettable green-bonding experience, giving a close-up look at the landscape through the eyes of the Northwest's most renowned outdoor photographer.

This is no ordinary guidebook. *Best Wildflower Hikes in Washington* brings you the region's foremost experts to help you explore the state from ocean to mountaintop, from meadow to desert, on arguably the best trails around chosen for their floral abundance and variety, to celebrate that most delicate and fascinating of living jewels—the wildflower.

Begin the journey.

Christine Clifton-Thornton
Editor

WILDFLOWER HABITATS: THEIR ECOLOGIES AND NATURAL HISTORIES

Wildflowers gloriously ornament nearly every land-based place in the greater Pacific Northwest. In Washington State we encounter their beauty and generous diversity from sea level to the alpine summits of the Cascades and Olympics. Let us start our love affair with their places in Nature by offering some thoughts on their biological status and ecological niches in the terrestrial landscape of our region.

First off, just what is a wildflower? Generosity provokes a broad definition: any native flowering plant with showy flowers. Many shrubs and some trees with showy flowers are captured in some wildflower books. So it is that some authors will embrace such trees as Pacific flowering dogwood, madrone, and many shrubs like red-flowering currant, salmonberry and mockorange as wildflowers. But here we narrow the floral field to herbs, plants that can grace the forest floor, meadow, or rocky alpine slopes for years—"perennial." The "wild-" of wildflower asserts pride-of-place; they were here as natives in pre-Columbian times. Not a few "wildlings" are imports by Euroman from the Old World: foxglove, toad-flax, and herb Robert (a.k.a. "Stinking Bob"), though showy in flower, are aliens . . . yes, weeds. Weeds are best defined in biological terms: plants that thrive under human disturbance. We will have none of them in this book!

The native herbaceous perennials we are calling wildflowers thrive in a multitude of habitats. What better way to savor this rich tapestry of wildflower fields than to imagine crossing our state from seacoast to the Columbia River? Our virtual travelogue takes us through several dominant vegetation types; these are what the ecologist calls *life zones*, named for their dominant plant life, mostly trees.

Westside Life Zones

The Sitka Spruce Zone. Forest grows right down to the sea's splash zone on the west side of the Olympic Peninsula. It has the grandest conifers of any temperate region in the world: towering, massive boles of Sitka spruce, side by side with western hemlock, western redcedar and Douglas fir. Under this forest canopy, look for a rich carpet of wildflowers on the shaded forest floor. Many of them we will meet in the chapter "Wildflower Portraits." To name just a few: bunchberry or dwarf dogwood, queen's cup or bead lily, vanilla leaf, foamflower, bleeding heart, Dutchman's breeches, wild ginger, and a gaggle of ground orchids like coralroot and calypso. Wetlands

Opposite: *Magenta paintbrush, golden fleabane, phlox, saxifrage, and penstemon fill a mountain crevice.*

in this and other lowland life zones display the majestic aroid, skunk cabbage (better called swamp lantern), the white bog orchid, and others happy with damp feet. Should we have started on a sandy beach at ebb tide, we would find a rich beach-and-dune wildflower flora: beach strawberry, sand verbena, beach morning glory, and searocket. The Olympic National Park ocean strip is the choice place for these beach denizens.

The Western Hemlock Zone. Lowland forest spreads in a vast swath east from Sitka spruce country to the slopes of the Cascades and Olympics; Sitka spruce is mostly left behind. The vast interior lowland of western Washington was dominated by western hemlock, western redcedar, and Douglas fir nearly as an unbroken old-growth forest in pre-Columbian times . . . before we came along in the early nineteenth century. In those

FIRST PEOPLE'S TRYST WITH SHORELINE FLORA

Plants of the ocean shore gave coastal First Peoples food, fiber, structural materials, and even ornaments. Foremost were the cone-bearing trees, especially western redcedar. Almost every possible domestic use was made of cedar: foliage, bark, and especially the heartwood, the latter used to build longhouses, canoes, and the like. A novel use of western hemlock was to place leafy branches in estuaries for the capture of edible fish roe. Willows, like Hooker's willow, were used in a variety of ways: for example, debarked and split to make rope and other fishing gear. Obvious edibles were the fruits of the evergreen huckleberry *(Vaccinium ovatum)*. Of the several members of the parsley family *(Umbelliferae)* occurring on the coast, some were edibles used in First Peoples' times. The roots of Pacific hemlock parsley *(Conioselinum pacificum)* were carrotlike edibles when cooked. The tall cow parsnip *(Heracleum lanatum)* was a favorite green vegetable. Ethnobotanist Dr. Nancy Turner sounds a vital warning: Because some members of the parsley family are highly poisonous, caution is voiced. Some of these toxic plants look like the edibles. One guesses that aboriginous peoples learned (the hard way?) to tell the good from the bad. Poisonous hemlock *(Conium maculatum),* introduced from Europe, may not have been a problem for pre-European native peoples. But the native water hemlock, *Cicuta* species, could have been a problem.

Another beach plant, the beach lupine, furnished edible roots for coastal harvesters. They must be baked in fire pits to detoxify them. As expected, the fruits of the beach strawberry were favored morsels, eaten fresh. There seems to be no record of First Peoples using such common shore plants as the wax-myrtle, beach morning glory, or the searocket. ■ A. R. K.

remaining stands of old growth, expect to find many of the same forest floor wildflower herbs of the Sitka spruce zone, plus such wildflowers as fringecup, youth-on-age, and carpets of woodland sorrel. Massively reduced by humanity, old-growth western hemlock forest persists only in national parks and rare patches in national forest. Dense stands of second-growth Douglas fir offer little in the wildflower domain, so densely shaded is the forest floor. In time, dense second growth gives way to late-successional forest with a more open ground layer and a return of some shade-tolerant wildflowers.

Be not surprised that the lowland forest type is, or even was in pre-Columbian times, not everywhere in the Puget lowlands west of the Cascades. Early naturalists such as Archibald Menzies and David Douglas found a mosaic of habitats that supported forest, plus bogs, coastal headlands, prairies, and oak savannah. Each nonforested habitat had its particular bouquet of wildflowers. The most familiar and elegant replacements of forest are the extensive grassland prairies and oak thickets in southern Puget Sound country. These stretches of open land caught the eye of many an early explorer. The Canadian itinerant artist Paul Kane sketched and painted this unique landscape, as did Lieutenant Alfred Agate of the Wilkes

Western redcedar and lady fern in the western hemlock zone

Lowland forest dominated by western hemlock and rich flora in the under-story; Skokomish River at Staircase, Olympic Peninsula

Expedition in the midnineteenth century. They would have encountered a choice array of wildflowers underfoot. The diversity is impressive; a sampling must feature both the edible blue camas and the yellow-flowered death camas, the showy yellow "heads" of the desert sunflower or balsamroot and the graceful chocolate lily. By circling the perimeter of Fort Lewis, the seeker of wildflowers can savor the flora of the prairies and Garry oak woodlands. The biggest surprise of all in Pierce and Thurston Counties is to witness mounded prairies—the Mima Mounds—seen at their best just west of Little Rock. Here they are preserved by the State, where an interpretive center gives the visitor a taste of their mysterious origin. Many of the same wildflowers of level prairies hold sway here. Alas, though, much of this remarkable prairie, both level and mounded, has been usurped by aliens—weedy invasives like Scotch broom, dandelion, cat's ears, and a host of human camp followers; they can often dominate the prairie landscape.

The Pacific Silver Fir Zone. In both the western Cascades and the Olympics, increase in elevation brings increase in precipitation both as rain and snow, as well as a shorter growing season. By 3000 feet at Snoqualmie Pass, the lowland hemlock–cedar forest has been replaced by a new forest dominant, Pacific silver fir (*Abies amabilis*). This superb true fir can form pure stands of old growth at this elevation and upward to 4500 feet. Its understory is rich in shrubs, mostly huckleberries, and in openings, wildflowers aplenty: dwarf dogwood, queen's cup or bead lily, twinflower, evergreen violet, and the imposing white-flowered stalks of bear grass or Indian basket grass. In wet sites, watch for the showy marsh marigold, with large white flowers, and the white-flowered bog orchid. Sun-splashed rock outcrops display penstemons, rock-hugging phlox, and parsley fern.

The Mountain Hemlock Zone. The uppermost continuous forest type is dominated by mountain hemlock, at 5000 to 6000 feet. This lovely hemlock may occur in pure stands or cohabit with Alaska cedar and Pacific silver fir. Its rich understory shrubs are mostly members of the heather family: thickets of waist-high huckleberry, the lovely cream-white Cascade azalea, and the first of the mountain heathers appear. Mingling with this family of heather kin, the hiker will delight in encountering mountain ash bushes, with its upper branches laden in fall with clusters of red to orange berries (actually little "apples," like fruits of garden cotoneasters or firethorn). Some of the same forest floor wildflowers persist here: besides bunchberry, vanilla leaf, and bear grass, expect to find mountain heliotrope, avalanche lily, and woodland lousewort. The mountain hemlock zone thrives under a regime of high moisture, mostly as deep snows; the snowpack may reach depths of up to 25 feet. A special feature of the upper forested hemlock zone is the spectacular display of snow avalanche tracks. When avalanches "run" most every year, forest is replaced by dense thickets of slide alder.

Nature's next higher and grandest display of plant life is just beyond the continuous mountain hemlock forest. It is the most captivating landscape in our part of the world: the parkland vegetation type. Hikers along the Pacific Crest Trail wander in and out of it for miles at a time. Here, forest trees persist only in isolated clusters, surrounded by vast open stretches of mountain meadow. Ecologists call this the parkland subzone of the mountain hemlock zone. A more telling term for this near-timberline type is "timbered atolls"—tree clumps in a sea of mountain meadow. The parkland landscape evokes its own place names in Mount Rainier National Park: Grand Park, Spray Park, Yakima Park, et cetera. Drive to Yakima Park, now Sunrise, or to Paradise on Mount Rainier to enter a grand sample of this parkland vegetation. The "timbered atolls" are mostly stocked with several subalpine trees: mountain hemlock, Alaska cedar, or, in drier sites, subalpine fir and whitebark pine. The "islands" of conifers will be encircled by skirts of shrubs and herbs, notably the low-statured huckleberries, willows, mountain ashes, and Cascade azalea. Showy herbs give color to this shrub skirt in the brief subalpine summer: yellow and lavender louseworts, mountain heliotrope, and the green-flowered majestic false hellebore or corn lily. Between the tree clumps stretch eye-catching expanses of treeless mountain meadows. Here the full glory of high mountain wildflowers holds sway. Heathers and huckleberries and prostrate juniper dominate

Upper montane (the timberline and alpine zones) with a field of bear grass;
Dark Divide, Olympic Peninsula

the shrub cover in the meadows. Most appealing are the three heathers, one yellow and one purple and the white-flowered cassiope or moss heather. They can form dense low patches in the meadowy swales. Late summer brings forth the grand display of innumerable herbaceous perennials: yellow and white avalanche lilies, penstemons, phlox, mountain daisies, partridgefoot, and a host of others. Indeed, the parkland scene is the choicest jewel in Washington's floral crown.

The Timberline and Alpine Zones. Both a few hundred upward feet of elevation and on exposed ridges above parkland, the most intrepid scattered conifers take on dwarfed and gnarled forms. This naturalists call *Krummholz* (German for "crooked wood"), a landscape that boldly tells of tree life at its stressful limits. Harsh winds, deep snow, and short growing season all conspire to limit tree growth to the Krummholz life form. Subalpine fir and whitebark pine are the two that can endure in shrub form here. Upward from timberline, "wood is a luxury" in the highest, alpine zone. So, no more trees, but plant life persists. All three heathers make out in the alpine, as do the dwarf juniper and the surprise of all, prostrate willows. Yet the alpine can be a richly colorful flower garden. Along rivulets below snowbanks, look for the showy elephant's head lousewort, red and yellow monkeyflowers, as well as marsh marigold and alpine willow-herb. In drier sites find Indian paintbrush, alpine lupine, cinquefoils, alpine bistort, cushiony daisies, and a host of other ground-hugging herbs.

Krummholz form of whitebark pine

The Crest of the Cascades and Eastward. Wherever one stands on the crest of the Cascades—at Goat Rocks, Cascade Pass, or Sunrise—vast stretches of mountainous terrain persist eastward. But a big change will appear; the eastern slopes are drier, feeling the effects of the mountain rainshadow—less moisture on the leeward side of the crest. There is a timberline still just east of the summits. Three conifers make out in this demanding habitat: subalpine fir, whitebark pine, and that remarkable deciduous cone-bearer, Lyall's larch. Here, the montane country displays this version of timberline eloquently, just as it does on the upper west slopes. Any backpacker reaching The Enchantments high above Leavenworth and Icicle Creek gets in mid-October the fall's golden hues of the deciduous larch in lavish measure.

Eastside Life Zones

East of the Cascade Crest, we descend from subalpine dry forest through a succession of three life zones, two forested and one in the dry interior of Washington—the broad belt of sagebrush and bunchgrass.

The Grand Fir–Douglas Fir Zone. Along the eastern midmontane slopes a diversely endowed forest greets the traveler. Besides the two dominants, grand fir and Douglas fir, other conifers grace these drier slopes. Two pines are frequent: western white pine (five-needled) and lodgepole pine (two-needled). The latter may occur in dense, even-aged stands, especially after fire. At the upper edges of this zone, we may encounter the huge trunks of Engelmann spruce, often in pure stands. In cool moist ravines, two westside conifers reappear, western redcedar and western yew, and occasionally even western hemlock. Not uncommon is the imposing deciduous conifer, western larch, so distinctive in its fall golden stage. Look east from Chinook Pass in October to be rewarded with the fall color of this tall larch dotting the dark green of the other forest trees. Understory shrubs of this zone include the two evergreens, Oregon boxwood and snowbrush or sticky laurel; also find several deciduous shrubs: snowberry, ninebark, oceanspray, and mockorange. Often the open forest floor is densely paved with bright green pine grass. Herbs aplenty, too, in this zone: arnicas, daisies, buckwheats, lupines; numerous rock outcrops harbor penstemons, lewisias, phlox, and flat cushions of yellow buckwheat. Trails most everywhere in this zone from Okanogan to Skamania Counties gain entry to this dry but floriferous forest zone. Ecologists assert that it is more wildflower blessed than any equivalent zone on the west side.

The Ponderosa Pine Zone. Unmistakable are old-growth stands of this majestic three-needle pine. Widely spaced massive trunks of ponderosa pine are clothed with bold plates of buff to yellow bark, which emit a savory vanilla scent in the heat of the day. Ponderosa pine stands are intermittent along the lower east side of the Cascades and are especially common between Leavenworth and Cle Elum. Local habitats that shift to a moister regime will favor most of the conifers of the grand fir–Douglas fir zone. Deciduous broad-leafed trees appear frequently in ponderosa pine country. Easily spotted are the dense thickets of aspen, with leaves quivering in the wind. Our only oak, *Quercus garryana*, reappears in the dry east pine country. Look for it along the midreaches of the Yakima River and Naches River and abundantly clothing the lower hillsides along the Satus

Shrub–steppe zone dominated by sagebrush and Columbia Plateau lava; Frenchmans Coulee, just above the Columbia River advantage

Pass Highway (US 97). A variety of shrubs track moist to dry open pine stands. The driest favors bitterbrush (or antelope brush), rabbitbrush, Indian currant, and snowbrush. In moister sites, find snowberry, ninebark, oceanspray, mockorange, and serviceberry. No shortage of wildflowers here: balsamroot, phlox, larkspur, lupines again, buckwheats, desert parsley (or biscuit root), as well as the showy ephemerals like shootingstar and prairie star. This dry, open terrain greets the eye with amazing bounty.

The Shrub–Steppe Zone. By the time the naturalist-traveler reaches the Columbia River at Vantage, Wenatchee, or Hanford, he or she has passed down out of the "lower timberline" of ponderosa pine into sagebrush country. Often called the sagebrush–bunchgrass vegetation type, it is (or was before irrigation agriculture) a vast expanse of the chest-high gray sagebrush and its native companion, blue-bunch wheatgrass. Companion shrubs include bitterbrush, Indian currant, and the late summer yellow-flowered rabbitbrush. Shrub–steppe country is far from a homogeneous sagebrush plain. Coulees and draws, walled in by massive shelves and cliffs of ancient lava, create habitats for other vegetation types. Common on the dry rock-strewn talus below the basalt walls are colonies of serviceberry, mockorange,and bitter cherry. On bare rock outcrops with little or no soil, the sole shrubs may be purple sage and a low, silvery sagebrush. Water courses in this "dry interior" (so called by our Canadian neighbors) are decked out in red-osier dogwood, willow, cottonwood, and often the water birch. Old US 10, east of Ellensburg to Vantage, at the Columbia River, gives grand views of sagebrush country.

Wildflowers of the East Slopes

Across the crest of the Cascades, in spring through late summer, there is a decidedly greater abundance of wildflowers on the east than is found on the western slopes. The drier, more open forested slopes create greater habitat diversity for a wealth of showy perennials. It is in the grand fir–Douglas fir zone that new flowers appear in dazzling variety. Early season bloom offers impressive bouquets of spring beauty: camas, prairie star, bluebell, shootingstar, alumroot, and the ever-present balsamroot or desert sunflower. Common forest-floor flowers range in color from the yellows of heart-leaved arnica and Oregon sunshine to the reds of scarlet bugler and rock penstemon to the purples of other penstemons and larkspur. On rock outcrops, captivating flower gardens grace the scene: more penstemons, lewisias, buckwheats, stonecrops—the roster is bountiful. Wet places in the midmontane forest have their own floral delights; white rein-orchid, purple monkshood, trapper's tea, elephant's head lousewort, and cotton grass, among many others.

Our magic carpet traverse from the Pacific Coast, across the Olympic peaks, into lowland western Washington, across the Cascade Mountains to the Columbia River, speaks to the accessible glory of Washington's wildflowers. Have at it! ■ A. R. K.

Marsh marigold

THE NAMING OF PLANTS

The use of Latin names in this book for native wildflowers has not been simply a display of erudition; common names have been used, too. But the Latin name is the "lingua franca," the universal mode of communication among people of all tongues when dealing with the catalog of life on our planet. Common names turn out to be unreliable in several ways. Over and over we find cases where one organism may have many different common names, often in different languages. Common names may give rise to erroneous ideas about the affinity of an organism; for example, several unrelated plants have the word "cedar" in their common name. Then, common names are unusable on a worldwide basis. Or they may not exist for a large number of organisms; countless obscure locoweeds and sunflowers have no particular ("specific") common name.

Common versus Latin Names

Initial encounters with Latin names are usually painfully unrewarding. To confront the Latin name *Gaultheria shallon* for the first time is bad enough, but if you are an easterner, the common name, "salal," is not much better. It is simply that a strange name has no inherent informational content. But being shown a specimen with its name tag fulfills the information gap. Both names now have meaning. Then why not use common names exclusively? If each kind of plant were unique—without a sign of kinship to any other kind—then a simple common name might do. But within Nature's array of diversity there is also the strong element of relatedness. Thus two kinds of *Gaultheria*, when called by their common names, "salal" and "wintergreen," are forever separated. But their Latin names, *Gaultheria shallon* and *Gaultheria procumbens*, reflect their bond of kinship in *Gaultheria*.

Common names are relegated to subordinate usage for other reasons. First, they lack universality. Common names are usually indigenous to a single country, or even only to one part of a county (in Europe the inhabitants of a single village or valley may have passed on a local name for generations). The bipolar shrublet *Empetrum nigrum* is a simple case: Americans call it "crowberry," Russians "odyanika," and Germans "Krahenbeere" or "Tauschbeere." For more aggravating and picturesque examples, we can turn to the flora of rural England where we find lavish use of common names for one and the same plant. In that delightful work by Geoffrey Grigson, *The Englishman's Flora*, I counted nearly a hundred different common—and often very local names—for *Caltha palustris*: marsh marigold, bachelor's buttons, cups and saucers, and water goggles. Second, the same common name may apply to several very different plants. The name "May flower" has been given to *Podophyllum* in the Midwest; to a member of the heath family in New England; to the hawthorn, marsh marigold, and cuckoo flower in

England; and to a legume in the West Indies. Though such examples could be repeated endlessly, I cannot resist a third to further the proof of confusion in common names. A handsome member of the sunflower family was called "Venus's paintbrush" when it first appeared in America; later, as it proved to an aggressive, noxious weed, it became known as the "Devil's paintbrush."

Finally, there is the case of corrupted meaning through centuries of usage. Plants of the dogwood genus *Cornus* were once called "dagwood," because "dags" were made of its wood for use as skewers. To be historically correct, you should call our native "dagwood" the skewerwood, rather than dogwood!

The use of common names often becomes ludicrous when they are "manufactured." "Tweedy's rattleweed" does not add much to the binomial *Astragalus tweedyi.* Are you any better off knowing that *Tropicarpum capparideum* can also be called "caper-fruited tropicarpum"? Enough said of common names—established as well as contrived—except to say that, when in wide popular use, they should be retained and used with Latin names for conducting the international business of scientific botany and zoology.

The Binomial or Latin Name

There really is nothing scientific about the so-called scientific name in biological nomenclature. It is derived neither by experiment nor by observation, only by what it stands for—systems of populations of organisms that can be tested like a hypothesis. Yet it is the only valid "handle" that can be attached to organisms. The scientific name is a compound of two Latin or Latinized words, the generic and the specific: This double epithet is the species name. Thus, the binomial *Pinus ponderosa* is applied to a particular kind of pine, one with a distinctive ensemble of structural features and one that occurs in self-reproducing populations throughout a wide but delimited geographic and ecological range.

Other species of pines, each with their distinct attributes, are given particular species names: *Pinus monticola* for the western white pine, *P. contorta* for the lodgepole or beach pine, *P. albicaulis* for whitebark pine, and so on. Note that all these species and the eighty or so others of pine reveal by the binomial of each their kinship in the genus name, *Pinus*, the collective name for all major pine variants.

What variations on plant names do we encounter all within the framework of the binomial? There are essentially four classes of generic and specific names. Take, for example, *Gaultheria,* a commemorative genus honoring a little-known French-Canadian physician and botanist, Jean Pierre Gaultier. Kings, rogues, botanists, patrons, lovers—all have been memorialized in this way. The addition of "-ia" to a personal name is a sure route to immortality: *Linnaea, Kalmia, Lewisia, Kolkwitzia, Magnolia, Jepsonia, Jeffersonia,* and so on through floras and faunas of the world. *Linnaea*, the delightful trailing twinflower of our woods, is named for Carolus Linnaeus, the father of systematic botany. *Kalmia,* the mountain laurel, is named for one of Linnaeus' students, Peter Kalm. You would be certain to recognize that *Lewisia* is named for Meriwether Lewis of the Lewis and Clark expedition; William Clark is commemorated in the genus *Clarkia,* a group of colorful annuals common in the spring floras of the Pacific Coast.

A more "academic" class of generic epithets is the classical descriptive name. Here, Greek or Latin, or sometimes a mismatch of both ancient tongues, is used to depict some characteristic of the genus in question. Thus the genus *Liriodendron* is translated from the classic language as "lily tree"; *Xanthorhiza* means "yellow root"; *Oxydendrum* means "sour tree"; *Cladothamnus* means "branched shrub"; *Enkianthus* means "pregnant flower"; et cetera.

Occasionally, generic names have been derived from the original native word. A botanist in the tropics would find that many of the genera there are Latinized versions of the original native name. Two examples from the Asiatic flora are *Tsuga,* which is the Japanese name for hemlock, and *Gingko,* the Chinese name for that famous and sacred tree of temple gardens.

The last category of generic names is both an amusing and intriguing one, the so-called fanciful, poetical, or mythological name. Here are four names that typify this kind of generic epithet: *Dodecatheon* means "twelve gods"; *Theobroma,* the generic name for the cocoa plant, means "god's food"; *Phyllodoce* means "sea nymph"; *Calypso* and *Narcissus* are characters in Greek mythology.

Of the four categories of species names, the descriptive and commemorative are the most common. *Rubra* (red), *nana* (dwarf), *repens* (prostrate growth), *saxatilis* (growing in rocks), et cetera, are descriptive adjectives. Sometimes the descriptive adjective is compound, as in *angustifolia* ("narrow" and "leaf"), *cordifolia* ("heart-shaped leaf"), *racemiflora* (flowers in a racemose inflorescence). Occasionally, a specific name is taken from the generic name in another group; thus we find the specific name *bignonioides,* which means "like bignonia," or *acerifolia* ("leaves like the maple"). A great many of the more recent specific epithets are simply commemorative. Thus, you would find on almost any page of Hitchcock and Cronquist's *Flora of the Pacific Northwest* plants with proper names as the specific epithet, such names as *douglasii, menziesii, lyallii, thompsonii, piperi, barrettiae.* Whereas in the past, commemorative specific names have been capitalized, the current recommendation of the International Rules is to lower case both commemorative and place names (although this is largely left to the discretion of the user). The last group consists of species names that indeed are nouns, such as *Pyrus Malus* and *Prunus Laurocerasus.* Usually such names were formerly generic; thus the species in question, which was once placed in another genus, now uses the former genus name as a specific epithet.

Adapted from Kruckeberg, A. R. *Natural History of Puget Sound Country.* Seattle: University of Washington Press, 1991.

ABOUT THIS BOOK

If you have ever watched a flower garden grow from spring through summer and autumn and then fade away into winter, you have a small vision of the excitement that occurs in the life of a bobbing patch of wildflowers. Unlike the cultivated variety, where plants are carefully chosen and planted, in a wild garden every day an unexpected blossom arrives; on every breeze a new seed is borne. Each month can seem an entirely different season in the ever-changing life of a field of wildflowers.

The "Wildflower Portraits" section in the latter part of this book contains stunning color photographs and notes on forty-five forest and montane meadow flowers, which can be found in season on the hikes in this book that wander the appropriate habitats. In addition, you can seek out some of your favorite flowers that might be found on the hikes by searching by common or scientific name in the index, as all wildflowers mentioned in the hikes are listed there. However, the hike descriptions in this book do not by any means list every flower species one might find while strolling along on each hike; that would spoil the fun. A list of Dr. Kruckeberg's favorite wildflower field guides and other related references is included in the bibliography, sure to enhance the enjoyment of the hikes. For those who would like a more complete Washington trails plant list, the Washington Native Plant Society offers such information to members and friends. Contact information can be found in the "Useful References and Other Resources" section at the back of this book.

Camping

Camping is allowed—yes, even encouraged—in many places throughout the state of Washington. The hikes in this book are arranged loosely west to east, north to south. It seems reasonable that you might wish to complete more than one hike in any given part of the state if you have traveled from another part of the state to get there. Camping is a pleasant way to accomplish this.

Commercial and other campgrounds are convenient and afford the lowest-impact option for camping. But what can compare to a day spent wandering high alpine meadows, noting shades of pinks and scarlets and blues—blues!—you've never seen before in wildflowers along the way and then spending an evening under the stars, far from the everyday troubles of life?

If you choose to camp off-trail—backcountry camping, which usually requires a permit—take care of your camping area: Use established sites whenever possible, or where none is available, use the "dispersal" method of camping—find your own quiet spot to set up your tent, away from others, to disperse the potential damage to the environment. Keep tents off meadows and other delicate areas, and at least 100 feet away from water sources. Use established backcountry toilets when available. Don't bury toilet paper; pack it out. Build campfires only in established fire rings, and use only dead and down wood, away from the campsite; where no fire rings are available, use only camp stoves. For information on both camping availability and campfires, contact the ranger station for the area you intend to explore.

At-a-Glance Hiking Information

Each hike begins with a quick-reference list of information about the hike.

Round trip or **Loop trip:** Indicates in miles the total length of the hike, whether the trip is out and back (round trip) or a loop.

Difficulty: The abilities of hikers vary as dramatically as do the inherent difficulties of trails. All things being equal, these ratings apply to an "average" hiker. An *Easy* trail has little or no elevation gain. A *Moderate* trail may

Camping above timberline on Ptarmigan Ridge, Mount Baker

include a stream crossing or two as well as significant elevation gain. A *Strenuous* trail may indicate a poorly graded, physically demanding trail; routefinding skills may be required. Read the route descriptions carefully and be willing to turn around if the trail is beyond your abilities. Bad weather or late snow on the trail can increase the usual difficulty of a hike.

Best flowers: The months you'll most likely find flowers at their peak. Although we've done our best to pinpoint each location with as much accuracy as possible, this may vary according to the whims of nature.

Hikable: This category indicates the months during which the trail tends to be relatively free of snow. Note, however, that in some parts of the state, snowstorms can and do happen in every month. Always check weather conditions before you leave for the trail.

High point: This indicates the highest elevation the trail—and therefore you—will reach.

Elevation gain: Indicates the rough cumulative elevation gain you can expect to acquire—in other words, how many feet uphill you'll need to go to complete the hike. Be sure to note the elevation gain of the hike you plan to take in combination with the distance: A 3-mile hike with 2000 feet in elevation gain can be much more strenuous than a 6-mile hike with 2000 feet in elevation gain.

Getting there: Driving directions are provided to the trailhead of each hike. We strive to provide the most accurate and up-to-date information possible, but during the life of a guidebook, changes to trailhead accesses can occur; it's always a good idea to call for current information.

Maps: Whenever possible, trail maps are listed for each hike. Most often noted are Green Trails and USGS maps, which generally can be purchased at mountain equipment and map shops. They also carry the quite accurate national forest recreation maps, which can also be obtained for a small fee at ranger stations. National forest recreation maps are highly recommended to help you find the back roads that lead to many of the hikes in this book; state road maps usually will not get you there. *Note that the maps found in this book are for orientation only; additional maps are essential for navigating both roads and trails.*

Information: Ranger station phone numbers are provided for each hike; always call to get current information on your trail before you leave home. *Note:* Some phone numbers in the Wenatchee Ranger District might change. For information regarding possible phone changes in that district, call (509) 664-9200.

Trail Care

The terrain covered in this book is so vast that generalities, for the most part, must suffice: Step lightly. Keep pets at home. Be kind to the environment. In especially fragile areas such as eastern Washington's shrub–steppe country, where wide-open spaces beckon to carefree meandering, it is sometimes easy to forget that even the most prickly desert cactus is at heart a fragile blossom. In many of the places featured in this guidebook, hiking cross-country is allowed; however, when possible, stay on trails—even game trails—to avoid damaging tender plants.

Water

If you're hiking, you'll need water; that's a fact. If you're camping and there's a nearby reliable water source, and you have a fire source—*voila!* Boiling water thoroughly produces steam plus potable water. Water filters are a popular option for creating drinkable water from a natural source; iodine tablets are another option. However, few water sources in nature are entirely reliable year-round, and many areas in this book have no water available of any kind. Be safe: Bring with you the water you need and then bring extra.

The Ten Essentials

Hikes in this guidebook vary from a gentle 1-mile easy stroll to a 27-mile backpack. Your interests may vary from that of a studious flower watcher with a preference for Pojar and MacKinnon and jars of fresh lemonade to a 9-minute-miler on the hunt for coralroot orchids. What you bring with you will be dictated by many factors: among other things, your location, the climate, the duration of your excursion, and your personal preferences. Other books can better guide you in choosing the outdoor gear best suited to your needs. In addition, on all hikes, The Mountaineers recommends bringing the Ten Essentials.

1. Navigation (map and compass)
2. Sun protection (sunglasses and sunscreen)
3. Insulation (extra clothing)
4. Illumination (headlamp or flashlight)
5. First-aid supplies
6. Fire (firestarter and matches/lighter)
7. Repair kit and tools (including knife)
8. Nutrition (extra food)
9. Hydration (extra water)
10. Emergency shelter

Flooding, Fees, and Other Natural Disasters

Fall of 2003 brought disastrous flooding to the Northwest region. As we go to press, it is unknown if the flooding caused serious damage to any of the hikes in this book or, if so, whether any such damage might remain by spring of 2004. Flooding and other fluctuations in nature can alter accesses, trails, river crossings, and other recreational facilities. Always call for current information regarding the trail you plan to hike before you leave.

For many years hikers enjoyed the backcountry with no cost other than the fuel it took to get there. Unfortunately, with increased trail usage, increased cost of maintenance, the financial straits of government agency budgets, and no other options in sight, it has become necessary to charge fees for backcountry use. If a pass or permit is required at a trailhead, it is noted in the driving directions. However, these regulations may change; contact the ranger station to ask about fees before you leave home.

- A Vehicle Use Permit ($10 a season, cost included with a hunting or fishing license) is required at all sites managed by the Washington State Department Fish and Wildlife. For information, call (360) 902-2434 or visit their website at *www.wa.gov/wdfs*.
- A Northwest Forest Pass ($30 annually, $5 for a day pass) is required for parking at some trailheads. To purchase a pass or for more information, call (800) 270-7504 or visit the Northwest Forest Pass website at *www.fs.fed.us/r6/feedemo/*.
- An entrance pass ($10 per vehicle or $5 per individual for a 7-day pass) is required at Mount Rainier National Park, Olympic National Park, and Mount St. Helens National Mounument. For information, call Olympic National Park Wilderness Information Center at (360) 565-3130 or (360) 565-3131, Mount Rainier National Park at (360) 569-2211, or Mount St. Helens National Volcanic Monument at (360) 449-7800 or visit the website at *www.nps.gov*.

For frequent users of national parks and forests, a variety of annual passes are available that are more cost effective and convenient than purchasing short-term passes; inquire at the forest service or national park website or on-site information centers. ■ C. C. T.

A NOTE ABOUT SAFETY

Safety is an important concern in all outdoor activities. No guidebook can alert you to every hazard or anticipate the limitations of every reader. Therefore, the descriptions of roads, trails, routes, and natural features in this book are not representations that a particular place or excursion will be safe for your party. When you follow any of the routes described in this book, you assume responsibility for your own safety. Under normal conditions, such excursions require the usual attention to traffic, road and trail conditions, weather, terrain, the capabilities of your party, and other factors. Keeping informed on current conditions and exercising common sense are the keys to a safe, enjoyable outing.

The Mountaineers Books

Opposite: *A meadow filled with lupine at Hurricane Ridge (Hike 3)*

OLYMPIC PENINSULA

1
RIALTO BEACH

Round trip	■	**3 miles**
Difficulty	■	Easy
Best flowers	■	Summer
Hikable	■	Year-round
High point	■	100 feet
Elevation gain	■	100 feet

Getting there ■ From Seattle, take an Edmonds or Bremerton ferry or drive around (Interstate 5 to access US 101) to Forks. If coming from Hoquiam, drive to Forks and at 2 miles beyond Forks turn north (left) onto LaPush Road. If coming from Port Angeles, 2 miles before Forks turn north (right) onto LaPush Road. Drive 8 miles on LaPush Road, then turn right on Mora Road and continue 5 miles to the parking lot, picnic area, and facilities. A Park Service backcountry use permit is required for an overnight stay.

Maps ■ Custom Correct Ozette Beach Loop, Green Trails No. 130S Ozette

Information ■ Olympic National Park Wilderness Information Center, phone (360) 565-3130

You don't have to hike a great distance to experience one of the most scenic areas along the Pacific Coast. From the parking area, turn right (north) and hike the beach as little or as far as you want. This long stretch of wilderness beach stretches north and south from the Quillayute River.

There are several hikes along the coast, but this one is easier than others: The creek crossings are not difficult, and there is only one headland that cannot be hiked around at low tide. The terrain is generally easy to walk on and consists of sand and cobblestones. In general, the walking is easier at low tide—otherwise you may be scrambling over slippery rocks, driftwood, and soft sand.

If you are going beyond Hole-in-the-Wall, be sure you carry a tide chart so you don't get stranded. Backpackers must also carry an animal-resistant food storage container. Bears are not generally a problem but smaller mammals, such as raccoons, are intelligent and can easily open packs and food caches hanging from ropes. These aare required along some sections of the coast. Check with the Wilderness Information Center before setting out if you are backpacking. Mora Campground is just off Mora Road; camping is also allowed at Ellen Creek and the Chilean Memorial, and many campsites can be found in between.

I've never thought of the beach as being a place to look for flowers, and indeed, a beach is not primarily a flower walk. Yet there are many flowers and kinds of vegetation that grow along the shore. Flowers that you may

Sea stacks on Rialto Beach

see in late August are pearly everlasting, yarrow, goldenrod, daisies, and an assortment of grasses growing near the trailhead and small streams and bordering the tide line where driftwood washes up. Plants you may see earlier in the summer are beach morning glory and searocket. Look for other plants and vegetation such as bull kelp and sea lettuce (marine algae) that washes ashore. The tidepools are also teeming with life. Apparently only two genera of aquatics are found in the ocean—common eel grass and Scouler's surfgrass. Most aquatic plants in our region grow in fresh water. A guidebook to aquatic plants will help you locate and identify these. One such book is by Patricia K. Lichen, called *Brittle Stars and Mudbugs: An Uncommon Field Guide to Northwest Shorelines and Wetlands.*

From the parking lot, head north (right) and in about ½ mile cross Ellen Creek on a logjam or cross at low tide. Incidentally, the tea-colored water of Ellen Creek is from bark tannin. The water is safe to drink if treated or boiled. By late summer, Ellen Creek can be a mere trickle in a dry year.

Before you get to Hole-in-the-Wall, you'll hike past two large sea stacks—these also are teeming with life. On sea stacks such as these, look for trees growing on the top (hemlock, fir, spruce) and you may also spot huckleberry, salal, licorice ferns, and other shrubs and flowers in season.

Hole-in-the-Wall is a favorite of photographers, and most hikers I know have had their photograph taken there at one time or another. The first headland where you need a tidal chart is just beyond Hole-in-the-Wall— and you will need a low tide to know when to cross it safely. This area around Hole-in-the Wall is best seen at low tide, when you can prowl the rocky shore and peer into tidepools where green anemones, starfish, barnacles, and other life forms are seen (do not handle them). By the way, if you've seen one barnacle, you haven't seen them all—there actually is a variety of them. When barnacles are first hatched, they swim and only adhere to the rocks after they have gone through several molts. Their meals are delivered to them on currents and tides.

Listen to seagulls scream, and on sea stacks farther out at sea you may see sea lions and other sea birds. Deer often are spotted along the shores, and raccoons also are seen, sometimes too often. The ocean is a noisy place, but it is strangely calming: You will be followed by the roar of the ocean and the cries of gulls every step of the way.

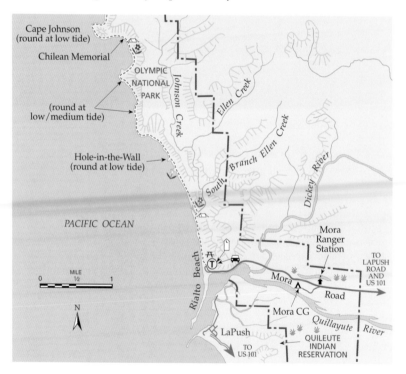

Salal blossoms give way to dark purple berries in the fall.

Another good destination for a day or overnight is the Chilean Memorial, at 2½ miles. Hikers going beyond that point will need a low tide to round Cape Johnson at 3 miles (there is no trail over the top).

If you stay for the sunset, you may encounter groups of photographers bristling with tripods and long lenses. And why not? This is an incredibly beautiful place to be for a sunset or any time of the day, any season of the year. ■ K. S.

Art's Notes

The mini-islands just offshore along our Olympic Peninsula coast, called sea stacks, are fragments of an inexorable change in coastlines. The eternal fluctuation in sea level over geologic time either isolates these fragments or welds them to the shoreline. Plant life on sea stacks are mini-samples of mainland coastal vegetation. Most sea stacks are clad with familiar conifers, hemlock, spruce, and Douglas fir. Understory shrubs are also mainlanders: common are salal and huckleberry. Yet there can be subtle differences. On the steep, exposed slopes of a sea stack, expect to find nodding onion *(Allium cernuum)* and licorice fern *(Polypodium glycyrrhiza)*. Some of these mini-islands might be visited by kayak or even on foot at lowest tides. But don't tarry! Isolating high tides are just around the corner to strand the visitor.

GEOLOGY OF THE OLYMPIC MOUNTAINS

Just as in the Cascades and Wenatchees, geology on the Olympic Peninsula takes command over where plants may thrive. The lofty Olympics, reaching more than 8000 feet at Mount Olympus, act as a massive barrier for rainfall coming in from the Pacific. The difference between Forks (250 cm/100 inches) and Sequim, at the northeast base of the range (45 cm/18 inches) dramatically portrays the classic rainshadow effect. Mountains faithfully create this abrupt drop in precipitation wherever they stand athwart a prevailing weather flow. The effects on plant life are striking: Old-growth rain forest of Sitka spruce, western hemlock, and western redcedar forests on the westerly (windward) perimeter are replaced by Garry oak savannah on the leeward, east side.

Topography within the Olympics also affects the quality of plant cover. Valleys, ridge tops, direction (aspect) of mountain slope (north facing vs. south facing) exact their influence on what grows where. Just compare Hurricane Ridge with the Hoh River rain forest: Expanses of flowers bedeck the subalpine meadows on the ridge, in contrast to the massive boles of old-growth conifers and bigleaf maples festooned with moss, lichens, and ferns in the western rain forest drainages. Land forms created by geology exert a powerful influence on floras.

The bedrock geology of the Olympics differs markedly from that of the Cascades. The eastern and northern perimeter of the range consists of an arc of pillow lavas (basalt) once formed under the sea and later (25 M.Y.A.) thrust upward (the Crescent formation). Looking west from the Puget basin, the imposing eastern rampart of the Olympics displays the lava shield prominently, accentuated by the high peaks of Mount Constance, The Brothers, and Mount Jupiter. The central core of the range is also of oceanic origin, but all sea floor sediments—sandstones, shales, limestone, and conglomerates—squeezed into tilted, even vertical, slabs of rock. When these rocks weather to make soil on gentle slopes or basins, plants make out well. But on steep slopes, soil is in short supply; weathering of the rock makes shards: talus and scree. Some of the most colorful cushion plants thrive on these unstable rocky to gravelly slopes. On talus and scree, look for phlox, drabas, Olympic onion, sandworts, lewisias, and a host of other rock garden delights, making out on ever-moving slopes. The star of them all on scree must be Piper's bellflower, expansive mats of foliage topped with large blue saucer-shaped bells. It is found only in the Olympics. Other choice wildflowers restricted (endemic) to the range are Flett's violet, hugging rocky crevices; Olympic milkvetch; and Henderson's rock spirea, its prostrate mats of grayish leaves bearing short spikes of white flowers.

Geology imposes its will on Olympic flora in yet another fashion. The very isolation of the range and its wet-to-dry climatic extremes have fostered the evolution of several plants found only in the Olympics. The mystery of mysteries is the veronicalike *Synthyris schizantha*; besides its local occurrence in the Humptulips drainage, it also pops up in the Little Rockies above Elbe and in Oregon on Saddle Mountain. For a thorough account of the Olympics flora and geologic history, *Flora of the Olympic Peninsula,* by Nelsa Buckingham, et al. (1995), is a must. ■ A. R. K.

Hurricane Ridge and the Elwha River valley

2 HOH RIVER NATURE TRAILS AND HAPPY FOUR CAMP

Round trip ■	Happy Four Camp, 11½ miles; ¾-mile and 1¾-mile nature trails
Difficulty ■	Easy to moderate
Best flowers ■	May through August
Hikable ■	Year-round
High point ■	800 feet
Elevation gain ■	230 feet

Getting there ■ Drive US 101 south of Forks to the Hoh River Road. Turn east and continue 18 miles to the Hoh River Visitor Center and campground, elevation 578 feet. A Park Service Backcountry Permit is required for camping.

Maps ■ Custom Correct Seven Lakes Basin–Hoh, Green Trails Nos. 133 Mount Tom and 134 Mount Olympus

Information ■ Olympic National Park Wilderness Information Center, phone (360) 565-3130 or (360) 565-3131

The nature trails and the Hoh River trail all depart from the Hoh River Ranger Station on a single trail. The trail immediately crosses a marshy

Two flowers of the forest: foamflower, left, and woodnymph, right

creek and climbs to a split. Before you leave the creek, spend a few moments looking at the aquatics of the stream, which is a brilliant green abstract of rushing water and billowing grasses. Most impressive is a sedge, the small-flowered bulrush.

The split is shortly beyond the creek and is well signed. Turn left for the Hall of Mosses Nature Trail. The Spruce Nature Trail (another short loop) and the Hoh River trail are to the right. Photographers and naturalists can easily spend a couple of hours on the Hall of Mosses alone.

Whether you hike the short loops or continue on the Hoh River trail, you will see that the rain forest is predominated with Sitka spruce, followed by fire-resistant Douglas firs and western redcedar. Bigleaf maples, often festooned with licorice ferns, and vine maple add to the splendor any season of the year. A discussion of the mosses, liverworts, and lichens found along these trails are beyond the scope of this brief trail description, but nature guides can help you identify them.

You will also find several ferns along the trail, including sword fern and deer fern. Another point of interest is the "nurse log," which acts as a nursery in which other trees take root. When you notice several trees lined up in a straight line, you can bet they took root in a nurse log. Over time, the nurse log breaks down and the trees remain to compete for light and nutrients.

In late August the mosses were dry, a result of a long summer without rain. A few late-summer flowers were hanging on, but not many—foamflower and a few yellow composites could still be seen along the trail. Also seen along the nature trail were vanilla leaf and false lily-of-the-valley, though none were flowering.

If you hike farther along the Hoh River trail, you will see that Douglas fir becomes the dominant tree. Hikers and backpackers often continue to Happy Four Camp, at 5¾ miles. Don't rule this out as a winter hike: That may be the only time of the year to experience solitude here before tourists

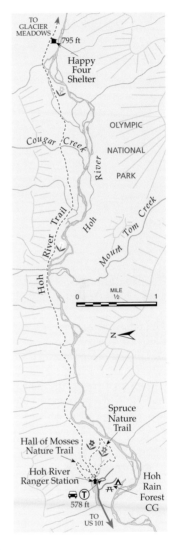

An understory of moss, oxalis, and fern in the Hoh rain forest

and casual hikers arrive in summer. If you do visit on a summer weekend, plan to get a very early start.

The trail travels through groves of trees, with the Hoh River, rapids, and gravel bars often in view. There are occasional views to Mount Tom and Mount Carrie, and if you do come in winter you may see herds of Roosevelt elk. ■ K. S.

Art's Notes

At many places along the Olympic Strip sector of the park, be charmed (or amazed) by the forest daring to reach the water's edge. This nearly pristine stretch of forested coastline must be little different from ancient times when seen by the Spanish exploring expedition under Bodega y Quadra and viewed from offshore by Captain Vancouver in the late 1700s. All the conifers of the Hoh rain forest reach the water's edge here: Sitka spruce, western hemlock, western redcedar, and even Douglas fir.

A special fern can appear in rocky places, just above the splash zone: Scouler's fern *(Polypodium scouleri)* has a dark, leathery texture to its 8-inch divided fronds. It is named for John Scouler, a botanical companion of David Douglas during their stay at Fort Vancouver in the 1830s.

THE RAIN FOREST

When naturalists and ecologists conjure up the idea of a rain forest, the first image likely would be somewhere in the tropics—the Amazon Basin, Indonesia, or the African Congo. Yet temperate rain forests, like those of the Hoh, Queets, and Quinault Rivers, do have some similarity to rain forests of the tropics: high rainfall and moderate annual temperatures foster year-round growth, culminating in high arboreal splendor—trees of gigantic size and number. This temperate rain forest in Washington terminates southward into coastal Oregon and reaches grand proportions in southeastern Alaska. Exuberant growth of mosses, ferns, and lichens nestled in the canopy is another temperate rain forest attribute. These nonflowering plants are everywhere: covering the forest floor, on tree trunks, and well into the upper canopy of trees, especially bigleaf maple. Similar displays of luxuriance appear in temperate rain forests elsewhere, like the west coast of the South Island of New Zealand and the southern coasts of Chile.

The mats and cushions of mosses and ferns in upper canopies of trees were once thought to be mostly passive—freeholders. But then an intrepid forest botanist, Nalini Nadkarni, ascending into the upper reaches of trees, took a close look at the nature of the host tree's linkage to these cushions. She made a remarkable discovery: The host tree, in its topmost branches, is induced by the damp moss-fern cushions to put out feeder roots into the cushions. Nadkarni and now others have found this same symbiosis elsewhere, especially in the tropics. The host roots penetrating the epiphytic mats give the host tree added nutrients and moisture. The moss-fern cushions catch airborne dust and rain, serving as spongy reservoirs of nutrients for the host tree.

On the Hoh River trail you are in the very heart of rain forest country. With more than 100 inches of rain per year at nearly sea level, exuberant growth occurs nearly year-round in Olympic National Park. Where old growth prevails, widely spaced two- to three-hundred-year-old Sitka spruce, western hemlock, western redcedar, and Douglas fir form the colossal canopy of a rich shrub stratum and even a diverse forest floor. Besides massive old-growth conifers, the premium hardwood, bigleaf maple (*Acer macrophyllum*), can reach well into the upper conifer canopy. This magnificent maple is host to a rich aerial flora of mosses, lichens, and ferns, the epiphytes that choose bigleaf maple for a host tree. It is this luxuriant aerial growth of epiphytes that epitomizes the "rain forest" name. Yet it is temperate rain forest, the nearest thing to the tropical rain forest.

Most any of the rivers running off the west slope of the Olympics

The Hall of Mosses Nature Trail

offer—or did offer—the awesome experience of temperate rain forest. Yet only those rivers in the park still have good samples of this world-class forest. Outside the park, rain forest is now stumps or monotonous second growth. Within the park, other rain forest rivers merit exploration: the Quinault, the Queets, and the Bogachiel. My favorite is the Queets River, for the added blessing of solitude. You may have to ford the river near the trailhead (not difficult in late summer) to gain the valley-bottom trail. Frequent extensive clearings in the forest valleys are evidence of early homesteads, before Olympic National Park was established.

It may not be apparent why any of these rain forest valleys have such exceptional visibility, at eye level. Though the hiker may not ever see elk or deer, they have done their work: They have browsed understory herbage so extensively as to create corridors of vista.

A unique river-bottom habitat is the alder sandbar and flats, where the rivers have left to change course. These open habitats allow for sand and sun lovers to establish—wild strawberry and an occasional high-country flower like the pink monkeyflower, from seed washed down from higher elevations. ■ A. R. K.

3 | HURRICANE HILL

Round trip ■ **3 miles**
Difficulty ■ Moderate
Best flowers ■ July through August
Hikable ■ Late June through October
High point ■ 5757 feet
Elevation gain ■ About 750 feet

Getting there ■ From west on US 101 in Port Angeles, turn left (south) at the sign for Hurricane Ridge near the city center and follow the signs as the road curves left (the Wilderness Information Center is to the right). Continue into the park (5 miles) and to Hurricane Ridge, 17.5 miles from Port Angeles. The Hurricane Ridge Visitor Center has rest rooms, interpretive displays, guided walks during peak season, and a gift shop. Drive roughly another 1.3 miles from the Visitor Center to the end of the Hurricane Ridge Road and the Hurricane Hill trailhead, 5000 feet. There are also picnic areas along this section of the road.

Map ■ Custom Correct Hurricane Ridge

Information ■ Olympic National Park Wilderness Information Center, phone (360) 565-3130 or (360) 565-3131

This trail is an old forest service road that provided access to the Hurricane Hill lookout when it was in use. The paved trail is wide and easy to follow, staying level for the first ½ mile. It is another easy mile to the summit, with

Fleabane along the Hurricane Ridge road

Senecio neowebsteri *(endemic to the Olympics) and* Elmera racemosa

moderate elevation gain—but carry water. The trail does not cross any streams.

There are actually two ways to reach Hurricane Hill, but most hikers will prefer the approach from Hurricane Ridge. The other approach is a steep, 6-mile climb from the Elwha Ranger Station on the Elwha River trail (it is sometimes referred to as the Hurricane Hill trail). The Elwha River trail junction (5640 feet) is located near the summit of Hurricane Hill and is well signed.

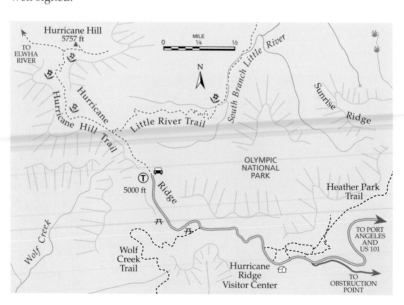

The Hurricane Hill trail from Hurricane Ridge is easy and scenic, so be prepared to share this trail with other hikers. The Little River trail is another trail that descends to the Elwha. That junction is at ½ mile and is well signed.

The trail offers great views the entire way. Mount Angeles (east) and Mount Olympus, with its multiple summits, are hard to miss on a clear day. In less than ¼ mile the Little River trail descends steeply (right). There are good views of the Bailey Range across the valley.

The trail bears right, and long switchbacks climb through meadows toward Hurricane Hill. On a clear day there are good views of Port Angeles,

Art's Notes

So much of the high country in the Olympics is reached only by miles of "valley pounding," hiking long stretches of low-elevation trails in rain-drenched forest. It is only at Hurricane Ridge that the subalpine country can be reached with ease—by car. Besides this easy access to Hurricane Ridge and Hill, there are other great destinations from the ridge area. North from the Big Meadows parking lot at the ridge, find the Lake Angeles–Klahane Ridge trail. It leads to the high north peak, Mount Angeles. In mid-July, floras abound. Watch especially for the rock-hugging *Douglasia laevigata*, with cushiony foliage and deep rose-pink flowers. Another rock crevice plant is the amazing rock spirea or Olympic rock mat, *Petrophytum hendersonii*. The other stellar Olympiads, piper's harebell *(Campanula piperi)* and Flett's violet *(Viola flettii),* should be watched for.

Obstruction Point is another destination, going east by gravel road from Hurricane Ridge. En route, watch for that ground-hugging larkspur with purple flowers, *Delphinium glareosum*. At Obstruction Point's parking lot, you are in typical "crooked wood": Krummholz conifers, mostly dwarfed subalpine fir. Rocky places sport a gaggle of low alpine species: a favorite Olympic endemic, the gray-leaved kitten tails *(Synthyris pinnatafida* var. *lanuginosa)*, with perky, erect lavender flower tassels. Near late melting snowbanks, find the yellow daisy, *Senecio neowebsteri*, also an Olympic endemic. Scrambling among the rock crevices, you may find my namesake, Kruckeberg's holly fern *(Polystichum kruckebergii)*. It was first described from these rocky sites.

Several trails lead away from Obstruction Point. Ridge running can take you all the way to Deer Park. Or go downhill to the verdant meadows of Badger Valley.

An unforgettable vista at Obstruction Point is to look northeast to a "sea" of Krummholz, windswept, shrubby subalpine fir covering slopes above Grand Creek. Should you venture out on the upper Grand Ridge trail to Deer Park from Obstruction Point, be aware that a steep snowbank covers the trail into midsummer. Traverse with caution.

Fawns in Big Meadow, Hurricane Ridge

Vancouver Island, and the Strait of Juan de Fuca. At about 1¼ miles (5640 feet), the Elwha trail descends (left). Near the summit of Hurricane Hill (right) a short, unpaved loop weaves through small meadows, clumps of subalpine trees, and rocky outcroppings along the summit ridge. Here is a better chance of solitude. From the summit there are views down to the canyons of the Elwha, Mount Constance, Mount Anderson, and The Needles. A map will help you identify them.

Marmots may be seen in the meadows and along the trail, though you are more likely to hear them than see them. Black-tailed deer are also common here, and on warm afternoons you find them seeking shelter among trees. I saw a buck in late August, but female deer are most often seen; bucks tend to be loners.

Mid-July is generally peak time for flowers on Hurricane Ridge. In midsummer, look for lance-leaved spring beauty, glacier lilies, Columbia (tiger) lilies, thread-leafed sandwort, bistort, lomatium, broad-leafed arnica, fanleaf cinquefoil, Indian paintbrush, and wandering fleabane. In late August, most of the flowers had gone to seed but a few yellow composites—harebells, asters, and masses of pearly everlasting—were still in bloom. I also saw lupine and elephant's head louseworts (gone to seed), and Indian thistle, a native thistle. Thistles at lower elevations are considered weeds. Trees included subalpine fir, mountain hemlock, and Alaska yellow cedar, with occasional Douglas fir and western white pines.

As summer progresses, one species of wildflower replaces another—grasses and sedges begin to dry and meadows turn brown as winter approaches. ■ K. S.

4 ┊ MARMOT PASS VIA BIG QUILCENE TRAIL

Round trip ■ **10½ miles**
Difficulty ■ Strenuous
Best flowers ■ Late June through August
Hikable ■ Late June through October
High point ■ 5990 feet
Elevation gain ■ 3590 feet

Getting there ■ From US 101, drive 0.9 mile south of the Quilcene Ranger Station and turn right onto Penny Creek Road. At 1.4 miles, turn left at an unsigned junction—it should be signed "Big Quilcene River Road," but in 2003 the sign was gone. This becomes Road No. 27. Continue 7.5 miles and go left on Ten Mile Road (Road No. 2750) (signed); continue 5 miles to the trailhead (Big Quilcene trail No. 833.1), elevation 2400 feet. The trail is open to hikers and stock—mountain bikes are prohibited. A Northwest Forest Pass is required.

Map ■ Custom Correct Hurricane Ridge

Information ■ Olympic National Park Wilderness Information Center, phone (360) 565-3130 or (360) 565-3131

It's been said that the Garden of Eden is in Mesopotamia, but many hikers believe it can be found on the trail to Marmot Pass. However, if you live in the greater Seattle area, getting an early start is critical for this hike. Whether you drive around or take a ferry, plan on a long day. The trail is situated in the Buckhorn Wilderness and features some of the best scenery and flowers the Olympics have to offer. For the best flowers, July may be the best bet. When I was there in early August, many of the flowers were already going to seed.

The Big Quilcene trail No. 833.1 begins at 2400 feet and almost immediately enters the Buckhorn Wilderness. The first 2½ miles are in cool forest

Lupine and paintbrush at Marmot Pass

as the trail follows along and near the Big Quilcene River to Shelter Rock Camp, 3700 feet. The camp is not signed but it is hard to miss it. Fill your water bottles here—the next water is 2 steep miles away.

From Shelter Rock Camp, the trail alternates between forest and open areas with Buckhorn and Iron Mountains coming into view on the right side of the trail. Meadows predominate as the trail gains elevation; turn around for a view of Glacier Peak on a clear day. From Shelter Rock Camp, it is 2 miles to Camp Mystery (5400 feet), a popular destination for the Boy Scouts.

That 2-mile stretch before Camp Mystery became known as the "Poop-Out Drag" to the Scouts. The hard work was over by the time they made it to Camp Mystery. It is good that memories of beautiful places last longer than tired legs and aching shoulders, but make no mistake—this is not an easy hike. The good news is that the trail is in good condition and there are no difficulties other than elevation gain.

On open slopes and in the meadows between Shelter Rock Camp and Camp Mystery, look for tiger lilies, arnica, a variety of paintbrush (magenta paintbrush at higher elevations), fireweed, phlox, lupine, asters, agoseris, harebells, cow parsnip, pearly everlasting, and yarrow.

Though the greatest displays are beyond Shelter Rock Camp, the forest has a variety of flowers as well. Between the trailhead and open hillsides, look for rhododendrons, salmonberry, blueberries, pipsissewa, twinflower, common monkeyflowers, Canadian dogwood, wild ginger, vanilla leaf, rosy twistedstalk, bead lily, foamflower, and trilliums; by August, some plants had gone to seed. At the first meadow near a small stream, tall blue delphiniums were prevalent though starting to fade.

The trail levels out near Camp Mystery, 4½ miles from the trailhead. There are campsites and water from two nearby springs but no toilets. From Camp Mystery, the trail climbs, passes under a cliff, and crosses a meadow before climbing to Marmot Pass, 5990 feet. There are views in all directions—bring a map to identify the peaks. From Marmot Pass, trails connect

BUCKHORN PASS

Buckhorn Pass epitomizes the Olympics' rainshadow effects, but at high elevations. Similar summits to the west, like Mount Colonel Bob, have a rather modest wildflower display. But here on the east, rocky summits yield lavish drifts of showy plants. Here is a tempting sampler.

Notable Plants From Buckhorn Pass to Marmot Pass and Down to Boulder Shelter

E = endemic to the Olympics; +E = near endemic

BOTANICAL NAME	COMMON NAME	ENDEMIC
Aster paucicapitatus	white aster	+E
Campanula piperi	Piper's harebell	E
Collomia debilis	alpine collomia	
Douglasia laevigata	smooth douglasia	+E
Elmera racemosa	elmera	
Erigeron compositus	cut-leaved daisy	
Erysimum arenicola	wallflower	E
Geum triflorum var. campanulatum	avens	E
Lewisia columbiana var. rupicola	Columbia lewisia	+E
Phlox hendersonii	Henderson's phlox	E
Salix arctica	dwarf willow	
Salix nivalis	snow willow	
Saxifraga oppositifolia	purple mountain saxifrage	
Senecio neowebsteri	yellow daisy	E
Silene acaulis	moss campion	
Synthyris pinnatifida var. lanuginosa	gray-leaved kitten tails	E
Viola flettii	Flett's violet	E

Wallflower Erysimum arenicola, *endemic to the Olympics*

to the Upper Dungeness and Tubal Cain Mine trails, though there were no trail signs at the pass.

Turn left (south) at the pass and climb 300 feet to a knoll for views of Mount Fricaba, Mount Mystery, The Needles, and Gray Wolf Ridge. At Marmot Pass and the knoll, look for columbine, Sitka valerian, bistort, daisies, Cusick's speedwell, western pasque flower, magenta paintbrush, and more. The most unusual flower is mountain death camas—find it blooming along the trail between Marmot Pass and the knoll.

Strong hikers can also turn right (north) at the pass and follow a boot-beaten path to the west summit of Buckhorn Mountain (6956 feet) for views of Warrior Peak and Mount Constance. North is the Strait of Juan de Fuca and Vancouver Island. ■ K. S.

Art's Notes

I have reached Marmot Pass from the north, via Buckhorn Mountain and Buckhorn Pass, ridge running most of the way. This approach starts via the Copper Creek trail in the Dungeness River drainage, a trail adorned with our native rhododendron *(R. macrophyllum)*. Above the Tubal Cain Mine campground, the trail switchbacks through glorious fields of wildflowers before reaching Buckhorn Pass. And here at the pass is the finest of floral rock gardens. Watch for some of the Olympic Mountain endemics, like *Aster paucicapitatus* (a white aster), the exquisite *Campanula piperi,* and the showy lace pod, *Hedysarum occidentale.* The eastern flank of the Olympics seems to be favored with a greater floral richness than one finds in the western, wetter terrain. Just compare Mount Colonel Bob on the west with the richer flower gardens in the Marmot Pass area. Its kindred eastside locales such as Deer Park, Obstruction Point, and Mount Angeles are simply more floriferous. Causes of this contrast in floral richness may well be a combination of differences in precipitation and in soils. The eastern perimeter is in a rainshadow (lesser rainfall) and its soils are mostly derived from marine lava (pillow basalt).

5 | STAIRCASE

Camp Pleasant round trip	■	**14 miles**
Difficulty	■	Moderate
Hikable	■	May through November
High point	■	1600 feet
Elevation gain	■	800 feet

Staircase round trip	■	**Almost 2 miles**
Difficulty	■	Easy
Hikable	■	May through November
High point	■	950 feet
Elevation gain	■	150 feet

Home Sweet Home round trip	■	**27 miles**
Difficulty	■	Strenuous
Hikable	■	July through October
High point	■	4688 feet
Elevation gain	■	4000 feet in, 500 out

Best flowers	■	Late April through August

Getting there ■ Drive US 101 to the center of Hoodsport and turn west. Drive past Lake Cushman and 9.4 miles from Hoodsport go left on road No. 24, the North Fork Skokomish River road, signed "Staircase." In another 1.7 miles leave the pavement, and 16 miles from Hoodsport reach the road end at the Staircase Ranger Station, elevation 800 feet.

Maps ■ Custom Correct Mount Skokomish–Lake Cushman, Green Trails No. 167 Mount Steel

Information ■ Staircase Ranger Station, phone (360) 877-5569

Forest flowers galore, fairyslippers, vanilla leaf, dwarf salal, woodnymph, twinflower, devil's club. I could go on and on—but go see for yourself.

I promised Pat some fairyslippers for Mother's Day 2002. What better way to honor a mother, a grandmother, and a wife of fifty-three years than to show her some fairyslippers (commonly called calypso or ladyslippers). I knew I could lead her to them, for there had been lots of them back in the 1930s when my brother and I had made an annual springtime pilgrimage to Camp Pleasant, 7 miles up the North Fork Skokomish River from Staircase.

It was a beautiful day when we parked at Staircase and started up the trail lined with vanilla leaf and yellow Johnny jump-ups, plus a nice showing of trilliums. Some elk ran across the trail in front of us.

I was getting embarrassed. Where were the fairyslippers I had boasted

Douglas firs along the Staircase trail

about? Finally, about 1½ miles into the hike, I found one, and for the next 100 feet there were at least a hundred in bloom or just fading. We walked another mile and though the habitat looked the same, there were no more to be found.

My adventures at Staircase go back to 1931, when the road was built to Staircase and my father drove our family there. We often stayed in a cedar shake cabin at the Staircase Resort.

Where the name "Staircase" came from seems to have been lost. In 1890, Lieutenant Joseph P. O'Neil used Lake Cushman as a jumping-off place for his expedition across the Olympics. Most of the way was on easy valley bottom. At Staircase, though, the river butted up against a 400-foot cliff. During high water, when the river couldn't be waded, a route had to be found over the cliff—the "Devil's Staircase." Eventually the trail was blasted into the cliff.

CAMP PLEASANT. When we lived in Shelton when I was a boy, our family made a point of hiking this trail in early spring to see the bands of elk before they left for their summer browsing grounds in the high country. It was on these trips that I became acquainted with the fairyslipper and first boasted about seeing so many on this trail.

The trail starts from the parking space behind the ranger station on a long-abandoned road. This was the road that the CCC intended to cross the First Divide (4688 feet), drop to the Duckabush River valley, cross O'Neil Pass (4900 feet), and drop to Lake Quinault and the Pacific Ocean. What a loss of wilderness that would have been.

At 4½ miles the way narrows to honest-to-gosh trail. At 6 miles, pass Big Log Camp, a spacious area beside the river. At 6½ miles, a bridge crosses the river over a deep, quiet pool surrounded by moss-covered rocks. Immediately beyond is a junction; go right. The trail climbs gently to Camp Pleasant, 7 miles, 1520 feet, on a large maple flat, a very pleasant camp for springtime backpackers. The camp is generally snowfree in May.

STAIRCASE. Hike along a staircase of spectacular rapids through moss-draped groves of maples, alders, cedars, and Douglas firs.

From the ranger station parking area, cross the concrete bridge of the North Fork Skokomish River, following a well-worn path straight into a forest of huge maples, hemlocks, and cedars. In ¼ mile or so, take a marked spur trail left to the base of an 800-year-old western redcedar, 14 feet in diameter and 43 feet in circumference. It fell a few years ago but is still

Calypso, a.k.a. fairyslipper

impressive. Returning to the main path, continue above the noisy, small falls of the Staircase Rapids. Look for Johnny jump-ups, twinflower, vanilla leaf, and devil's club. In a scant mile, the trail passes through some house-size boulders and reaches the vacant piers of a footbridge that was lost in the 1999 flood. Eventually the bridge will be replaced. For now, return the way you came.

Home Sweet Home. For a real flower treat, come back to Staircase in late July and walk the 13½ miles from forest flowers to the flower-covered meadows at Home Sweet Home. The fairyslippers and trilliums will be gone, but the vanilla leaf will still be here, along with Indian pipe, woodnymph, twinflower, and pipsissewa, which should be in bloom. The first 9 miles are easy, but at Nine Stream the trail turns uphill, climbing into meadow flowers to its highest point, 4688-foot First Divide, 13 miles from the road. From here the trail descends to the large, lupine-covered Home Sweet Home meadow. ■ I. S.

Art's Notes

Ira's love affair with this demure woodland orchid led him into the thorny thicket of common-name profusion: fairyslipper, ladyslipper, calypso, et cetera. What to call it? My preference is to adopt the name calypso, borrowing from botany's binomial *Calypso bulbosa*. Calypso borrows from Greek mythology, referring to a sea nymph who bewitched Odysseus' sailors. Not only is calypso a scarce species (widespread but never abundant), it also capriciously disappears—or appears—from year to year. A capriciousness that botanists find mysterious!

Opposite: *Mount Shuksan and Highwood Lake along the Mount Baker Highway (Hike 7)*

THE NORTH CASCADES & HIGHWAY 20

6 : YELLOW ASTER BUTTE

Round trip ■ **8 miles**
Difficulty ■ Strenuous
Best flowers ■ July through August
Hikable ■ July through October
High point ■ 5800 feet
Elevation gain ■ 2200 feet

Getting there ■ From Seattle, go north on I-5 and take exit 255 at Bellingham for Mount Baker Highway (SR 542). Drive SR 542 through Maple Falls about 16 miles east to just beyond the Glacier Public Service Center and turn left on signed Twin Lakes Road No. 3065. This is a narrow, steep gravel road. At 4.5 miles, turn into the Tomyhoi Lake/Yellow Aster Butte trailhead, elevation 3600 feet. Parking is limited, especially on summer weekends. A Northwest Forest Pass is required.
Map ■ Green Trails No. 14 Mount Shuksan
Information ■ Glacier Public Service Center, phone (360) 599-2714

The focus of this book is wildflowers, but this hike is also spectacular in late summer or early fall when autumn colors appear and berries ripen. On a clear day the sky is deep blue, Mount Baker is at its best, and the meadows of Yellow Aster Butte are golden and dreamy. As for the flowers, there really aren't any yellow asters—the "yellow asters" are daisies. In addition to lots of daisies look for purple asters, Indian paintbrush, fireweed, bistort, penstemon, mertensia, rosy spirea, lupine, and anemone.

Golden fleabane might have inspired the name of Yellow Aster Butte.

The original trail to Yellow Aster Butte was the Keep Kool trail, but that trail is permanently closed. Today, the Yellow Aster Butte trail No. 686.1 starts out on the Tomyhoi Lake trail No. 686. Be prepared to encounter more hikers, since closing the Keep Kool trailhead has resulted in fewer trailheads and a growing number of hikers. Go midweek if possible to avoid human bottlenecks on this popular trail.

The hike begins on Tomyhoi Lake trail No. 686 for the first 1¼ miles as the route switchbacks through brush and avalanche slopes before entering timber. The trail breaks out and the grade levels off in a meadow with a trail junction at 1¼ miles (5200 feet). Turn left onto the Yellow Aster Butte trail No. 686.1 as it contours around Yellow Aster Butte with ups and downs. Red and white heather predominate here, and in the fall, the slope is red with blueberry shrubs. In 2⅓ miles more the trail ends at 5800 feet, 4 miles from the trailhead on the south side of the butte. If there are not too many hikers about, you may spot mountain goats or ptarmigan.

From here you can look down on a chain of tarns interspersed with mining artifacts. You can easily descend to the tarns for a closer look. These remnants of mining debris and equipment hint of tales of the miners who dreamed of gold and whose stories were never told.

Check with the Mount Baker Ranger District for camping regulations in this area. In general, backpackers are asked to camp on bare ground, rock, or sedge as meadows are fragile. Never camp on heather.

From the "end" of this trail at 4 miles, you can also look for an obvious scramble path that leads to the true summit of Yellow Aster Butte (6145 feet).

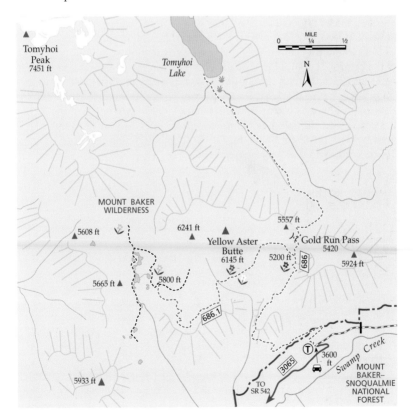

Meadows on Yellow Aster Butte, Mount Baker in the distance

You don't need to go all the way to the summit for the views; you can stop anywhere for those. Experienced hikers with routefinding skills can also look for a trail that climbs from the tarns and meadows and follows a ridge to the base of Tomyhoi Peak. The summit of Tomyhoi is off limits to hikers and is rated as a technical climb. Views from any high point here are extraordinary: to the north, American Border Peak and Mount Larrabee; Winchester Mountain is to the east; and beyond, the jagged peaks of the Picket Range. To the southeast is Goat Mountain, with Mount Shuksan rising above. South is Mount Baker, and if you climb high enough, you can look down to Tomyhoi Lake to the north. ▪ K. S.

Art's Notes

Don't expect to find any yellow asters on this trail or anywhere else on the planet. Strictly speaking, asters, in the genus *Aster*, have "flowers" mostly blue, purple, or even white. But let's hark back to "flowers." Asters and most other members of the sunflower or aster family (*Asteraceae*) bear their real, seed-producing flowers within the composite "flower." The "flower" is a collection of flowerlets (florets) that collectively simulate a "flower." So any aster "flower" is an aggregate of florets. An aster can have as many as thirty to fifty strap-shaped, radially placed florets, usually blue or purple; they surround a pincushion of tiny yellow disk florets. I doubt that Yellow Aster Butte gets its name from the central cluster of disk florets. I put my money on the possibility of the Yellow Aster name linked to the golden daisy, *Erigeron aureus*, sure to occur here and elsewhere on rocky subalpine ridges.

7 CHAIN LAKES LOOP

Round trip ■	**13 miles or 7-mile loop**
Difficulty ■	Moderate
Best flowers ■	July through August
Hikable ■	Late July through October
High point ■	5300 feet
Elevation gain ■	One way 600 feet gain, 1500 feet loss; loop 1500 feet gain, 1500 feet loss

Getting there ■ From Seattle, drive north on I-5 and get off at exit 255 for Mount Baker Highway (SR 542). Travel east on SR 542 to Glacier (about 33.5 miles) and just beyond, to the Glacier Public Service Center (a good stop for maps, current weather, trail and road conditions). From here continue 23.6 miles to the Artist Point and Chain Lakes trailhead, 5100 feet. Between the little town of Glacier and Artist Point, the highway is designated as a National Forest Scenic Byway. Accesssible rest rooms are located at Artist Point and at the Heather Meadows Visitor Center (the Heather Meadows Visitor Center is between the ski area and Artist Point, and is another opportunity to get trail and weather updates). A Northwest Forest Pass is required.

Map ■ Green Trails No. 14 Mount Shuksan

Information ■ Glacier Public Service Center, phone (360) 599-2714, or Mount Baker Ranger District, phone (360) 856-5700

There are few hikes that equal this one: Where else can you hike through an alpine setting with close-up views of two major Cascade peaks? If you start the loop from Artist Point, you are facing Mount Baker and on the return you will be facing Mount Shuksan. Best of all are the views from Herman Saddle, the high point (5300 feet) of both peaks as well as the north side of Table Mountain.

There are several options: If you don't want to make a loop or do a one-way hike, you can hike to Iceberg

Blueberry bushes at Mount Baker's Heather Meadows wear fall colors.

Glacier lilies emerging from snow

Lake and back for an easy 5-mile round trip. You can also hike to Herman Saddle from Artist Point or the Heather Meadows Visitor Center if you don't mind elevation gain (700 feet from the visitor center), but for the best scenery, the loop or a one-way hike is recommended.

Chain Lakes Loop trail No. 682 begins on the west side of the Artist Point parking area. Table Mountain trail No. 681 also starts from this trailhead. For Chain Lakes, turn left; the Table Mountain trail climbs uphill (right). In ½ mile, the trail enters the Mount Baker Wilderness. The first mile of trail is rocky as it contours around the south side of Table Mountain, and Mount Baker seems close enough to touch. In about a mile the junction for Ptarmigan Ridge trail No. 682.1 is reached. For

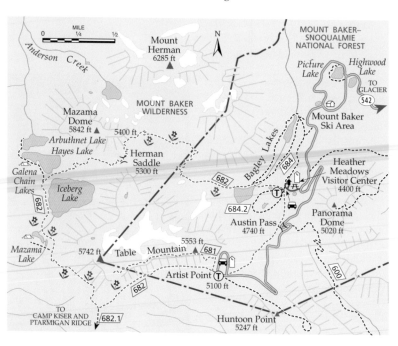

Mount Baker from the Chain Lakes trail

Chain Lakes, stay right as the trail descends 700 feet in ½ mile to Mazama Lake, the first of the Chain Lakes and designated campsites. Look for marmots sunning on the rocks near this lake.

From Mazama Lake, the trail climbs to an isthmus between Hayes and Iceberg Lakes. Iceberg Lake (4800 feet) is larger than Mazama Lake, and you may see icebergs floating on the lake—it does not melt out completely every year. Campers can find more designated camps at Galena Camps. Follow the signed trail around Hayes Lake to access them.

From Iceberg Lake, the trail climbs 600 feet to Herman Saddle, at 5300 feet. Several overlooks of the lake are found along the way. From the rocky pass, look west to Mount Baker and east to Mount Shuksan. As you descend, you'll see the attractive Heather Meadows Visitor Center above Bagley Lakes.

For the loop, the trail switchbacks and descends to Upper Bagley Lake then contours around the edge of the lake and crosses the outlet on a stone bridge. Turn right to the visitor center and parking area (a good place to leave a car for a one-way walk).

To complete the loop to Artist Point from the visitor center parking lot, find the Wild Goose trail just beyond the parking lot and climb 1 mile to Artist Point on a combination of trail and stairs (700 feet gain). You can also leave a car at Lower Bagley Lake near the ski area and hike to the visitor center.

In early August, the flowers were a bit past their peak but still were plentiful. Between Artist Point and Mazama Lake there were asters, lupine, partridgefoot, common monkeyflower, pussytoes, fireweed, heather, Sitka valerian, ferns, marsh marigolds, rosy spirea, orange agoseris, sulphur (white) paintbrush, arnica, mountain ash, false hellebore, bistort, and white rhododendron. I also saw leatherleaf saxifrage and elephant's head louseworts in meadows near Mazama Lake. Near Herman Saddle, look for phlox and western pasque flower.

About midway between Herman Saddle and Bagley Lakes, look for a moss-covered rock garden near a small stream with Lewis (pink) monkeyflowers and common (yellow) monkeyflowers sharing the same habitat. This is unusual; they usually do not share the same habitat. ■ K. S.

Art's Notes

Names on the land can be intriguing. Mount Baker, named by Captain George Vancouver in 1792 for his Lieutenant Joseph Baker, who first sighted the lofty volcanic peak, had two other names: Koma Kulshan was the First Peoples' (a.k.a. Indian's) name alluding to the mountain's eruptive behavior. The Spanish explorer Manuel Quimper called Baker Gran Muntaña del Carmelo. Nearby lofty Mount Shuksan, the highest nonvolcanic peak in our state (9131 feet), takes the Skagit First Peoples' name meaning "rocky and precipitous" (Phillips 1972). This hike does not quite gain the alpine zone—the "land above the trees." Rather you walk through open stands of Pacific silver fir (*Abies amabilis*) and mountain hemlock *(Tsuga mertensiana)*. Besides wildflowers galore—glacier lilies just emerging as the snow melts to mountain fleabane later in the season—watch for the uncommon shrub, a rhododendron relative, copperbush (*Cladothamnus pyroliflorus*), with a coppery bark and wintergreenlike flowers. It is locally common on the first stretches of the Lake Ann trail from Artist Point (Austin Pass). An alternate trail can take you to the flat dome of Table Mountain, a massive eminence of basaltic lava. Here look for the heatherlike crowberry (*Empetrum nigrum*).

8 RAILROAD GRADE VIA PARK BUTTE TRAIL

Round trip ■ 7 miles
Difficulty ■ Moderate
Best flowers ■ July through August
Hikable ■ Mid-July through October
High point ■ 5500 feet
Elevation gain ■ 2200 feet

Getting there ■ From I-5 at Mount Vernon, get off at the exit for SR 20. Turn right (east) and proceed through Sedro-Woolley on SR 20 to paved Baker Lake–Grandy Road, between mileposts 82 and 83. Turn left. Drive 12.1 miles to Forest Service Road No. 13 (Sulphur Creek Road), turn right, and continue 5.1 miles to Mount Baker National Recreation Area, elevation 3364 feet. A Northwest Forest Pass is required.
Map ■ Green Trails No. 45 Hamilton
Information ■ Mount Baker Ranger District, phone (360) 856-5700

Admire the floral displays of Morovitz Meadows, hike to the Park Butte lookout, or climb along the crest of a moraine created by the Easton Glacier on Mount Baker.

The magic begins on Park Butte trail No. 603—it begins just to the left of the rest room. The trail passes a picnic area and crosses Sulphur Creek on a sturdy bridge. Just beyond is a trail junction for Scott Paul trail No. 603.1. Turn left and continue on trail No. 603—partly on boardwalk—as it passes small ponds and marshes in Schriebers Meadows. Find pink heather and, later in the season, blueberries. Other flowers to look for in July are purple violets, rosy spirea, asters, mountain ash, buttercups, partridgefoot, and hellebore. At 1 mile Rocky Creek is crossed on a suspension bridge, and a little farther along is another crossing. (Note: One of the bridges at 1 mile at Rocky Creek was washed away by the floods of 2003. In late summer, fording may not be a problem for most hikers. Call the Mount Baker Ranger District for details.)

Buttercup

Mount Baker from Park Butte

This crossing is more challenging and may require boulder hopping or fording. There may be a footbridge in place a little farther upstream.

The trail climbs a long mile through forest and crosses Lower Morovitz Meadows—in mid-July, bead lily was predominant. The trail gains approximately 1000 feet of elevation to another junction with the Scott Paul trail—stay left at all junctions with the Scott Paul trail. Continue (left) toward Upper Morovitz Meadows, Park Butte, and Railroad Grade. Trail No. 603 emerges from forest into Upper Morovitz Meadows; in July, snow patches were still lingering in the meadows. Islands of subalpine trees are scattered throughout the meadows, and Mount Baker comes into view.

From the crossing of Rocky Creek to the upper meadows, look for yellow violets, bleeding hearts, rosy spirea, lupine, Sitka valerian, and bead lily. From the upper meadow, the trail climbs to a ridge crest and T-junction: The Park Butte trail (left) climbs another mile to Park Butte lookout. Turn right on Railroad Grade trail No. 603.2—this is also a climber's approach to Mount Baker. In early July, this ridge may be partially under snow, but the route is obvious and signs point your way to Railroad Grade, toilets, and water. There are designated campsites along the ridge tucked away in trees. Follow the ridge as it approaches the moraine. A short staircase leads to the ridge crest. Follow the line of the ridge as it climbs toward Mount Baker as the narrow, airy trail weaves a serpentine path above the moraine. The path is bordered on one side by clumps of pink and white heather, and if you can tear your eyes away from Mount Baker, look down into the moraine, a waterfall, and the squiggle of the Scott Paul trail below.

The trail continues along the moraine to High Camp (it is well signed). Stop at any point and enjoy the show. Glaciers are noisy places—you may hear the thunder of an avalanche or rock fall or the voices of climbers farther away. Most hikers should not venture beyond High Camp. Past that point, mountaineering skills are required. Along the moraine I saw white and pink heather, penstemon, mountain ash, valerian, fireweed, phlox, partridgefoot, and even one lone dandelion. ■ K. S.

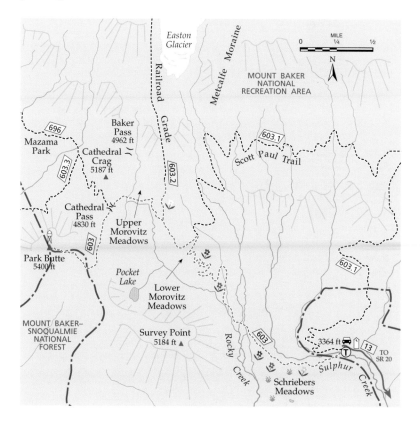

White and pink heather on Mount Baker

Art's Notes

Like other high country, the upper slopes of Mount Baker offer ample displays of heather meadows. The word "heather" calls for a quick botany lesson. Both words—heather and heath—refer to Old World species of two members of the heather family, *Ericaceae*. The single species of true heather, *Calluna vulgaris*, the Scot's heather, is famed in the lore of Scotland. Heath has two ancient Anglo-Saxon meanings: "wasteland," usually densely carpeted with some heathlike plant. The other meaning designates the vast clan, many species of *Erica*; all are heaths of Europe, and many of them are in southern Africa. To be sure, our Pacific Northwest heathers (or heaths) are in the heather family but are neither *Calluna* nor *Erica*. The commonest mountain heather in our high country is *Phyllodoce empetriformis*, with purple flowers. At higher and more exposed sites, look for a yellow heather, *Phyllodoce glanduliflora*. When the two mountain heathers are within pollination range of each other, expect to find a charming hybrid, *Phyllodoce intermedia*, with soft pink flowers. When your wildflower guidebooks refer to a white heather, it is *Cassiope mertensiana*, often intermixed with the purple heather. Unlike phyllodoces, with short needlelike leaves, the white heather has tiny scale leaves overlapping to form a squarish stem. Both genus names are out of Greek mythology: Phyllodoce was the sea nymph and Cassiope was the mother of Andromeda. And she also commemorates another heather, *Andromeda polifolia*. So there!

9 SAUK MOUNTAIN

Round trip	▪	**4 miles**
Difficulty	▪	Moderate
Best flowers	▪	Late June through September
Hikable	▪	Mid-June through October
High point	▪	5541 feet
Elevation gain	▪	1041 feet

Getting there ▪ Take exit 230 (SR 20, Cascade Loop) from I-5. From the exit, turn right and follow SR 20 through Sedro-Woolley and to Sauk Mountain Road No. 1030, on the left side of the highway, about 7 miles east of Concrete. Road No. 1030 is a steep, narrow, gravel road. Road junctions are not signed, but the main road is obvious. Stay right at an unmarked junction for Road No. 1036 at 7 miles and continue 0.5 mile to the parking area at 4500 feet. The trail begins on the east side of the parking lot; a rest room is located on the right side of the trail.

Maps ▪ Green Trails Nos. 78 Darrington and 46 Lake Shannon

Information ▪ Mount Baker Ranger District, phone (360) 856-5700

Get an early start for this hike—this is a popular trail, and July is the best time to see the wildflowers. In fact, the flowers will attract your attention before you even get to the trailhead. The last 2 miles of the road are bordered with Indian paintbrush, cow parsnip, and daisies. As the road continues to climb, the hanging meadows and rock towers of Sauk Mountain come into view.

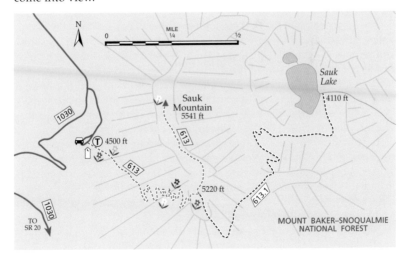

Fireweed on the Sauk Mountain trail above the Skagit River Valley

The views begin at the parking lot. For starters, look down to the Skagit Valley, almost a vertical mile below. Flowers begin immediately. Go slow and partake of both. There are close to thirty switchbacks on the trail as it climbs the southwest side of the mountain through steep flower meadows the first 1½ miles. Flowers line the trail as it continues toward the summit ridge. In fact, this trail can give you a false sense of security as it is so densely lined with vegetation. Keep in mind that this side of the mountain is an avalanche chute in winter, and in summer, rock fall is a potential hazard.

In mid-July, flowers to look for are: valerian, asters, cow parsnip, fireweed, mountain ash, Nootka rose, false hellebore, tiger lily, orange agoseris, penstemon, paintbrush, bistort, lupine, rosy spirea, columbine, lousewort, foamflower, wild strawberry, and vetch. At the higher elevations and near the summit, many of the same flowers can be seen but add to that list phlox, cinquefoil, and saxifrages.

The trail levels out on the southwest side of the peak before it veers left and follows the east side of the summit ridge toward the lookout site—the lookout was removed by the Forest Service a few years ago.

Once you are on the other side of the mountain, Sauk Lake comes into view. You'll come to an unsigned trail junction for Sauk Lake, a 1½-mile descent. Camping is allowed at Sauk Lake (4110 feet). Fishing is allowed—a Washington State fishing license is required.

From the Sauk Lake junction, the trail continues its rocky climb to the site of the lookout at 5541 feet. There are 360-degree views—Mount Baker is to the north, El Dorado is to the east, Sauk River and Pugh Mountain are to the south, to the southeast is Glacier Peak, and to the west, Puget Sound and the San Juan Islands. If you are up on your topography and/or have a map, you may be able to pick out the Park Butte lookout and the Railroad Grade on Mount Baker (Hike 8). All that remains of the lookout on Sauk Mountain are the views and clumps of saxifrage on the summit rocks.

Carry plenty of water. Other than snowmelt, there is none. In mid-July, one small snow patch lingered near the summit ridge, though ice axes were not needed. The Sauk Mountain trail is a hiker-only trail. ■ K. S.

Art's Notes

From such a richness of wildflowers, let me pick a pair to expound upon. False hellebore, a member of the lily family, is an exorbitant lily! In flower it can reach 6 feet tall, its many small green flowers surmounting a stem bearing deeply veined large leaves. This cornstalklike display prompts its other common name, corn lily. The green-flowered one of the high country is *Veratrum viride*. Its deeply buried corm (a large root stalk) produces a valued drug, a heart-depressant called veratrine. The underground corm had a remarkable tenacity on Mount St. Helens. Buried under many inches of tephra (volcanic ash), it survived to make a new season's flowering stalks the year after the 1980 eruption.

The familiar red-flowered paintbrush, *Castilleja miniata*, has, like most all other paintbrushes, an intriguing life history. They are semiparasites and need to penetrate, with their roots, a host plant. The tiny seeds, when germinated as seedlings, must find roots of a grass or other herb or they cannot survive. Though they can do the green-plant photosynthesis, they must make this initial parasitism to survive.

This curious phenomenon of partial parasitism in Indian paintbrushes must have evolved more than once. It occurs in other members of the snapdragon family *(Scrophulariaceae)* as well as in unrelated wildflowers. Indeed, we can find all degrees of linkages, plant to plant (as in mistletoes) or plant to fungus (mycorrhizal root connections to conifers, in coralroot orchids or Indian pipe) in the plant kingdom. Nature's interconnectedness is universal. As John Muir so aptly said: "When we try to pick out anything by itself, we find it hitched to everything else in the universe."

10 ┆ MAPLE PASS

Round trip ■	**7 miles**
Difficulty ■	Moderate
Best flowers ■	Mid-July to mid-August
Hikable ■	Mid-July to mid-October
High point ■	6970 feet
Elevation gain ■	2100 feet

Getting there ■ From Marblemount, travel east on SR 20 (North Cascades Scenic Highway) for 51 miles to the Rainy Pass Picnic Area, near milepost 158. From Winthrop, travel west 35 miles on SR 20. The trail begins from the south end of the picnic area near the Rainy Lake Nature Trail, elevation 4855 feet. A Northwest Forest Pass is required.

Maps ■ Green Trails Nos. 49 Mount Logan and 50 Washington Pass

Information ■ Methow Valley Ranger District, phone (509) 996-4000

There are no shortages of great hikes from the North Cascades Scenic Highway. The Maple Pass Loop rules supreme among them. In 7 short miles, this trail will treat you to old-growth forests, alpine lakes, alpine meadows, open ridges, and stunning North Cascades vistas. Throughout most of the summer, you will see along this trail a fantastic floral show as well.

I prefer to hike this loop counterclockwise. As the ascent is more gradual

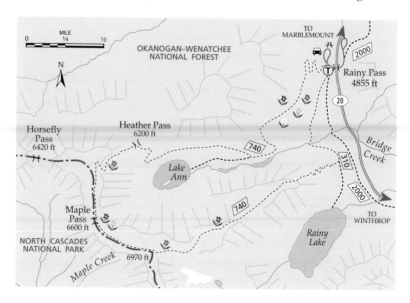

Lake Ann from the Maple Pass trail

this way, it allows me to slowly pass through the various zones. Without an abrupt transition from forest to meadow I'm given an extended arrangement of blooms and blossoms—and a longer time to appreciate them. However, the descent is steep via this direction, so adjust your hiking plans to your physical needs.

The well-beaten and well-maintained trail begins immediately in a stately, ancient forest of fir and hemlock. Huckleberry bushes crowd the understory. In early summer find the usual culprits: Twinflower, spring beauty, and vanilla leaf bring life to the forest floor. Elderberry, gooseberry, currant, hellebore, and thimbleberry make their presence known as well.

As you continue through the forest you'll pass several marshy areas saturated with columbine and marsh marigold. Within ½ mile you'll come to a large opening in the forest; let the flower show begin. By midsummer, meadow parsley, cow parsnip, fireweed, aster, thistle, yarrow, pearly everlasting, columbine, and bluebells are in full bloom.

Just beyond 1½ miles you'll reach a junction with the Lake Ann trail (5300 feet), a beautiful side trip. The loop trail continues upward, gradually gaining elevation and breaking out into the subalpine world. As you work your way around the Lake Ann cirque and cross Heather Pass (6200 feet) on the way to even higher Maple Pass (6600 feet), the flowers, along with the scenery, intensify.

In early summer, melting snowfields near Heather Pass unveil dazzling displays of glacier lilies. Later, the flowering heather steals the show. Lewis

Horse thistle

monkeyflower, paintbrush, and penstemon add reds and purples to the alpine landscape. In the jumbled rocks find arnicas and cinquefoil. The pikas will help point them out, along with their favorites, lupine.

Higher up along the ridge, aster, partridgefoot, valerian, harebells, spirea, anemone, lousewort, and bistort line the trail. In late summer, deep purple gentians burst from hiding. Alpine larches await their turn to add the final color before the snows fly.

The trail enters Maple Pass and then works its way to a 6970-foot high point. Respect the meadows here; lots of trampling has occurred. Stop and savor the views before making your descent. Glacier Peak and its icy neighbors dominate in the southwest. Corteo, Black, Frisco, Whistler, and Tower ring the immediate surroundings.

The loop makes a steep and rapid retreat off the ridge but not without first traversing yet more glorious meadows and flower gardens. It's then a quick descent through hemlock, heather, and huckleberry back to the start at Rainy Pass. ■ C. R.

Art's Notes

The completion of the North Cascades Highway (SR 20) in 1972, from Newhalem to Early Winters, opened up to easy road access some of the most spectacular high country in the West. Much of this grandeur has been captured in word and picture by an early protagonist of the highway's country, Dr. Fred Darvill Jr., of Mount Vernon. His latest encyclopedic *Hiking the North Cascades* (Stackpole Books 1998) is much more than a hiking guide. Darvill's introductory chapters delve deep into the geology, flora, and fauna of the region, from Snoqualmie Pass to the Canadian border. It can make a valuable companion to this guidebook.

Most everywhere at midaltitudes you will meet with a tall, showy thistle. Far from being a noxious alien weed, horse thistle, *Cirsium edule*, is a well-behaved native. It likes moister areas, along with Sitka valerian, corn lily (false hellebore), and red-flowered columbine. Flower heads of this prickly morsel are gingerly browsed by horses. It is said that they unfurl their lips and then snip off the tasty purple heads—"composite candy," no less.

11 SLATE PEAK

Round trip ■ **1 mile**
Difficulty ■ Easy
Best flowers ■ July through August
Hikable ■ July to mid-October
High point ■ 7100 feet
Elevation gain ■ 200 feet to Slate Peak lookout

Getting there ■ Drive to Mazama on SR 20 (11 miles west of Winthrop). Continue 1 mile to an intersection and turn left on Harts Pass Road (Forest Service Road No. 5400), also known as Lost Lake Road. Pass a general store and post office. Pavement ends at 7 miles. Pass a junction for the Riverbend Campground at 9 miles. About 2 miles past Riverbend is a 0.5-mile stretch that is rocky, narrow, and exposed. Continue to Harts Pass (6198 feet), 19 miles from Mazama, and turn right onto Slate Peak Road (Forest Service Road No. 5400-600). Drive 1.8 miles to the Slate Peak trailhead, 6900 feet. The road is gated a short distance from the lookout. All trailers are prohibited on Harts Pass Road. A Northwest Forest Pass is required.

Maps ■ Green Trails Nos. 49 Mount Logan and 50 Washington Pass
Information ■ Methow Valley Ranger District, phone (509) 996-4000

This is a long drive for a short hike, but it is worth it. Plan on at least 2 days if you can; 3 days is better. You can camp at Riverbend or Meadows Campgrounds or stay at a motel in Mazama or Winthrop.

Lupine

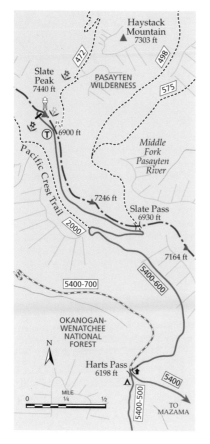

Harts Pass is on the crest of the Cascades, 20 miles south of the Canadian border, but winter comes early and this region is open for only a brief period after the snow melts and before winter brings fresh accumulations.

Slate Peak is more of a side trip than an actual hike, but you can hike other trails in the area for more mileage, including the Pacific Crest Trail in either direction. In a heavy snow year Slate Peak Road may be gated and you may need to walk a portion of the road. Look for flowers and snail fossils in outcroppings along the road.

The views from the summit of Slate Peak are excellent. The peaks of the North Cascades rise in every direction—Crater Mountain, Mount Baker, Jack Mountain, Azurite Peak, and Silver Star. Nestled below the peaks are deep-forested valleys of the West Fork of the Pasayten River and Slate Creek. An interpretative sign at the lookout helps identify the peaks.

You may run into members of an outdoor organization such as the North Cascades Institute near Slate Peak. They often conduct wildflower workshops and seminars at Harts Pass. The subalpine areas and meadows near Slate Peak are ideal for locating and identifying flowers and learning how living organisms adapt to changing and harsh conditions. For example, willows grow so close to the ground here you'll need to get down on your hands and knees to see them. It was in these very meadows that I learned that moss campion is not a moss but a flower.

On the road to Slate Peak, notice how small the trees and plants are at these high elevations. It takes them a long time to grow, and small trees can be hundreds of years old. Subalpine trees adapt to inhospitable growing conditions by spreading out across the ground.

In July the meadows near Slate Peak are lush with flowers—cinquefoil, spotted saxifrages, white bog orchids, and moss campion. Also look for western pasque flower, asters, paintbrush, bird's-beak lousewort, fleabanes, and speedwells. ■ K. S.

Mount Ballard near Harts Pass

Art's Notes

I first visited this impressive pass and peak in 1950, daring to pass over Dead Horse Turn, an eroding and precarious stretch of gravel road traversing a sheer drop-off. It is now a much safer traverse. But the country beyond was—and still is—a world-class splendor. In those days there was an active Forest Service lookout structure at Slate Peak, which is no longer there. Some of my students slept overnight, just outside the lookout, for the rapturous sunrise. The surrounding parkland is alive with flowers from mid-July as the heavy snows melt. Vivid is my memory of first sighting the yellow mountain avens, *Dryas drummondii*—rare in Washington. Look for it on the west-facing slope just below Slate Peak summit, a ground-hugging rock plant with deeply embossed leaves.

A surprise is in store for the hiker en route to Slate Peak. Look for rock outcrops with fossils—marine snails, no less. Yes, this high place was once below sea level eons ago.

The timbered atolls here have three conifers, whitebark pine, subalpine fir, and even Engelmann spruce. The low-growing common juniper *(Juniperus communis)* can be found hereabouts. Close to timberline, the Krummholz gnarled tree form reappears. Above tree line, woody plants persist, mostly as heathers and prostrate juniper. Look for another woody gem, the dwarf willow, *Salix arctica*; flat on the ground, it reveals its willow kinship with erect fluffy male or female flower stalks (catkins). For the ultimate in a quest for the unusual, seek the rare steer's head, *Dicentra uniflora*, a tiny relative of bleeding heart.

12 WINDY PASS VIA PACIFIC CREST TRAIL

Round trip ■	7 miles to Windy Pass
Difficulty ■	Moderate
Best flowers ■	July through August
Hikable ■	July through mid-October
High point ■	6900 feet (Windy Pass)
Elevation gain ■	500 feet in, 1000 feet out

Getting there ■ Drive to Mazama on SR 20 (11 miles west of Winthrop). Continue 1 mile to an intersection and turn left on Harts Pass Road (Forest Service Road No. 5400), also known as Lost Lake Road. Pass a general store and post office. Pavement ends at 7 miles. Pass a junction for the Riverbend Campground at 9 miles. In about 2 miles past Riverbend is a 0.5-mile stretch that is rocky, narrow, and exposed. Continue to Harts Pass (6198 feet) and turn right onto Slate Peak Road (Forest Service Road No. 5400-600). Find the Pacific Crest Trail trailhead and parking at a switchback (1.5 mile, elevation 6800 feet). All trailers are prohibited on Harts Pass Road beyond Ballard Campground. A Northwest Forest Pass is required.

Maps ■ Green Trails Nos. 50 Washington Pass and 18 Poseidon Peak

Information ■ Methow Ranger District, phone (509) 996-4003, or Methow Valley Visitor Center, phone (509) 996-4000

Since getting to Harts Pass involves a long drive on a narrow, winding road, you can combine this hike with a visit to Slate Peak (Hike 11) for a 2- or 3-day trip to make it even more worthwhile. I suggest car camping at Riverbend or Meadows Campgrounds and hiking to Windy Pass on one day and visiting Slate Peak the next. Harts Pass is on the crest of the Cascades, 20 miles south of the Canadian border, but this region is open for only a brief period after the snow melts and before winter brings new snow. It is not uncommon for the Harts Pass Guard Station (6198 feet) to close shortly after Labor Day, depending on conditions. By August, the mornings have a nip in the air and tarns may be frozen. Outdoor organizations such as the North Cascades Institute often conduct wildflower workshops and seminars in the meadows near Harts Pass and Slate Peak.

For the best flowers and hiking, Windy Pass is highly recommended. Some hikers swear it is one of the best flower walks in the Cascades. The hike begins on the Pacific Crest Trail and is accessed at the first switchback on Slate Peak Road, elevation 6800 feet. From the trailhead you will be heading north. In the first ½ mile, the PCT climbs a meadow shelf and contours the steep slope of Slate Peak before descending to Benson Basin and camps. You can see the scars of gold mining days from the north side of Slate Peak.

From Benson Basin, the trail climbs to a spur ridge and follows on and near the crest to Buffalo Pass (6550 feet) and onward to another spur and high point. The site of Barron is below Buffalo Pass. It is hard to imagine that a hundred years ago, thousands of people were living below in the town of Barron.

The trail descends to Windy Pass at 6257 feet, with views and campsites. There are flowers all along the trail and in the meadows during peak season. The meadows, in fact, extend for miles and miles. And so do the tamaracks.

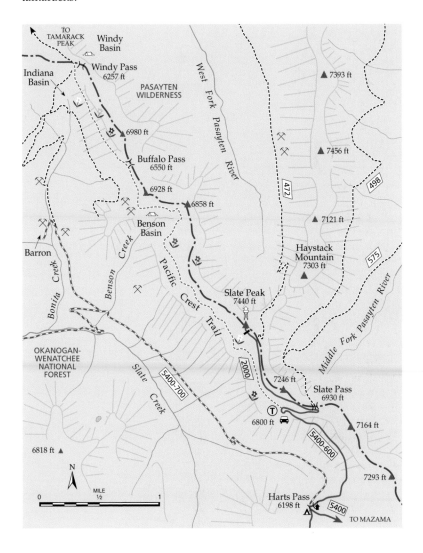

The Pacific Crest Trail near Windy Pass

You can take side trips into Indiana Basin, though some of that is still private property and has been bulldozed in the past (mining laws make it almost impossible for the Forest Service to protect the land). However, there is very little mining activity today on the old claims, and the forest is gradually reclaiming the town of Barron. Don't spend too much time here if you find it is depressing—perhaps it is better for your soul to explore other delights.

Continue north through flowers and meadows to Tamarack Peak and

Art's Notes

Northward from Harts Pass and Slate Peak, the Pacific Crest Trail passes through subalpine flower gardens of unending beauty. Nearly all those seen at Harts Pass follow you to Windy Pass and beyond—to Canada! The tamarack mentioned here is the elegant subalpine or Lyall's larch, *Larix lyallii*. It is only found in the subalpine country, a close kin to the midelevation western larch *(Larix occidentalis)*. Fall in larch country puts on a superb display of golden foliage before winter nudity sets in. Known to many alpine hikers is the autumnal larch panorama witnessed lavishly in the Alpine Lakes area of the Stuart Range.

great views at 7290 feet (an easy scramble), or continue on the PCT, descending to Windy Basin and more camps.

There are good views all along the trail, beginning with Gardner and Silver Star Mountains, Golden Horn, Azurite Peak, and Mount Ballard. Jack and Crater Mountains can be seen toward the west—even part of Mount Baker. Bring a map to identify them. Easterly is the high and remote country of the Pasayten Wilderness, and, of course, if you keep going on the PCT, you'll end up in Canada. ■ K. S.

POLLINATION IN THE HIGH COUNTRY

The spectacular floral displays in the high country bedazzle the human observer. Yet all this floral diversity and prodigality serves but one biological purpose—perpetuation of each species, generation after generation. Flowers are reproductive organs, designed to produce offspring via seeds. Two crucial events precede seed production: pollination and fertilization. Pollination is the transfer of pollen (male sex cells) to the egg-containing floral ovaries. Since most flowers have both pollen- and egg-yielding organs (stamens and ovary), the simplest act of pollination can occur within a single flower—self-pollination. Some mountain flowers indulge in this internal mating. But most often, cross-pollination (outbreeding) is the rule. Why the bias toward outcrossing? Simply put, it assures that greater hereditary variation passes to offspring for maintaining and enhancing adaptive survivability.

Cross-pollination is achieved by either wind transfer of pollen or by animals, mostly insects. Wind pollination is the mode for grasses and their kin (sedges and rushes); no showy flowers here, just sex organs freely exposed to the air for wafting pollen.

The rich mosaic of floral color and form is matched by a wealth of flower visitors—insects and some birds. The diversity of insects in the open parkland at Paradise, and elsewhere in the high country, runs the full gamut: from tiny gnats and mosquitoes to flies, bees, beetles, grasshoppers, and butterflies. Insect visitors to flowers seek either pollen or nectar—life-sustaining food. Some insects also rely on wildflower herbage for food; herbivory is easily observed. Leaves or flower stalks show obvious signs of being "preyed upon." The larval stages of lepidopterans (moths and butterflies, as caterpillars) rely on herbivory to prepare for adulthood.

Form and color of flowers often determine the kind of insect visitor. Buttercups and cinquefoils, with their yellow saucer-shaped regular flowers, tend to be visited by insect "generalists"—beetles and flies that flit from one kind of open flower to the next. When the flower is

Hello there! Grasshopper on a lupine petal

tubular and asymmetric (lower vs. upper lip), like that of penstemons or monkeyflowers (*Mimulus* species), bees, hoverflies, and butterflies are the likely pollinators, seeking nectar or pollen. Most specialized are the intricately twisted floral tubes of the louseworts (*Pedicularis* species). All five species on Mount Rainier are visited by several different bumblebees.

Anyone watching a patch of red columbines long enough will delight in the visits to these artfully contrived flowers (tubular, long nectar-spurs) by hummingbirds. The observer may even witness hummingbirds defending the columbine patch against other intruding hummers. These tiny nectar-feeders also visit the purple monkshood (*Aconitum columbianum*) and horse thistle (*Cirsium edule*). And these bird-visited flowers get cross-pollinated by pollen-laden bird beaks.

The pollination story in our high country is a piece of a larger drama. Ecologists now view the flower–pollinator linkage as a prime example of coevolution—both flower and animal visitor matching adaptively each other's structure and function. Such mutual pattern-matching is the result of a survival-driven adaptive evolution over stretches of deep time. For more on pollination ecology, see Kruckeberg 1991, chapter 8. ■ A. R. K.

13 TIFFANY MOUNTAIN

Round trip ■	**6 miles**
Difficulty ■	Moderate
Best flowers ■	July through early August
Hikable ■	Late June to mid-October
High point ■	8242 feet
Elevation gain ■	1740 feet

Getting there ■ From Winthrop, drive north on County Road 9137 (East Chewuch River Road). Drive 6.5 miles to just before the road crosses the river. Turn right here, on paved Forest Service Road No. 37. Enter national forest in 1 mile; pavement ends in 7.5 miles. After 13 miles, come to a junction with Forest Service Road No. 39. Turn left, and follow this washboard-ridden road for 3.2 miles to a cattle guard at Freezeout Pass, elevation 6500 feet. The trail begins on the east side of the road, with parking for about five vehicles along the road. A Northwest Forest Pass is required.

Map ■ Green Trails No. 53 Tiffany Mountain

Information ■ Tonasket Ranger District, phone (509) 486-2186

Perhaps nowhere else in the Cascades can a hiker saunter to an 8000-foot peak with such little effort. With a trailhead at 6500 feet, Tiffany Mountain requires very little sweat to make it to its 8242-foot summit. All the better, for you'll want to spend as much time as possible stopping and smelling the flowers along the way. The entire trail is lined with them, from forest to meadow to the grassy and rocky summit.

The trail begins on Freezeout Ridge in an open and mature forest of lodgepole and whitebark pine. Plenty of sunlight reaches the forest floor; come in late July, when the entire trail is lined with lupine, providing a purple pathway to the peak. Arnica and daisies add their golden touch. In time, clusters of valerian help whiten the forest floor.

As the forest thins along the lupine carpet, asters, louseworts, groundsel, and fireweed help diversify the colors. In 1 mile you'll enter a gorgeous parkland—buckwheat and other golden grasses and sedges engulf clumps of fir and pine. The summit cone of Tiffany comes into view as well as the surrounding highlands.

As you climb higher into the alpine meadows, on first inspection it may appear as if many of the flowering plants have made a retreat. Winds can be severe at these altitudes, and the western slope takes a pounding. But as you hike along this ever more breathtakingly beautiful trail, you'll begin to notice the tenacity of alpine flora. Protected behind lichen-encrusted boulders, and hiding in small depressions, are wildflowers. Scope them out.

Stonecrop

You'll spot bistorts, larkspur, yarrow, paintbrush, shootingstars, columbine, penstemon, pussytoes, saxifrage, and stonecrop. Look too for clumps of the showy, white mountain avens. Of course, the lupines are here, too. Being on the eastern fringe of the Cascades, where the sun shines more than the rain falls, Tiffany has its share of desert-steppe plants, too. Particularly striking are the clusters of junipers clinging to weather-beaten rocks and outcrops.

After 2½ miles you'll come to a junction (7700 feet). Take a left and head ½ mile to the airy summit. Now it's time to look at the budding landscape. You'll get a panorama of Pasayten peaks to the north. The golden Okanogan Highlands shine in the east. To the south and west are mountains for as far as you can see.

If you want, you can continue

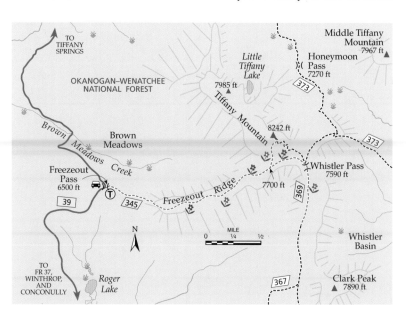

Hikers on the summit of Tiffany Mountain

hiking another mile to Whistler Pass and along the North Summit trail for 2 miles to Clark Peak's open slopes. The lupines will help point the way. ■ C. R.

Art's Notes

I'd come back here any time. Getting there is a good part of the sheer pleasure of this Okanogan country. After leaving the lower Chewuk (a.k.a. Chewak) River country, you will drive along a high plateau where lodgepole pine dominates. Bountiful along this stretch of road, just before the Tiffany Mountain trailhead, are the abundant shrubby cinquefoil *(Potentilla fruticosa)*. I know of nowhere else in our state where it is so abundant. It is easy to recognize, with its showy yellow flowers bedecking a 3–4-foot-high shrub. Up close, note the "cinquefoil" foliage, small leaves dissected into five "fingers"—narrow lobes. Like other cosmopolites in our flora (such as twinflower, moss campion, and bunchberry), shrubby cinquefoil spans the north temperate zone of the Old and New Worlds. And you may recognize it as an old garden friend: It is a popular ornamental for dry, sunny spots.

My place names book (Hitchman 1985) links the mountain's name with the famous New York Tiffany family. William Tiffany, with his two brothers, camped for two years at the base of the mountain. William was killed in the Spanish-American War.

Tiffany Mountain has been recognized by forest ecologists as representative of a high-elevation ecosystem and was accorded Research Natural Area status. Notable are the mature stands of subalpine fir and whitebark pine.

14 | DISAPPOINTMENT PEAK

Round trip ■ 5 miles
Difficulty ■ Moderate
Best flowers ■ Mid-May to mid-July
Hikable ■ May through October
High point ■ 7160 feet
Elevation gain ■ 1200 feet

Getting there ■ From downtown Tonasket, look for a sign saying "Many Lakes Recreation Area, Loomis, Nighthawk." Turn here (west) and follow the Loomis Highway for 16 miles, to the small village of Loomis. Turn right (north) on County Road 9425 (Loomis–Oroville Road) and follow it for 2 miles. Turn left on Forest Service Road No. 39 (Toats Coulee Road) and head west 7.7 miles to a Y intersection just beyond a cattle guard. Bear right (signed "Cold Springs Campground") onto a rough but drivable gravel road for 6.5 miles to Cold Springs Campground. On the way to the campground watch for unmarked road junctions. Bear right at the first intersection, left at the second intersection, and left again at the third intersection. Just beyond the campground and before the entrance to a picnic area, find trailhead parking on the right, elevation 6200 feet. The trail begins on an old gated mine road.

Map ■ Green Trails No. 21 Horseshoe Basin

Information ■ Washington State Department of Natural Resources—Colville, phone (509) 684-7474

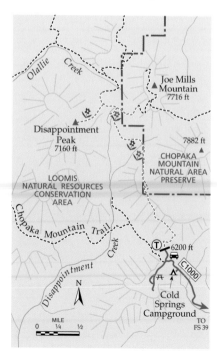

Until very recently, the Loomis State Forest was known by very few. Most of this wild country, which contains some of the best lynx habitat in the Lower 48, was slated to be logged. Thanks to a well-funded and well-publicized campaign by a coalition of conservationists, 25,000 acres of the Loomis has been saved,

Moss campion

reclassified as the Loomis Natural Resources Conservation Area.

Bordering the Pasayten Wilderness to the west and British Columbia's Snowy Mountain Provincial Park to the north, the Loomis is within good company and it deserves your attention. This is a land of incredible diversity—the transition zone between the Cascades and the Okanogan Highlands. Rare fauna, much flora, and a handful of endangered flowering plants can be found here.

One of the easiest and more rewarding hikes in the Loomis is the 2½-mile trip around the Disappointment Creek Basin. Despite the name, you won't be. Following an old mine road, the "trail" winds its way to a 7160-foot summit on the shoulder of Chopaka Mountain, referred to locally as Disappointment Peak.

En route, the "trail" traverses a special DNR Natural Area Preserve, where it is imperative that you do not leave the trail. On the summit of Disappointment, however, feel free to roam away.

The trail begins in high-altitude lodgepole pine forest. Views begin almost instantly to the high peaks of the Horseshoe Basin area. By midsummer the forest floor is streaked with colors. Hawksbill, paintbrush, lupine, and aster brighten your way.

You'll soon drop down about 200 feet to a damp area of seeps and springs, an oasis in a dry alpine area. Look here for gentians, cinquefoils, marsh marigolds, wild strawberries, and rare sedges and moonworts.

After a mile, you'll cross Disappointment Creek (6500 feet) and enter a forest of Engelmann spruce and whitebark pine. Soon afterward you'll break out into an open meadow lined with sagebrush. In the Loomis, sage meets fir: Sage creeps as high as 7500 feet here on southern exposures.

You'll now go from admiring bog plants to desert plants. Look for desert bluebells, sagebrush buttercups, desert parsley, and desert shootingstars.

In about 2 miles you'll come to a spring and a barbed wire fence (6850 feet). Turn left here and continue on the obvious road-trail. Reach a high saddle and leave the road-trail for tread leading to the open summit to your west, Disappointment Peak. From this Loomis Country lookout, admire the surrounding giants that not many people know: Chopaka, Hurley, Joe Mills, Goodenough, and Snowshoe. Admire, too, the special flowering flora of this unique area. ■ C. R.

Art's Notes

This has been a favorite high-country destination of mine for many years. On the summit, one feels somehow adrift between the Pasayten country of the North Cascades and the Okanogan Highlands and the Kettle Range to the east. Disappointment Peak (a.k.a. Chopaka Mountain) is isolated, yet its flora is a mix of Cascade and Northern Rockies plants. The treeless summit beckons the hiker to revel in the vast views: Horseshoe Basin is to the west and the valley of the Similkameen River is to the northeast. Then, at your feet find a gaggle of alpine lovelies. Moss campion *(Silene acaulis)*, which you can see at Harts Pass, has a snug home here. Nowhere else in my vagabonding in the Northwest have I seen trapper's tea *(Ledum glandulosum)* as a near-dominant low shrub; in the alpine, it is an evergreen relative of Labrador tea *(L. groenlandicum)*, with white flowers. *Phyllodoce empetriformis,* the purple-flowered one, can be found close by the *P. glanduliflora*, the yellow-flowered mountain heather. In this connubial tryst, expect to find their hybrid, *P. X intermedia.*

In the saddle between Chopaka Mountain and Joe Mills Mountain, I found a local outcrop of serpentine soil and rock (high in iron, magnesium, and nickel). I was immodestly pleased to find Kruckeberg's holly fern, *Polystichum kruckebergii,* nestled in its crevices.

So stay a while here; the campground at nearby Cold Springs is a fine base camp and will regale you after the hike with its own rich flora.

By the way, Chopaka means, in First Peoples' tongue, "high mountain."

15 COPPER BUTTE

Round trip	■	**9½ miles**
Difficulty	■	Moderate
Best flowers	■	Late May through July
Hikable	■	Mid-May through October
High point	■	7140 feet
Elevation gain	■	2390 feet

Getting there ■ From the junction of SR 20 and SR 21, 2.5 miles east of Republic, head north on SR 21. Follow it for just under 3 miles to a four-way junction. Turn right (east) on the gravel County Road 284 (Fish Hatchery Road). Just shy of 3 miles, come to a major junction; turn left. At the Echo Bay Mine, bear right on the less-obvious road, which soon becomes Forest Service Road No. 2152 upon entering the national forest. This is open-range country—watch for sauntering cattle. Follow this narrow but good gravel road for 3 miles to Forest Service Road No. 2040. Bear left and follow Forest Service Road No. 2040 for 5 miles to the junction with Forest Service Road No. 2040-250. Turn right here; a sign indicates the way to Marcus trail No. 8. In 1.5 miles, come to a small clearing; a former log yard is on your left. This is the trailhead, marked by a small sign. Ample parking space, elevation 4750 feet.

Map ■ USGS Copper Butte

Information ■ Republic Ranger District, phone (509) 775-3305

Rising more than 7000 feet in the sun-baked Okanogan Highlands are Washington's forgotten mountains, the Kettle Range. Named after the major river that snakes around them, the Kettles form an imposing wall midway between the craggy Cascades to the west and the rolling Selkirks to the east. Lofty but gentle, these mountains are graced with miles of trails.

Occupying the transition zones between the Cascades and Rockies, the steppe and interior highlands, the Kettles contain incredible biological diversity. A hike to the range's highest summit, 7140-foot Copper Butte, makes for a wonderful introduction to this isolated range. By way of the Marcus trail you'll traverse old-growth, fire-succession, and subalpine forests, as well as alpine meadows.

Especially meadows. Nearly half of the Marcus trail climbs gracefully through some of the largest and most prolific alpine meadows in the entire range. And where there are meadows, there are flowers—a score of varieties and a near-infinite number of blossoms.

The trail begins in an open forest of giant ponderosa pine and Douglas fir. Spring comes earlier to the Kettles than the Cascades, but it can still be wet. The warming sun, with ample May and June precipitation, creates

Larkspur

perfect conditions for producing wildflowers. Along the forest floor, look for arnica, wood violets, bedstraw, gooseberries, pearhip rose, bitterbrush, and ninebark.

After ½ mile you'll enter a large area that succumbed to a fire in the early 1990s. A miniforest of lodgepole pines is slowly gaining on the blackened and silver snags. By early summer, waist-high fireweeds bombard the burn with a profusion of purple. By midsummer, the fireweeds begin

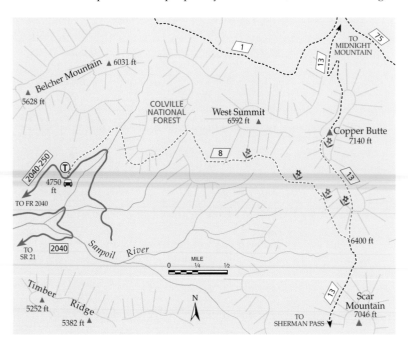

yielding to the pearly everlastings now whitening the charred forest floor. Shootingstars also brighten the area.

Re-enter mature forest, now dominated by larch and subalpine fir; look for arrow-leaved groundsel. By this time you'll have hiked nearly 2 miles and will find yourself at the beginning of those promised meadows. In early to midsummer you'll be hard-pressed to even notice the native grasses: They'll be overrun by the oranges, purples, yellows, and reds of a dazzling floral show. Here you'll find bistorts, lupines, yarrows, roses, golden peas, asters, buttercups, locoweed, bluebells, and paintbrush. If you miss the early show, the harebells perform late into the summer.

You'll share the meadows with some free-ranging and grazing cows, and they, too, appreciate the flowers. After 3½ miles, you'll come to an intersection with Kettle Crest trail No. 13 (6400 feet). Turn left and head north 1¼ easy miles to the summit of Copper Butte. Once home to a fire lookout, its far-reaching views still remain. If you can lift your head up from admiring the summit floral arrangement—gaze up and down the Kettle crest and realize there's an entire mountain range out there just waiting to be explored. ■ C. R.

Art's Notes

As long as you are this far northeast of most anywhere in our state, plan to stay a while, a night or two either in Forest Service campgrounds or lodging in Republic. Any naturalist visiting the Republic vicinity must pay homage to the plant life of "deep time." The Republic area is the epicenter of a rich fossil flora and fauna, where paleontologists have struck it rich. Early Tertiary times (60 M.Y.A.—million years ago) was an age when the first ancestors of modern plant and animal life emerged out of the earlier Dinosaur Ages of the late Mesozoic. The harvest of fossils hereabouts is on display at a museum in Republic. Also, there are places where you can delve into the semitropical past. With a geologist's pick-and-hammer you can dig into Eocene times for mementos of this subtropical past life. Most often your lucky strike with hammer will yield leaf impressions, mostly of trees that now live in eastern Asia: maples, alders, magnolias, and conifers, like dawn redwood. You may confirm your finds either at the fossil museum in Republic or back in Seattle at the Burke Museum on the University of Washington campus.

For identification of plants along the Copper Butte trail, there are two good guides: *Plants of Southern British Columbia*, a Lone Pine Publishing book by Parish, Coupe, and Lloyd. It works well for eastern Washington and adjacent Idaho. For the more determined naturalist, try "The Plants of the Kettle Range" by C. R. Annable and P. M. Peterson. It was published as an Occasional Paper of the Washington Native Plant Society, 1988.

16 ┊ WAPALOOSIE MOUNTAIN

Round trip ■	6 miles
Difficulty ■	Moderate
Best flowers ■	May to mid-July
Hikable ■	May through October
High point ■	7018 feet
Elevation gain ■	2000 feet

Getting there ■ From Republic, head east on SR 20 for 21 miles to Forest Service Road No. 2030 (Albion Hill Road). The road is located 4 miles past Sherman Pass on your left (north). (From the east, Forest Service Road No. 2030 is approximately 22 miles from Kettle Falls.) Follow Forest Service Road No. 2030, a winding but good gravel road, for 3.3 miles to the trailhead, elevation 5000 feet. The trailhead is well signed and begins in a small campground with a privy but no piped water.

Map ■ USGS Copper Butte

Information ■ Three Rivers Ranger District, phone (509) 738-7700

The finest meadows on the west slopes of the Kettle Range belong to Copper Mountain, but nearby Wapaloosie Mountain can lay claim to the best meadows on the east slope. Although the two peaks are separated by only one other summit along the Kettle crest, they are uniquely different.

Wapaloosie's eastern slope, which its trail ascends, has a southeastern exposure. It takes the full brunt of the Okanogan sun. Its soils are well

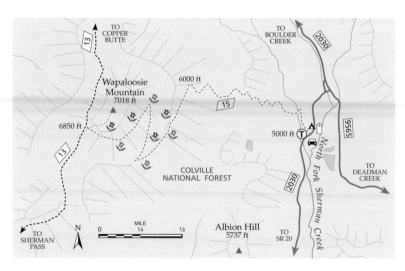

The Kettle Range

drained and gravelly. It is on this peak and this trail where a dramatic eco-system transition can be witnessed—where sagebrush meets lodgepole pine and subalpine fir. The eastern side of the Kettles sees little range activity, too—native fescue grasses proliferate.

You'll want to hike Wapaloosie for the early season blossoms. As soon as the snow melts by midspring, arrowleaf balsamroot speckles the mountainside bright yellow. Arnica, yellow violets, and mountain dandelions pitch in. In due time the floral guard is changed; alpine lupine takes over to punctuate the soft greens and flaxen yellows of the sedges and grasses with various shades of violet. Trailing harebells make sure that the meadows get one more dose of purple before turning drab by late summer.

Wapaloosie Mountain trail No. 15 is well maintained and easy to follow. It starts off through a uniform stand of lodgepole pine, quintessential interior montane forest. In ½ mile you'll skirt a large blown-down section of forest. Fireweed and other early succession species soak up the sunlight here from this hole in the canopy.

In another mile you'll break out of the canopy and begin your odyssey across Wapaloosie's sprawling meadows (6000 feet). The trail steepens at times but then eases, making long switchbacks across the broad slope. Views are fantastic, ranging from British Columbia's Rossland Range to the Abercrombie–Hooknose highlands. The Twin Sisters, Mack Mountain, and King Mountain stand out like emerald sentinels guarding the eastern flank of the Kettle crest. Of course, your nose may very well be too close to the ground to even notice.

Fireweed

Asters, lupine, fireweed, yarrow, and paintbrush create a mosaic of colors. Buckwheat, hawkweed, rabbitbrush, and spirea share space with clumps of sagebrush that creep toward the summit.

The Wapaloosie trail reaches the Kettle crest (6850 feet) in 2¾ miles. From this point you can venture north or south through an open forest of whitebark pine and subalpine fir along Kettle Crest trail No.13 or make the easy ascent to Wapaloosie's 7018-foot summit; just head northeast through the meadows. It's a 10-minute walk to the broad high point. Try not to step on any flowers on your way to the top. ■ C. R.

Art's Notes

Here in the high country of the dry interior of eastern Washington, a distinctive mix of plant life can occur. Sagebrush and rabbitbrush consort with pines and Douglas fir. Elsewhere in the Columbia Plateau these two shrubs dominate in treeless expanses at lower elevations.

In nearly every habitat east of the Cascades, expect to find one or more kinds of buckwheats. These wildlings in the genus *Eriogonum* are indeed kin to the Eurasian crop plant buckwheat *(Fagopyrum esculentum)* in the buckwheat family *(Polygonaceae)*. Our wild buckwheats can range in size from compact ground-hugging mounds to 3-foot-tall wands of flowering stalks. Two low-growing ones, the sulfur buckwheat *Eriogonum umbellatum* and the gray-leaved *E. ovalifolium,* like open rocky habitats (known as lithosols, "rock soils"). The tall *Eriogonum elatum,* reminding one of the garden baby's breath, also likes rocky shallow soils in openings in the woods. Flower colors are either yellow *(E. umbellatum)* or mostly white. These three buckwheats are herbaceous perennials but border on the habit of shrublets. First Peoples harvested for food their hard, triangular nutlets.

At first glance, the name of this preeminent Kettle Range peak should have an apt First Peoples origin and meaning. Yet it seems that a forest ranger used "wapa-loosie" for most any outstanding natural feature (Hitchman 1985).

Opposite: The North Cascades as seen from Mount Dickerman (Hike 20)

THE MOUNTAIN LOOP HIGHWAY & US 2

17 GREEN MOUNTAIN

Round trip ■	**8 miles**
Difficulty ■	Strenuous
Best flowers ■	July through August
Hikable ■	Late June through October
High point ■	6500 feet
Elevation gain ■	3000 feet

Getting there ■ From Seattle, drive north on I-5 and get off at the Arlington exit. Proceed to Arlington and take SR 530 to Darrington. Drive through town and turn left; pass the Darrington Ranger Station (left) and continue to the Sauk River bridge and turn off (right) onto Suiattle River Road No. 26. Drive about 20 miles to Green Mountain Road No. 2680 and turn north (left). Continue about 5 miles to the end of the steep gravel road and the trailhead, 3500 feet. A Northwest Forest Pass is required.

Map ■ Green Trails No. 80 Cascade Pass

Information ■ Darrington Ranger District, phone (360) 436-1155

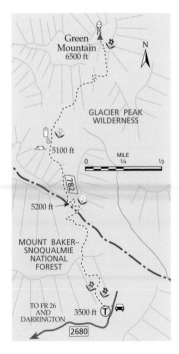

There are several Green Mountains in the Northwest, but most hikers agree this one is greenest. The color is the first thing you may notice when you arrive at the trailhead. As for flowers, you will be hiking through them much of the way, even later in the season when lower meadows are thick with fireweed and bracken. In midsummer, look for lupine, columbine, buttercup, bistort, bleeding hearts, glacier lilies, Sitka valerian, Indian paintbrush, cow parsnip, cinquefoil, tiger lilies, and more.

This is a steep trail that leads to the site of a lookout built in 1933. Badly in need of restoration, the Green Mountain lookout was removed piece by piece and was flown out by helicopter. It is under restoration. Work includes repairing window frames, reglazing panes of glass, and repairing the structure's siding and framing. The lookout is scheduled to be back in place in 2004. The

Marmot

Green Mountain lookout is listed on the National Register of Historic Places.

The first mile will give you a chance to warm up your muscles as the trail climbs through old-growth forest. Near the edge of the forest is a dark campsite with a spring that is sometimes used by hunters in the fall. At 1 mile the trail enters the Glacier Peak Wilderness.

As the trail breaks out of the trees it begins a series of switchbacks through a hillside of thigh-high bracken and subalpine plants, but growing views will compensate for the sweat and toil on a hot day. In late summer, feast on blueberries found along the higher switchbacks and views of Glacier Peak, White Chuck Mountain, and forests of the Suiattle valley. The Green Trails map will help you identify these peaks and others, Mount Pugh and Sloan Peak rising beyond Lime Mountain.

At 2 miles (5200 feet), the trail goes around a corner, contours a hillside, and descends 100 feet or so to small tarns in flower gardens and meadows, 2½ miles from the trailhead. Campers can find designated camps, a toilet, and a water source. Camping is not allowed beyond this point. These meadows live up to their reputation as being "buggy," especially in midsummer. The Forest Service asks hikers to stay on the trail and not cut switchbacks, as they are trying to restore the vegetation in this sensitive basin.

From the basin, it is still a steep climb to the summit of Green Mountain. Climb the final switchbacks through late summer flowers to the summit and lookout site at 6500 feet (of course, the last mile of the trail is the steepest). Pull out the map again to locate Dome and Formidable, peaks of the Ptarmigan Traverse, and more. Look and listen for marmots. ■ K. S.

Bleeding heart

Art's Notes

Easy to recognize is the elegant bleeding heart in full bloom. Copious goblet- to heart-shaped pink flowers, pendant above a lush and ferny foliage, steely blue-gray in hue. The inverted heart-shaped flowers inspired the plant's common name. *Dicentra formosa* is so named for the spurlike appendages in the two outer petals (thus *Di-* and *centra*); and *formosa* means "beautiful," most apt for this charmer. Bleeding heart seed have a unique stratagem for their dispersal. Each seed has a tiny food body (the elaiosome) on its surface, eagerly sought by ants. The ants pack this morsel and seed to their dens and lo!—the next generation is started, well away from the parent plant.

Two other dicentras occur in Washington: the diminutive steer's head, *Dicentra uniflora*, infrequent at mid- to high elevations. The other one, *D. cucullaria*, is an occasional white to pink beauty in the Columbia Gorge country. I've seen it on the Dog Mountain trail.

Kin to the dicentras is the lush, tall Dutchman's breeches, *Corydalis scouleri*. It is frequent in moist places in forests. We have met the species name *scouleri* before, honoring John Scouler, a companion of the Douglas of the fir, David Douglas.

On nearly every trail in the high country, encounter fields of Sitka valerian, *Valeriana sitchensis*, tallish (2-foot) stalks of small white flowers in dense clusters. In late summer, its flowers will have turned to tiny parachutes, fluffy airborne seeds. Its dark green compound leaves often have a strong odor when crushed. Also called mountain heliotrope, it is a dominant along Heliotrope Ridge on the north slope of Mount Baker.

18 | WALT BAILEY TRAIL

Round trip ■	**8 miles**
Difficulty ■	Moderate
Best flowers ■	July through August
Hikable ■	July through November
High point ■	4500 feet
Elevation gain ■	1500 feet

Getting there ■ Drive to the town of Granite Falls, which is northeast of Everett on SR 92. Go through town (straight) on East Stanley Street and turn left onto the signed Mountain Loop Highway. Continue on the Mountain Loop 7.1 miles past Verlot and turn right on Mallardy Ridge Road No. 4030. The road forks at 1.5 miles; turn right on Forest Service Road No. 4032. The road climbs to a saddle; here, go left and descend to the end of the road and the small trailhead at 5.7 miles, elevation 3000 feet. If the parking area is full, backtrack 0.3 mile and park at the saddle.

Maps ■ Green Trails Nos.110 Silverton and 142 Index

Information ■ Darrington Ranger Station, phone (360) 436-1155

There are about a dozen Cutthroat Lakes scattered like rare coins through the meadows below Bald Mountain, although I am not certain where one draws the line between large tarns and small lakes. No matter: This is a great destination in the summer and into fall, when the blueberries are ripe. There is something for everyone—wildflower enthusiasts, hikers, backpackers—and even a tough scramble of Bald Mountain for those with mountaineering skills. Hikers who enjoy a challenge can also approach the lakes from Ashland Lakes, but it is a longer route and the middle stretch, the Bald Mountain trail, is seldom hiked, overgrown, and hard to follow.

The trail is a labor of love built by Walt Bailey, a former Civilian Conservation Corps (CCC) employee, and other volunteers. It is known to some

Corn lily, or false hellebore

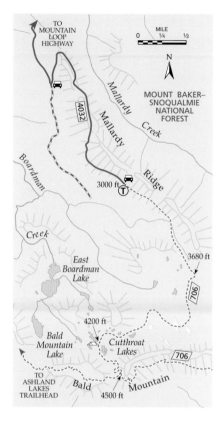

as the Mallardy Ridge trail, though most trail historians may disagree. The true Mallardy Ridge trail is long abandoned and, for all practical purposes today, nonexistent. Though the Walt Bailey trail does not meet Forest Service standards, there are no particular difficulties. The trail was constructed to avoid obstacles; some sections can be muddy or steep and narrow.

From the trailhead, the route heads uphill, and the first mile is steep as it climbs through a recovering clear-cut followed by old-growth forest. Notice a huge boulder split down the middle with a tree growing out of it at the end of a switchback. Shortly beyond the boulder, the trail levels out to cross a small stream and wanders with ups and downs to a high point (3680 feet) in heather and blueberries. At about 1½ miles, the trail descends to a large meadow and stream crossing, a good turn-around or lunch spot. In August look for shootingstars and marsh marigolds. You may also spot bead lily, with its single white bloom or dark berry, depending on the season. The trail enters forest again and contours through evergreens interspersed with meadows. In August, the false hellebore is waist high and lush.

The trail descends, crosses a rock slide, and then climbs steeply to the first tarns at 3 miles, 4200 feet. Sperry Peak, Big Four Mountain, and other Monte Cristo peaks come into view. In fall the tarns are framed by colorful foliage and evergreens. The trail continues climbing above lower Cutthroat Lake and then to the upper lake, about 3½ miles. There are campsites at the lakes, some with old fire rings. A path continues climbing to the junction for the Bald Mountain trail at 4 miles (it may not be signed). For views of Spada Lake, Bald Mountain, and Mount Rainier, continue ¼ mile to the ridge crest (4500 feet).

Wherever you stop on the Walt Bailey trail there is plenty of room to roam, look for flowers, graze on berries, or gaze Narcissus-like at your reflection in the still water of a lonesome tarn. ■ K. S.

Blueberries—Vaccinium deliciosum

Art's Notes

Here we are, back in wet, spongy, Stillaguamish River country. It should be dry in late summer and early fall, a time for berry picking. Our state is blessed with many different kinds of huckleberries, all in the genus *Vaccinium*. Those of choice edibility are in three distinct species. At midmontane elevations, the dark purple berries of *Vaccinium membranaceum* are on waist-high bushes in easy reach along most any trail on either side of the Cascades and Olympics. At higher elevations, often in the glorious parkland of timbered atolls in among swaths of mountain meadow, is the berry needing belly-level picking from the prostrate bushlets: Here are the steely blue-gray berries of *Vaccinium deliciosum*—the botanists got it right with this apt name! At low elevations on the Kitsap and Olympic Peninsulas, the evergreen *Vaccinium ovatum* can be covered with its buckshot-size purplish-black berries. Delicious mouthfuls, they also make wonderful pancake syrup, cooked with a little sugar. Just a notch below these three is the red huckleberry, *Vaccinium parvifolium*, a bit tart and not too plentiful, but prized by some berry pickers. A favorite haunt of this bush is on top of stumps in old logged-over forest, a living proof that birds like them.

19 ┊ BIG FOUR ICE CAVES TRAIL

Round trip ■ **2 miles**
Difficulty ■ Easy
Best flowers ■ June through August
Hikable ■ May through November
High point ■ 1900 feet
Elevation gain ■ 200 feet

Getting there ■ Drive to the town of Granite Falls, which is northeast of Everett on SR 92. Go through town (straight) on East Stanley Street and turn left onto the Mountain Loop Highway (signed). Continue on the Mountain Loop 25.2 miles from Granite Falls to the Big Four Picnic Area, or start from the Ice Cave trailhead, 0.5 mile farther east of the picnic area (more parking here), elevation 1700 feet. The new wheelchair-accessible loop does not show on the Green Trails Map. A Northwest Forest Pass is required.
Map ■ Green Trails No. 110 Silverton
Information ■ Darrington Ranger District, phone (360) 436-1155

This trail is best known for the "ice caves" that form at the base of Big Four Mountain. These are not true ice caves but rather accumulations of snow from avalanches that occur in the winter and spring: As the temperature warms up, the snow melts out from underneath, and this is what causes

Salmonberry

the "caves" to form. The caves are hazardous and signs warn hikers to stay out of them.

The Ice Cave trail connects to the Big Four Ice Caves trail near the boardwalk and provides an accessible loop for wheelchairs (beyond the boardwalk, the trail is not disabled accessible).

The Big Four Ice Caves trail starts from the picnic area near Big Four Mountain. This is the site of the Big Four Inn that burned down in 1949; all that remains of the inn today is the old chimney.

From the picnic area, the trail heads toward Big Four Mountain and crosses a marsh on a boardwalk ½ mile before crossing the South Fork of the Stillaguamish River on a bridge and entering the forest. Near the marsh you may observe wildlife: Beavers have left their mark on gnawed trees and branches, and you may see birds near the marshes, including hairy woodpeckers, nuthatches, and kingfishers.

As for the flowers, you are likely to see fireweed, thimbleberry, elderberry, foamflower, devil's club, bleeding heart, skunk cabbage, and a variety of ferns, mosses and lichens. In the forest I also saw bead lily, salmonberry, and false lily-of-the-valley, with its graceful heart-shaped leaves. False hellebore, cow parsnip, Canadian dogwood, and rosy spirea were also present but already going to seed. Mountain ash, elderberry, devil's club, and rosy twistedstalk were already producing berries in late July.

Benches that invite introspection are scattered along the trail, though you are unlikely to find solitude here. This trail is easy enough for everyone in the family, and Big Four is sometimes the destination of school outings.

The trail breaks out of the forest in about a mile—in late July, the summer flowers and fall flowers were starting to overlap. I saw fireweed, pearly everlasting, bleeding heart, harebells, and goatsbeard. Near the base of Big Four Mountain and the ice caves there are gorgeous displays of Lewis monkeyflowers. ■ K. S.

Skunk cabbage—a.k.a. swamp lantern—blooms along the Stillaguamish River near Big Four Mountain while snow is still on the ground.

Art's Notes

This hike witnesses a rare drama in habitat change. At first you traverse a forest of Pacific silver fir and associated understory shrubs and herbs. Then, as the forest gives way to the meadowy scene at the base of Big Four Mountain, you are suddenly "elevated" to a higher life zone. The local climate at the Ice Caves has fostered a typically higher vegetation type, dominated by young mountain hemlock and its associated plant life. This spectacularly abrupt shift in vegetation is rarely seen in our mountains. The local drop in temperature and shortness of growing season created by the permanent snowbank is the probable cause.

20 MOUNT DICKERMAN TRAIL

Round trip ■	**8½ miles**
Difficulty ■	Strenuous
Best flowers ■	July through August
Hikable ■	Late June through October
High point ■	5723 feet
Elevation gain ■	3898 feet

Getting there ■ Drive to the town of Granite Falls, which is northeast of Everett on SR 92. Go through town (straight) on East Stanley Street then turn left onto the Mountain Loop Highway (signed). Continue on the Mountain Loop 25.2 miles from Granite Falls to the Mount Dickerman trailhead (left), rest room, and parking lot, almost opposite the Big Four Picnic Area, 1825 feet. A Northwest Forest Pass is required.

Map ■ Green Trails No. 111 Sloan Peak

Information ■ Darrington Ranger District, phone (360) 436-1155

This hike has several attractions that draw hikers of all persuasions: one of the largest huckleberry patches in the region, spectacular views of the Monte Cristo Peaks, and, last but not least, a variety of wildflowers, as this trail passes through several life zones. The trail was built by the Forest Service in the 1920s to serve as a recreational trail for visitors staying at Big Four Inn, which burned down in 1949.

Though the focus of this book is flowers, keep this hike in mind for fall, when the trail is vivid with the bright hues of vine maple, mountain ash, and huckleberry shrubs. The trail can sometimes be hiked partway well into November, as long as the Mountain Loop Highway is not gated at Deer Creek, which occurs when snow accumulates on the road. In November the forest is lush and beautiful with evergreens and a tapestry of moss, lichens, and large boulders

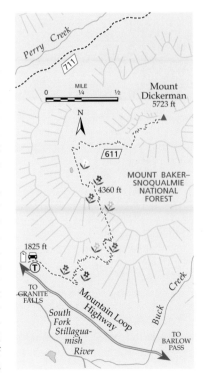

Mountain ash in fall

festooned with licorice ferns. As for the views of Stillaguamish Peak, Mount Forgotten, Glacier Peak, Sloan Peak, Big Four Mountain, and others—all gorgeous, any season.

True, you'll have to work up a sweat to see all the flowers, but this hike is worth the effort. Fortunately, you don't have to climb to the summit for flowers or views. Many flowers—and views—are found in meadows well below the summit.

The trail starts out climbing steeply through forest. In the forest look for twinflower, foamflower, Oregon grape, maidenhair fern, deer fern, and self-heal. Big Four Mountain comes into view at about ½ mile and Sperry Peak comes into view in another mile. As the trail gains elevation, look for Solomon's seal, goatsbeard, queen's cup, marsh marigolds, tiger lilies, pearly everlasting, and star flower.

Just past 2 miles, the trail passes under an overhang of basalt and enters an open area at the base of a cliff. The trail skirts the cliff and passes two gullies, switchbacks to the base of another cliff, and crosses a stream (4360 feet). Arnica and phlox begin to appear. The trail climbs to the top of a ravine; here you may spot false hellebore, heather, and marsh marigolds near the small stream. Climb a bit farther, to a large meadow rumored to be one of the largest huckleberry patches in the area. The trail is level for a while.

At an unsigned junction, stay right as the trail resumes climbing and the trees thin out. Lupine, mountain ash, and subalpine plants appear. As the trail follows along and near the ridge crest, several of the Monte Cristo peaks come into view: Mount Forgotten, Stillaguamish Peak, and Mount Pugh. To the south is Morningstar Peak and Del Campo.

Other hikers will swear that the last mile to the top is the steepest mile of all. Don't get too close to the edge; the north face of Mount Dickerman is a sheer drop of 450 feet. From the summit (5723 feet) there are scattered stands of evergreens but not enough to obscure the big views of more Monte Cristo peaks (Sheep, Cadet, and Columbia). Glacier Peak is to the east. A map will help you identify the peaks. ■ K. S.

Art's Notes

Since much of the trail is in old-growth forest, revel in the rich diversity of the forest floor flora. Unlike second-growth forest, where dense, even-aged stands of trees shut out light for the ground layer, old growth, with widely spaced large trees, gives the forest floor "elbow room." Given the elevation change from the trailhead (1825 feet) to the summit (5723 feet), the hiker is rewarded with an upward trek through two life zones: the lower western hemlock–western redcedar and the Douglas fir, merging upward into a Pacific silver fir forest with scattered Alaska cedar and mountain hemlock.

The South Fork of the Stillaguamish River luxuriates in an abundance of rainfall. En route to the trailhead, just feel the moisture in the air and watch for that indicator of high rainfall, Sitka spruce *(Picea sitchensis)* and bigleaf maple *(Acer macrophyllum)* festooned with mosses, lichens, and even licorice fern all along the lower river canyon. Another gift of high rainfall is a wealth of ferns. Just west of the Mount Dickerman trailhead is Perry Creek, which I once called "a fern-watcher's El Dorado." This ultramoist yet rocky drainage has been known for years as the richest fern paradise in the Pacific Northwest. In 1996, the Forest Service, with my persistent urging, created the Perry Creek Research Natural Area, yet kept the ferny trail open to hikers. Another day you must add this hike to your Dickerman ascent: The reward is truly amazing. For instance, it was along the Perry trail that the ace pteridologist (fern expert) Warren H. Wagner found a rare hybrid fern: both its parents occur together (sympatrically), common sword fern and Anderson's sword fern.

21 | SCORPION MOUNTAIN VIA JOHNSON RIDGE

Round trip ■ 9 miles
Difficulty ■ Strenuous
Best flowers ■ Late June through September
Hikable ■ June through October
High point ■ 5540 feet
Elevation gain ■ 2900 feet

Getting there ■ From the west, take US 2 to Skykomish, and near milepost 49, turn left onto Beckler River Road No. 65. Drive 7 miles then turn right on gravel Forest Service Road No. 6520. Don't confuse this with Road No. 6530, the Rapid River Road, which also is a right turn in the same area. The sign for Johnson Ridge may be missing, but you'll spot the road number sign if you look carefully. Drive another 1.75 miles to where Road No. 6520 splits; go left (straight) and continue to another fork, where you turn right on Road No. 6526 to the end of drivable road and the signed trailhead, at the end of a switchback, 3660 feet. A Northwest Forest Pass is required.

Maps ■ Green Trails Nos. 143 Monte Cristo and 144 Benchmark Mountain
Information ■ Skykomish Ranger District, phone (360) 677-2414

This lonesome trail is not as famous for flowers as other trails between Skykomish and Stevens Pass, but it is not one to miss. It can be a little tricky

Tiger lily

to find the trailhead—especially if signs are missing—so be sure you have maps, and get an update from the Skykomish Ranger Station before you set out.

After negotiating the road system, the Johnson Ridge trail begins on Forest Service Road No. 6526. Walk ½ mile on the road and where the road continues right, look for a rough track climbing uphill (left) through blueberry shrubs. After going through shrubs, the trail enters forest and follows along a broad ridge crest. The trail gets steep at about 2 miles and climbs to the top of Sunrise Mountain (5056 feet). The trail drops from Sunrise Mountain, losing 300 feet of elevation as it continues to follow the ridge crest.

The next mile is more scenic as forest alternates with flower meadows. Stay on the main trail as it continues toward the gentle summit of Scorpion Mountain at 5540 feet. Just below the summit, the trail traverses a short way through flower meadows to a lower point on the ridge before it descends 400 feet to Joan Lake (5000 feet) and the end of the maintained trail. Joan Lake was still mostly under snow when I was there in July.

Look for carpets of glacier lilies in late June on or near the summit. In mid-July, the glacier lilies were on their way out and the meadows were sweet with the scent of Sitka valerian. As the summer progresses, you'll see generous displays of lupine, tiger lilies, fireweed, Indian paintbrush, tall penstemon, pearly everlasting, false hellebore, lousewort, arnica, heather, mountain ash, and asters. In late August, look for harebells.

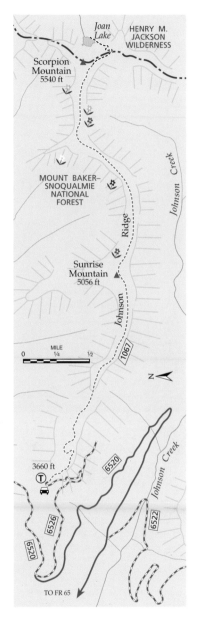

On a clear day, there are views of Captain Point, Glacier Peak, and Mount Fernow. ■ K. S.

Glacier lily

Glacier lilies, both yellow and white, are the ever-present hallmarks of our high country. They often emerge to flower through a melting snowbank. The yellow one is *Erythronium grandiflorum;* its white kin is *E. montanum.* Common names abound for these elegant lilies: besides glacier lily, find in your field guide avalanche lily, fawn lily, and even dog's tooth violet. At lower elevations here and there around Puget Sound country and the San Juan Islands, two fawn lilies decorate the woodland forest floor: *Erythronium oregonum,* with white flowers, and *E. revolutum,* with pink flowers. Both have speckled or mottled foliage, adding to their charm. All these lily relatives are early spring bloomers, mostly with a pair of basal leaves and a leafless flower stalk bearing one to several flowers.

22 ¦ JOSEPHINE LAKE VIA PACIFIC CREST TRAIL

Round trip ■	9 miles
Difficulty ■	Moderate
Best flowers ■	July through September
Hikable ■	Late June through October
High point ■	5200 feet
Elevation gain ■	1600 feet in, 900 feet out

Getting there ■ From the west, take US 2 to Stevens Pass. Just beyond the ski center, turn right into a large parking lot and find the Pacific Crest trailhead at 4056 feet. A Northwest Forest Pass is required.
Map ■ Green Trails No. 176 Stevens Pass
Information ■ Skykomish Ranger Station, phone (360) 677-2414

The Pacific Crest Trail 2000 (PCT) is one of the most challenging and beautiful trails in the United States, spanning border to border from Mexico to Canada—including the length of Washington State—but many hikers do not have the time, experience, or energy to spend weeks on the trail. Fortunately, you can hike the trail in "pieces" or sample a short stretch near an access point.

Several interesting destinations in the region that can be reached from the PCT trailhead at Stevens Pass are well within the reach of day hikers, such as Josephine Lake, only 4½ miles south of Stevens Pass.

From the trailhead at Stevens Pass, Pacific Crest Trail 2000 switchbacks upward, at times skirting the edge of the ski runs. Despite the trail's proximity to civilization, flowers are thriving and the area is lush with vegetation. Between 4000 to 5000 feet I saw mertensia, Sitka valerian, yellow violets, lupine, foamflower, bead lily, heather, rosy spirea, and tiger lilies. As the trail approaches the high point of the ridge (5200 feet), bistort, phlox, and mountain ash begin to appear. From the ridge crest, the trail descends on a series of long switchbacks that zigzag down to colorful flower meadows.

Rosy spirea

If there are no other hikers on the trail, you may encounter wildlife—I saw a young buck near the trail and a marmot sunning itself on a rock between the ridge crest and the meadows. Here, the trail levels out and wanders through flowers, rock gardens, and small streams. In the meadows, marsh marigold and occasional groupings of shootingstars were in bloom.

The trail continues to Lake Susan Jane and campsites at 4595 feet, 3½ miles from the trailhead. If you are not camping at the lake, continue on the PCT as it climbs away from Lake Susan Jane through a steep meadow of Sitka valerian and false hellebore to a ridge and a signed trail junction at 5000 feet (4 miles). At the trail junction, the PCT continues south (right). For Josephine Lake, turn left on Icicle Creek trail No. 1551 and descend to the lake (4681 feet) and points beyond. Before the trail drops, it follows the ridge line and provides a view through evergreens to the lake and out to peaks of the Stuart

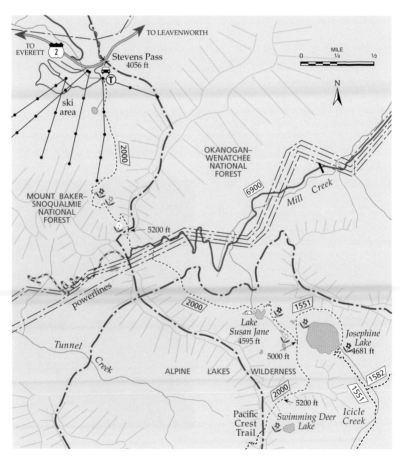

Red columbine

Range. Take time to enjoy the ridge before descending to the lake—scattered along the ridge are several lonesome tarns and meadows.

For more views of the high country and a view of Swimming Deer Lake, turn right at the 5000-foot junction and continue on the PCT (south) another mile to an open ridge at 5200 feet. Or farther, if you like. ■ K. S.

Art's Notes

The commonest columbine in our mountains, *Aquilegia formosa*, has glorious red flowers, held upside-down. With this orientation, the flowers are accessible only to hovering hummingbirds. When red columbines are abundant in a moist site, it's intriguing to observe the intense territorial behavior of the hummers, protecting their patch from interlopers. The long-spurred flowers yield a rich reward of nectar for the birds. And they pollinate the next flower! Less common is a yellow, similarly long-spurred columbine, *Aquilegia flavescens*. I've seen it most abundantly in the wooded trail to that floral mecca, Red Top Lookout. Columbines are notoriously promiscuous; most species can hybridize with most any other. Even the Old World short-spurred ones (*A. vulgaris* and kin) can make fertile hybrids with our long-spurred Northwest ones . . . only in gardens, though. The spur length of columbine flowers has coevolved with mouth parts (beaks or other nectar-sippers) of floral visitors—bumblebees seek pollen and nectar from short-spurred species, while hummingbirds and even hawk moths are adapted to service long-spurred species of the New World. Coevolution? Darwin first recognized the mutual adaptedness of a plant for a special animal. This remarkable reciprocal adaptation system is a universal outcome of natural selection.

23 ROUND MOUNTAIN TRAIL TO NASON RIDGE

Round trip	■	**10 miles**
Difficulty	■	Strenuous
Best flowers	■	July through September
Hikable	■	June through October
High point	■	6235 feet
Elevation gain	■	2335 feet

Getting there ■ From the west, take US 2 east to Stevens Pass and continue a short distance past the Nason Creek Rest Area. In 0.3 mile past the rest area, look for a driveway (left)—this is not the road. It is the next road on the left, Butcher Creek Road (Forest Service Road No. 6910). It also looks like a driveway and is easy to miss, as the sign is small. Continue 4.5 miles, passing private homes, to spur road No. 170. Go right and drive 0.2 mile on the spur to the signed trailhead, elevation 3900 feet, 4.7 miles from US 2. Butcher Creek Road is worse than it looks. The road is a washboard and some sections are narrow and exposed. A Northwest Forest Pass is required.

Map ■ Green Trails No. 145 Wenatchee Lake

Information ■ Lake Wenatchee Ranger Station, phone (509) 763-3103

Penstemon

Nason Ridge is a long ridge that rises on the north side of US 2. A trail runs the length of the ridge between Rainy Pass and Lake Wenatchee, though the section from the Smith Brook Road at Rainy Pass is abandoned, overgrown, and not recommended. The climax of this trail is Alpine Lookout (6235 feet) on Nason Ridge, one of the few remaining lookouts that is staffed during the summer. It can be accessed from other trailheads, but the Round Mountain trail approach is recommended if you have only a day.

Though Alpine Lookout is the usual destination of hikers, you don't need to hike that far to experience the flowers and views. You will see plenty of flowers on the Round Mountain trail, a hiker-only trail that is closed to motorized vehicles. One interesting feature of this approach is the opportunity to walk through a "ghost forest," recovering from a forest fire in 1994.

The Round Mountain trail is steep, and the first 1400 feet of elevation are gained in the first 1½ miles. The trail reaches the edge of the ghost forest and burn at ½ mile and the beginning of views. You may want to linger here with a flower guide, map, and/or camera. This outdoor classroom is a good place to observe how the vegetation recovers in a setting of white snags, some charred black from fire. The hillside is lush and green with fresh vegetation. In late June, fireweed was blooming and the slope was covered with mats of penstemon, the most I've seen in one location. Lupine and Indian paintbrush are beginning to return to this setting. Earlier in the season you may spot clumps of peach-colored *Lewisia tweedyi*.

At 1½ miles, the Round Mountain trail joins the Nason Ridge trail No. 1583 at 5300 feet. If you are not going to the lookout, the trail junction at 5300 feet is a good turnaround, and if you are camping, there are unofficial campsites tucked away in sheltering evergreens. From this junction, the trail is open to motorized vehicles except for a short wheel-free spur leading to the lookout. In addition to views and displays of wildflowers, there is more—mountain goats are sometimes seen near the lookout and along the ridge. Carry plenty of water—this is a dry trail.

If you are going to the lookout, the Nason Ridge trail climbs from the

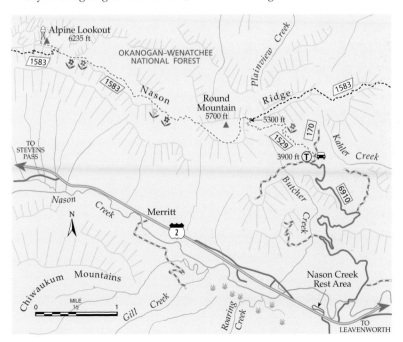

Paintbrush edges the trail to Nason Ridge

junction to views of Glacier Peak and down to Lake Wenatchee. The trail turns sharply to the right (west) and contours beneath Round Mountain before breaking out into the open country again. As you continue toward the lookout, you'll get views of the Stuart Range and the Chiwaukum Mountains to the south and Glacier Peak to the north.

Some hikers prefer to do this as a one-way hike of 11 miles between this trailhead and the Merritt Lake trailhead. To leave a car at the Merritt Lake trailhead, turn left (north) onto Forest Service Road No. 657 (11 miles east from Stevens Pass on US 2) and drive 1.6 miles to the end of road and Merritt Lake trailhead (trail No. 1588), at 3000 feet. ■ K. S.

Art's Notes

My fascination with place names led me to wonder about Nason, both the ridge and the creek of that name. According to Hitchman (1985), our place-name bible, Nason was the "white" surname of Charlie Nason, a Wenatchee Indian settler who lived in the lower reaches of Nason Creek. His Indian name was "Maw-mo-nas-et." The original Indian name for Nason Creek was "Natopac," now a name for a nearby mountain.

24 CHIWAUKUM CREEK

Round trip ■ **11 miles**
Difficulty ■ Moderate
Best flowers ■ Late May through July
Hikable ■ June through October
High point ■ 3360 feet
Elevation gain ■ 1560 feet

Getting there ■ From the west, take US 2 to Stevens Pass and continue 25 miles east. Just past milepost 89, turn right on Chiwaukum Creek Road (No. 7908). Drive a short distance to a junction and turn right. Continue about 0.5 mile to the parking area, rest room, and trailhead at 1800 feet. A Northwest Forest Pass is required.

Maps ■ Green Trails Nos. 178 Leavenworth and 177 Chiwaukum Mtns

Information ■ Leavenworth Ranger District, phone (509) 548-6977

Hikers who weary of winter and hunger for flowers will appreciate early flower displays found along Chiwaukum Creek, east of Stevens Pass, in late spring. The flowers begin in late May and continue through the summer, but June is ideal. The Chiwaukum Creek trail is a long valley trail with several options for backpackers, but day hikers can hike as much or

Johnny jump-ups, or yellow violets

as little as they choose. There are generous displays of *Lewisia tweedyi* at several points along the trail, and in June the path is lined with lupine.

In addition to flowers with which many hikers likely are already familiar, I found a display of showy ladyslipper (mountain ladyslipper) a few feet off the trail at about 3 miles. It's a good thing they were blooming off-trail because it takes these flowers fifteen years to produce a flower, and they are becoming increasingly rare as a result of being overcollected.

Trail No. 1571 starts at a gated road. Some hikers begrudge a road-walk, but clusters of *Lewisia tweedyi* along the 1½-mile road will help compensate. This road ends where the trailhead used to be. In the early 1980s hikers could drive to that point, but private ownership has changed all that and closed the road to public vehicles.

From the end of the road, the trail follows along and near Chiwaukum Creek with gentle ups and downs. Near the beginning of the trail you will see *Lewisia tweedyi*, lupine, mertensia, Solomon's seal, bead lily, and twinflower. Early in the season you'll find trilliums and yellow violets, some of the first flowers to bloom after the snow melts. As for the rare mountain ladyslipper, you may have to venture off-trail to find one, and that is not a guarantee.

Chiwaukum Creek is a pretty creek—several side paths descend to potential picnic or camp spots along the way. At about 4 miles, the trail passes through a section that was logged before the area was included in the Alpine Lakes Wilderness. From there, the trail re-enters old-growth forest and continues to a trail junction at 5½ miles (3360 feet). This will be far enough for most day hikers, but backpackers can continue from this junction on the North Fork Chiwaukum trail No. 1591 (right), to Larch Lake and Chiwaukum Lake, when the snow melts out at higher elevations. ■ K. S.

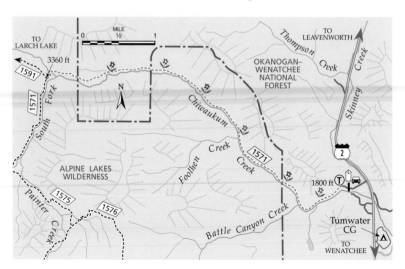

Tweedy's lewisia

Art's Notes

The stunning wildflower encountered early on the trail is the showy lewisia, *Lewisia tweedyi*, a.k.a. "Tweedy's lewisia"—a rather redundant common name. This low-growing herbaceous perennial with broad fleshy leaves can have as many as dozens of large salmon to apricot flowers. We thank the stars that it was not named the state flower of Washington, for collectors might have brought it to extinction. It thrives in rocky openings in the forest and is restricted to Kittitas and Chelan Counties, with outliers in the mountains bordering the Methow Valley and even in Manning Park, British Columbia. Of course, *Lewisia* commemorates Meriwether Lewis, who collected the other, *Lewisia rediviva*, the bitterroot, back in 1803. But what about Tweedy? Frank Tweedy, the botanist with the Pacific Railroad Survey, discovered this gem in the Wenatchee Mountains in the 1880s. Tweedy's colorful career will be recounted in *Plant Hunters of the Pacific Northwest* (Kruckeberg and Love, forthcoming).

25 TUMWATER PIPELINE TRAIL

Round trip ■ 2½ miles
Difficulty ■ Easy
Best flowers ■ May through July
Hikable ■ April through October
High point ■ 1400 feet
Elevation gain ■ None

Getting there ■ From Everett, go east on US 2 over Stevens Pass and look for a metal bridge about 2 miles east of "The Alps" gift and candy shop (1.7 miles west of Leavenworth). Park along US 2 in one of the several parking areas where rock climbers park. Cross US 2 carefully and walk a short distance to the bridge, elevation 1400 feet. You can also drive to the bridge and site of a powerhouse on a spur road just east of the bridge, but the road is difficult to spot when coming from the west. There is a portable toilet between the site of the powerhouse and the penstock bridge. A Northwest Forest Pass is not required.

Map ■ Green Trails No. 178 Leavenworth (shown as Penstock trail No. 0706)
Information ■ Leavenworth Ranger Station, phone (509) 548-6977

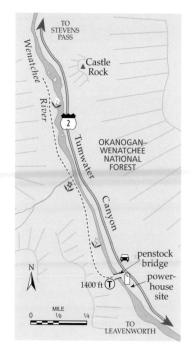

This is a short and easy hike, and some hikers may choose to combine it with another hike in the Leavenworth area. The trail is not well publicized but you may have noticed an old metal bridge spanning Tumwater Canyon just before you get to Leavenworth and wondered about it. I stopped and discovered a trail on the other side of the bridge that makes a pleasant spring hike. You are more likely to encounter locals here than hikers from the west side, as the trail is close to Leavenworth and is a local favorite. It is also suitable for family outings.

The hike begins on the other side of the bridge. From the highway, follow a short path down to the bridge or hike from the spur. From the end of the spur road, turn right (west) and walk a short distance along the Wenatchee River to

Fall color along the Wenatchee River

the bridge (less than ⅛ mile). Pick up the trail on the other side of the bridge and hike west along the Wenatchee River.

The trail is known by several names: It is sometimes referred to as the Old Pipeline trail or the Penstock trail, as it follows the route of a penstock pipeline that carried water to power electricity for the Great Northern Railroad.

In 1893 Great Northern built a line over Stevens Pass, but the grade was so steep that it was necessary to build switchbacks for the trains. There were other problems as well, and that stretch was abandoned when the Cascade Tunnel opened in 1900. The tunnel had problems, too: As trains climbed the steep grade, the tunnel filled with smoke and passengers and crew became ill. Great Northern resolved that problem by utilizing electric trains and constructed the powerhouse to power the trains. A dam was built upstream to drive the generators, and a wooden pipeline carried water from the dam to the power station. This system served the Great Northern until the power plant was sold and the roadbed became part of US 2.

The trail provides a pleasant walk most of the year. Side trails lead to hidden sandy beaches and calm pools, where you can idle away the hours on a summer day. April and May are best for wildflower displays, but you can come back in the fall when the trail through the canyon is colorful with vine maple. As you hike along the trail you will see evidence of a forest fire that ravaged the area a few years ago.

In spring there is a variety of flowers including some seldom seen, such as white shootingstars and mariposa lilies near the bridge. In addition to

123

Blue anemones found in Tumwater Canyon

the flower show, there are unobstructed views of Castle Rock at about a third of the way, where you can watch the climbers practice their airy craft.

Along the trail, historical artifacts are mixed in with the vegetation and boulders. At 1¼ miles, the trail comes to an end at an unsigned junction where a small tree lies across the upper trail (the lower trail descends to the river and a good turnaround). Beyond that point the main trail loses its trail-like status and becomes more of a scramble route as it rounds a rocky buttress above the river. This is an exposed spot and hikers should stop here. ■ K. S.

Art's Notes

Between the Wenatchee River bridge and east to Leavenworth on US 2, one drives through the spectacular Tumwater Canyon. Fall color in the two native maples, vine and bigleaf, enrich the narrow canyon's landscape, with occasional glimpses of the gorgeous bitterroot relative *Lewisia tweedyi*. If you've done the Chiwaukum Creek trail just west of Tumwater Canyon (Hike 24) and have seen this exquisite apricot- to salmon-flowered perennial, you will know what to look for. One of the rarest Washington wildflowers is restricted to the Tumwater Canyon area: It is the showy white-flowered stickseed, *Hackelia venusta*. Chances are that the roadside seeker of wildflowers will not see it. Rest assured that this local rarity (a narrow endemic) is being watched closely for it to survive as an endangered species. Now, place-name time! "Tumwater" means "rough water," most fitting for the boiling whitewater of the Wenatchee River. We also know another Tumwater, the town just south of Olympia. As for "Wenatchee," the name given to a city, a river, and the grand mountain range in Kittitas and Chelan Counties: It is another Indian word (originally We-na-tchi), meaning "river issuing from a canyon."

Opposite: *The Stuart Range from Navaho Pass (Hike 30)*

INTERSTATE 90 & EAST

26 IRA SPRING MEMORIAL TRAIL

Round trip	■	6⅘ miles
Difficulty	■	Moderate
Best flowers	■	June through August
Hikable	■	Late May through October
High point	■	4380 feet
Elevation gain	■	2100 feet

Getting there ■ From Seattle, take I-90 east and get off at exit 45, signed "Road No. 9030." At the stop sign turn left, go under the freeway to Road No. 9030, and at a split in about half a mile continue straight on Forest Service Road No. 9031. Continue about 3.5 miles to the Mason Lake trailhead, parking, and facilities, elevation 2280 feet. A Northwest Forest Pass is required.
Map ■ Green Trails No. 206 Bandera
Information ■ North Bend Ranger District, phone (425) 888-1421

For many years the Mason Lake trail had a reputation of being steep and mean. In addition, hikers had to negotiate a large boulder field before getting to the lake. Thanks to Ira Spring's urging, the Forest Service, with help from Volunteers for Outdoor Washington, have closed the old trail and

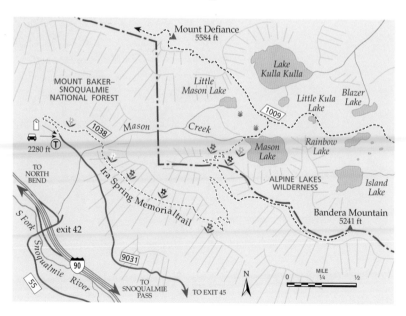

Bear grass on Bandera Mountain; Mount Rainier in the distance

constructed a new trail that avoids those obstacles. This trail is destined to become one of the most popular trails along the I-90 corridor. The new route provides a more scenic way to lakes within the Alpine Lakes Wilderness. Having hiked it, I was impressed with the hard work that has gone into the trail, and it is more aesthetically pleasing, with views most of the way. The original trail was built in 1958 so fire crews could reach and battle a forest fire northeast of Mason Lake, and hard-core hikers continued to use the trail.

Though some may refer to it as the new Bandera Mountain trail, in spring of 2004 the trail will be dedicated and designated as the Ira Spring Memorial trail. The Spring name is ideal for this trail, as it will soon gain recognition as a springtime "flower walk."

The trailhead is at 2280 feet, with a large parking area and a rest room. Pick up a trail permit for the Alpine Lakes Wilderness at the trailhead. As of September 2003, the trailhead sign states "the New Mason Lake trail is open but not complete." However, there are no obstacles and junctions are signed. The trail begins on the abandoned fire road turned trail, crosses Little Mason Creek (source of a waterfall), and climbs 400 feet to the "old" Mason Lake junction. The old trail is closed. Stay straight on the alder-lined road; the ground cover here is a dense carpet of twinflower in spring. It is about 2 miles from the trailhead to the end of the old road, which continues east and becomes part of a long switchback. At the end of the road, the trail continues east and the terrain begins to open up. McClellan Butte and I-90 are directly below and across the way.

More switchbacks lead to a trail junction at about 4180 feet. Turn left (west) for Mason Lake, and as you climb there are views to the west of Mount Defiance (5584 feet) and the long rocky ridge leading to West Defiance. For Bandera Mountain (5241 feet), turn right at the junction.

The trail climbs to its high point at 4380 feet. Here the trail enters the Alpine Lake Wilderness and levels off (you can't see the lake from the high point). For Mason Lake, continue as the trail descends, contouring across lichen-encrusted boulders and through a forested stretch where the old trail comes in and is marked by flagging. The trails merge and continue to Mason Lake, 4200 feet. It is a 180-foot descent from the high point to the lake, according to the altimeter. From Mason Lake, more lakes in the Alpine Lakes region beckon—look at a map and dream.

Twinflower, left, and common dwarf dogwood, right

Wildflower enthusiasts will spot flowers along the road to the trailhead. In September the road was lined with tansy, fireweed, goldenrod, and pearly everlasting. Along the first 2 miles of the trail, in early September there were still a few flowers in bloom: hedge-nettle, asters, fireweed, pearly everlasting, and goldenrod. Trees and shrubs included alders, evergreens, vine maple, willows, and oceanspray. Also seen (though not in bloom) were creeping raspberry, thimbleberry, large-leaved avens, foxgloves, mullein, vanilla leaf, bead lily, twistedstalk, wild ginger, and Canadian dogwood (fruiting).

By September, most flowers have gone to seed but here a few were still blooming along upper switchbacks, including Indian paintbrush, penstemon, and salal. During peak flower season (July), look for bear grass, tiger lilies, spirea, larkspur, bistort, Sitka valerian, Indian paintbrush, cow parsnip, and lupine. Along the upper switchbacks there were plenty of blueberries, wizened but sweet. On a clear day without haze, there are good views of Mount Rainier when the trail breaks out of the trees. ■ K. S.

Art's Notes

It is most fitting that this improved trail be named in honor and memory of Ira Spring. Countless hikers have known Ira through the many trails books—*100 Hikes* to most hikers anywhere in the Northwest—that he illustrated with his outstanding photos. Yet users of these guidebooks couldn't help but sense from the photos Ira's deep commitment to the wilderness ethic—a reverence for nature. And that ethic was so deeply ingrained in him that it promoted his devotion to the preservation of wild places. As a guiding light in the Washington Trails Association, Ira influenced the preservation and volunteer work of maintaining and improving trails.

This wildflower trails guide was to be the capstone work of Ira's long career. To its production he brought superb close-up portraits of wildflowers as well as dramatic scenery. I am emboldened to offer, in his memory, word portraits of two of his favorite flowers. Twinflower, plentiful along this trail, is a perky evergreen ground cover, in spring bearing showy pairs of lavender flowers. *Linnaea borealis*, its botanical binomial, commemorates the father of modern plant naming (taxonomy), Carolus Linnaeus; he is shown in an eighteenth-century portrait as a young man just returning from Lapland, bearing a flowering twig of the north temperate zone, cosmopolite. Another of Ira's favorites was a native ground cover, bunchberry or dwarf dogwood, *Cornus canadensis.* It can form dense ground-hugging carpets on the forest floor. Its four white "petals" are actually showy bracts surrounding tiny flowers. It is conspicuous in fruit with clusters of red berries. It, too, has a cosmopolitan distribution, flourishing in Eurasia and in North America.

27 ‖ KENDALL GARDEN KATWALK

Round trip ■	**10½ miles**
Difficulty ■	Moderate
Best flowers ■	Mid-July to mid-August
Hikable ■	Mid-July to early October
High point ■	5400 feet
Elevation gain ■	2700 feet in, 300 feet out

Getting there ■ Leave I-90 at Snoqualmie Pass exit 52 (exit 53 if driving from the east) and turn onto the frontage road, signed to "Alpental." In a few hundred feet the Pacific Crest Trail 2000 parking lot is on the right, elevation about 3030 feet. A Northwest Forest Pass is required.

Map ■ Green Trails No. 207 Snoqualmie Pass

Information ■ Forest Service/National Park Service Outdoor Recreation Information Center, phone (206) 470-4060

This is a popular bit of the Pacific Crest Trail 2000, climbing from forest to heather meadows, and in between rich flower fields on the steep side of Kendall Peak.

The trail immediately enters cool forest and you are hiking in pristine,

Pacific Crest Trail near Kendall Peak; Mount Rainier in the distance

old-growth forest. After about 2 miles, there is a frustrating loss of 250 feet in elevation as the trail drops below a boulder field and then passes a side trail to Commonwealth Basin and starts climbing again, regaining the 250 feet and a lot more. With long switchbacks the trail traverses the steep hillside, first in forest, and then finally enters Kendall Garden below the cliffs of Kendall Peak. Still upward the trail leads to the wooded crest of Kendall Ridge at 5¼ miles, 5400 feet, at the "Katwalk." The Katwalk is a walkway that was blasted across the face of an almost (well, it seems that way) vertical cliff. A good place to call it a day.

Most people go on. Here is a place you should watch your step and forget those interesting, tiny plants tucked in cracks above the trail. The trail generally is wide and safe enough for a pack horse, but do not attempt it if a snowbank blocks the way. There has been at least one fatality caused by a person trying to cross a snowbank here.

Once you are safely across, the vegetation ranges from storm-shaped trees, heather, and blueberries to patches of flowers. At 6½ miles, reach Ridge Lake surrounded by heather and look down on well-named Gravel Lake, a long day's outing.

For backpackers, there are more flowers along the next 10 miles of airy trail that traverse under 5524-foot Huckleberry Mountain and Chikamin Peak to Spectacle Point. ■ I. S. & A. R. K.

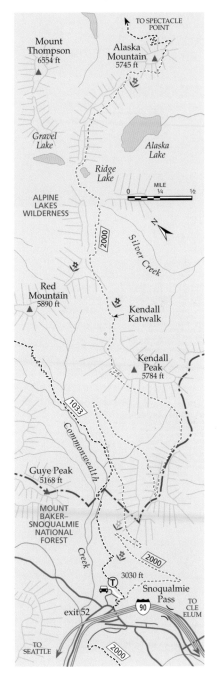

Fairybells

Art's Notes

Here you are hiking in pristine, old-growth forest dominated by Pacific silver fir *(Abies amabilis)*; it is the defining tree of the Pacific silver fir zone (2500–3500 feet). Besides spotting wildflowers, "know thy conifers." After all, it is the conifer forest that creates habitat for wildflowers on the forest floor. Pacific silver fir can easily be identified by inspecting a leafy twig. Along with the flat sprays of ¾–1-inch-long needles, an additional rank of shorter needles slantingly extend from the top of the twig, much like the hair on an aroused dog's back. The undersides of the leafy branches' leaves are waxy white.

Besides this elegant fir, look for an occasional mountain hemlock *(Tsuga mertensiana)* and Alaska cedar *(Chamaecyparis nootkatensis)*. The zone's understory shrubs can be dominated by heather relatives: huckleberries (mostly *Vaccinium membranaceum*) and fool's huckleberry *(Menziesia ferruginea)*. The forest floor can be carpeted with bunchberry *(Cornus canadensis)* and that diminutive relative of salal *(Gaultheria ovatifolia)*. Expect to find herbaceous kin of saxifrages, like mitrewort *(Mitella breweri)*, foamflower *(Tiarella trifoliata)*, and real saxifrages *(Saxifraga ferruginea* and *S. arguta)*. The forest floor's rich layer of organic duff and a subterranean web of fungus filaments support a variety of partial to full parasites: one or more wintergreens *(Pyrola secunda, P. asarifolia)* and pipsissewa *(Chimaphila umbellata* and *C. menziesii)*. Ground orchids flourish in the forest floor microcosm: calypso, rein-orchids *(Piperia* and *Platanthera* species), and the glory of them all, the coralroot orchid (species of *Corallorhiza)*—these beauties totally lack green pigment (chlorophyll), living off their host fungi, yet they flaunt the most gorgeous shades of pink to purple flowers.

28 LODGE LAKE

Round trip ■	3 miles
Difficulty ■	Easy
Best flowers ■	June through August
Hikable ■	Late June through October
High point ■	3500 feet
Elevation gain ■	500 feet in, 375 feet out

Getting there ■ From the west, drive to Snoqualmie Pass on I-90. Get off at exit 52 and turn right toward the ski area at Snoqualmie Summit Inn. Turn right (if you get to the visitor center you've gone too far) onto the first gravel road you come to, signed for the Pacific Crest Trail (the sign is small and easy to overlook). Follow this road (bear right) as it approaches the west edge of the ski area around 0.2 mile to a large parking area for the Pacific Crest Trail, elevation 3000 feet. A Northwest Forest Pass is required.

Map ■ Green Trails No. 207 Snoqualmie Pass

Information ■ North Bend Ranger District, phone (425) 888-1421

I will be honest—this section of the Pacific Crest Trail 2000 (PCT) is not the most scenic trail near Snoqualmie Pass. Most hikers are heading toward popular trails in the Alpine Lakes Wilderness on the other side of I-90.

The PCT heads south under the ski lifts and in summer the slopes are bare—at least at first glance. Day hikers often spurn this stretch of the trail as it is never far from the I-90 corridor, the ski lifts, and the blight of clear-cuts. What makes this hike interesting for wildflower enthusiasts is finding the different flowers and shrubs that grow in disturbed habitats and comparing it to habitat that has not been disturbed by Man. The habitat under the ski lifts provides an interesting cast of floral characters: You may find some floral villains mixed in with subalpine plants. Relief from civilization is at hand; once you have hiked beyond the ski slopes, solitude is almost a given.

Spring beauty

The first ¼ mile of the PCT goes through forest before it crosses slopes under the chairlifts. In early August, the slope was a haze of purple fireweed, meadow goldenrod, Indian paintbrush, and pearly everlasting. In August, look for foxgloves (an intruder), rosy spirea, mountain daisies, and mountain ash in the clearing under the lifts. Running clubmoss can be found near Beaver Lake. In ¾ mile the trail rises to a saddle and the highest elevation of this hike, 3500 feet. Clear-cuts and ski slopes are forgotten and the racket from the interstate is muffled by evergreens as the trail skirts the edge of Beaver Lake, 1 mile from the trailhead.

Progress may be slow from this point as salmonberries, thimbleberries, and blueberries are ripe and ready to eat. In the forest, look for false lily-of-the-valley, false hellebore, marsh marigold, Canadian dogwood, bead lily, vanilla leaf, rosy twistedstalk, devil's club, vine maple, and red elderberry.

From Beaver Lake, the trail descends through forest to a trail junction for Lodge Lake at 2 miles. If Lodge Lake is your destination, turn right and continue ¼ mile to the lake, at 3200 feet. The lake was named for the Snoqualmie Lodge, built by Seattle Mountaineers in 1914 and used as a popular base camp for mountaineering and skiing endeavors. The terrain around the lake hasn't changed much since then, though the lodge burned down in 1940.

There was no interstate highway then; getting to the lodge involved catching a train from Seattle. The Mountaineers got off the train and climbed a trail to the lodge by candle lanterns. All that is gone; all that remains are the stately evergreens, white snags, and the quiet lake. There are campsites near the lake.

You can extend your hike by continuing south as far as time and energy allow. A marshy pond is located a bit south of the Lodge Lake trail junction. Each year the pond becomes a little harder to spot as the vegetation is

Rosy twistedstalk

growing fast and tall. In August the pond was bordered by grasses and aquatic plants. Rockdale Creek is a good turnaround, 3 miles from the trailhead. The PCT proceeds to Stampede Pass and points beyond. ■ K. S.

Art's Notes

A bit more history: Years before I-90, the old Sunset Highway (US 10) passed the trailhead to Lodge Lake, about 2 miles west of Snoqualmie Pass. It was an uphill jaunt for my young family. Hardly any sign of this old trail persists. Now, the initial leg of the trail competes with ski lifts and their inevitable loss of forest. In this human-disturbed landscape, alien weeds and sun-loving natives compete for space. In a detached way, we should be a bit tolerant of alien plants; they are the planet's obvious biological successes, thriving where native flora cannot cope. Though most of us think of weeds as undesirables, invaders from other lands, the ecological definition is more apt. It captures their essential attribute: "Weeds are plants that thrive under human disturbance." Epitomizing this tenacious quality are such aliens as foxglove, sheep sorrel, knapweed, toad-flax, and other European waifs. Yet even some native wildflowers vie for a place on these sunny ski slopes: fireweed, pearly everlasting, and other natives listed above. At Lodge Lake and other boggy ground at the pass, watch for the dainty sundew *(Drosera rotundifolia)*, an insect-eating wetlander.

29 ESMERELDA BASIN

Esmerelda Basin round trip	■	**4½ miles**
Difficulty	■	Moderate
High point	■	4600 feet
Elevation gain	■	400 feet
Fortune Creek Pass round trip	■	**7 miles**
Difficulty	■	Moderate
High point	■	5960 feet
Elevation gain	■	1750 feet
Esmerelda Peaks loop trip	■	**15 miles**
Difficulty	■	Moderate
High point	■	5960 feet
Elevation gain	■	3000 feet
Best flowers	■	June to August
Hikable	■	Mid-June to mid-November

Getting there ■ For Esmerelda Basin, drive SR 970 east from Cle Elum. In 6.6 miles turn north on North Fork Teanaway Road (Forest Service Road No. 9737). The end of pavement is reached in 13 miles; continue on the unpaved road and in 10 miles more reach the road-end parking area, elevation 4243 feet. For the start of the Esmerelda Loop, after reaching the end of the pavement drive 8.3 miles more and go left on a road signed "Trail 1392." In 0.3 mile find Boulder–De Roux trail No. 1392, elevation 3800 feet. A Northwest Forest Pass is required.

Map ■ Green Trails No. 209 Mount Stuart

Information ■ Cle Elum Ranger Station, phone (509) 674-4411

A favorite spot for flower watchers who are aware of its variety of species is the varied terrain surrounding the 6477-foot Esmerelda Peaks. A dividend is its location in the eastside rainshadow, where in theory it rarely rains—but as we can attest, theory is no match for reality.

ESMERELDA BASIN. From the parking lot, a short, steep, abandoned miners' road-become-trail climbs beside noisy cataracts passing between craggy peaks, gaining about 250 feet of elevation in ¼ mile before easing off at the basin's entrance.

In a short ½ mile the trail splits; the right fork goes to Longs Pass and Ingalls Lake. Keep straight ahead, crossing several small streams and little flower fields. In about ¾ mile reach the special flower fields. Here in a wet area are two not rare but often-overlooked plants, the cotton grass and one of our carnivorous plants, the butterwort, with leaves that digest small insects. Nearby are bog orchids, shootingstars, and elephant's head louseworts.

There is more. Farther on the ground becomes dryer and scarlet gilia brightens the meadow. In about 2 miles the trail enters forest, a good turnaround point.

FORTUNE CREEK PASS. For Fortune Creek Pass, continue on from Esmerelda Basin another 1½ miles,

Elephant's head lousewort

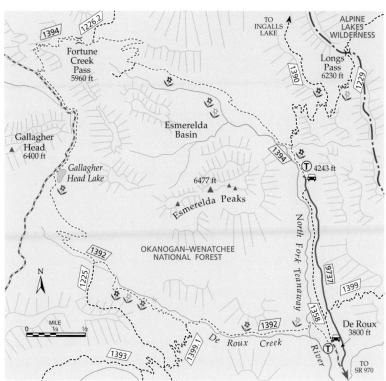

Gallagher Head Lake and false hellebore

alternating between forest and little meadows with lupine and forest plants to the rocky pass. Here you may find douglasia with its red flowers.

At Fortune Creek Pass, all is serpentine—a scattering of whitebark pines, but mostly a scantily clad serpentine barren. Here is where plant life finds it tough going, given the shortness of the growing season and the demands of serpentine soils.

ESMERELDA PEAKS LOOP. When the Springs were scouting trails for a new hiking guide, they had no trouble exploring this loop in one day. However, in late July a friend took his sleeping bag, a tarp, and a cold sandwich here and took 2 whole days just to identify the flowers. A couple of overnights would scarcely be enough. He counted in those 2 days more than 150 species—flowers of subalpine forests, dry meadows and bogs, cliffs and rock slides, Cascade Crest and rainshadow.

The loop starts at the end of the road in what formerly was the De Roux Creek Campground, on trail No. 1392. In ¼ mile cross the North Fork Teanaway River, dwindled mostly to creek here. The way starts in forest, with coralroot orchid, violets, woodnymph, wintergreen, and pipsissewa nearby. In about ¾ mile is a junction; stay right and start switchbacking along De Roux Creek as it passes a falls over a rock buttress pink with Columbia lewisia, one of our friend's favorite flowers. Above the falls the grade eases off and at 2¼ miles crosses the creek and enters in ½ mile a green vale. More switchbacks climb to the open basin of Gallagher Head Lake at 4 miles, elevation 5600 feet.

The shallow lake is surrounded by Hawkins Mountain, Gallagher Head, Esmerelda Peaks, and an old miners' road now open to ORVs. Before the Forest Service put a stop to it, the surrounding wet meadow was their playground, and even after twenty years their deep tracks can still be seen.

Follow the Fortune Creek "jeep" trail northward 1 mile, losing 450 feet in elevation. Turn left onto trail No. 1394 and climb almost 1000 feet to Fortune Creek Pass. Descend through Esmerelda Basin to the road end and a final 2 miles to the Boulder–De Roux trailhead.

Did you keep score? Did you beat our friend's 150? ■ I. S.

Art's Notes

In the Esmerelda Basin, two dramatically different geologies meet to exact their influences on the plant life. The precipitous Esmerelda Peaks, in the south border of the basin, are solid altered volcanics (metadiabase), as is their high eastern twin, Teanaway Mountain. But intermittently, all along the basin trail, one encounters the telltale reddish-brown (iron–magnesium rich) rock called serpentinized peridotite, along with its distinctive plants. Along the steep pitch just above the trailhead parking lot, watch for, on the right, a gaggle of penstemons and lewisias on the altered volcanic rock. This dazzling rock garden also sports phlox, rock ferns, and saxifrages. At the first permanent creek crossing is the wet place to look for the insectivorous butterwort (*Pinguicula vulgaris*), with its showy purple tubular flowers and glutinous ("fly-paper") leaves.

Well into Esmerelda Basin, the open forest of fir and pine offers a galaxy of wildflowers: yellow arnicas and senecios, creeping phlox and deep lavender lupines. In wet meadows, just below the trail, look for cotton grass, white bog orchid, elephant's head lousewort (*Pedicularis groenlandica*), and shootingstar. Just before reaching the rim of the basin at Fortune Creek Pass, we again enter the "red rock" country, where serpentines prevail. The red, iron-rich soil supports its own rich array of herbs: the two serpentine ferns—rock brake (*Aspidotis densa*) and serpentine holly fern (*Polystichum lemmonii*)—and other herbs that thrive on serpentine—the deep reddish purple-flowered douglasia (*Douglasia nivalis* var. *dentata*), kin to primroses, two buckwheats (*Eriogonum compositum*—both white and yellow flowers, and *E. pyrolaefolium*), and the local cream-yellow paintbrush (*Castilleja elmeri*).

Should you prefer a quicker exposure to the varied flora of the basin, try the "grunt" up the Ingalls Lake or Longs Pass trails. You traverse serpentine slopes all the way to the ridge tops. An added bonus on the Ingalls Lake trail is to find glorious alpine larch just over the top. And along the way, watch for the creamy-yellow paintbrush (*Castilleja elmeri*), the wintergreen-leaved buckwheat (*Eriogonum pyrolaefolium*), mats of the fleeceflower (*Polygonum newberryi*), the dwarfish Oregon sunshine (*Eriophyllum lanatum*), as well as all the other serpentine wildflowers seen in the upper Esmerelda Basin.

30 Navaho Pass

Navaho Pass round trip ■ **11 miles**
Difficulty ■ Moderate
High point ■ 6040 feet
Elevation gain ■ 2940 feet

Bean Basin round trip ■ **5 miles**
Difficulty ■ Moderate
High point ■ 5600 feet
Elevation gain ■ 2000 feet

Best flowers ■ Late June to mid-July
Hikable ■ Mid-June to November

Getting there ■ Drive SR 970 east from Cle Elum. In 6.6 miles turn north on North Fork Teanaway Road (Forest Service Road No. 9737). The end of pavement is reached in 13 miles at a major junction. For Navaho Pass, from the junction go right 1.3 miles on unpaved road No. 9737, then at a Y go right on Stafford Creek road No. 9703. In 2.5 miles more cross Stafford Creek and reach Stafford Creek trail No. 1359, elevation 3100 feet. For Bean Basin, at the Y intersection stay left on road No. 9737 and continue for an additional 2.5 miles to Beverly Creek. Just before crossing the creek, turn right and go 0.9 mile on Beverly Creek road No. 9737-112 to the road end, elevation 3640 feet, and the start of the Beverly–Turnpike trail No. 1391. A Northwest Forest Pass is required.

Map ■ Green Trails No. 209 Mount Stuart
Information ■ Cle Elum Ranger Station, phone (509) 674-4411

Navaho Pass. On this hike, along with a textbook procession of conifer communities from start (low) to finish (high), there are two special rewards for flower watchers: The first, at 4 miles (and a 1900-foot elevation gain), is a large, lush meadow fed by springs, with a range of flowers at its lower end and elephant's head louseworts to paintbrushes and lupines at its upper end. The second treat is the view of the Stuart Range from Navaho Pass, at 5½ miles.

While the main rewards are still miles away, other treats entice as the trail ascends moderately along Stafford Creek in airy old ponderosa pine, standing tall and aloof above a sparse forest floor with occasional patches of tiger lilies, columbine, pipsissewa, twinflower, and pine grass. The next community is of Douglas fir, a scattering of enormous relicts. Many are truly elderly, sure to die any century now. Others are mortally ill from the ravages of a lethal crown fire that must have opened up the forest within the past century, giving breathing room for young silver firs and lodgepole pines.

The trail swings away from the creek into lodgepole and western white pine, western hemlock, silver fir, Engelmann spruce, and still more Douglas fir relicts astonishingly ancient.

At 4 miles reach the first of the rewards. In the center of the big flower meadow, Standup Creek trail No. 1369 heads left. Go right on a trail signed "County Line Trail 2." Giant firs inhabit a long switchbacking ascent, dwindling to stunted lodgepole and subalpine fir in dry meadows.

Forget-me-not

THE WENATCHEE MOUNTAINS—A GEOLOGICAL WONDERLAND

The several wildflower trails featured here lie within that southeast-trending spur of the Cascades—the ancient Wenatchee Mountains. The loftiest spur—the western Wenatchees—is roughly delineated by three major streams, the Cle Elum River, the Teanaway River, and Icicle Creek. Then from Blewett and Swauk Passes (accessed via US 97) and east to the city of Wenatchee lies the high basalt lava plateau of Table Mountain and Mission Peak. The western Wenatchees are a vast jumble of many different rock types: Swauk sandstone, Teanaway basalts, the altered volcanics (metadiabase) of Hawkins Mountain and Esmeralda Peak, and the serpentine and periodotites of upper Esmeralda Basin, Longs Pass, Ingalls Lake, and Iron Peak. Topping it all is the awesome sawtooth summits of the Mount Stuart Range granites. Encircling the southern perimeter of the Stuart Range in a lazy horseshoe is the surprise rock of them all: iron–magnesium-rich serpentine and kindred rocks. This grand geologic diversity exerts deep effects on plant life, creating, by weathering, soils with specific nutrient levels. Of all the Wenatchee rock types, the serpentines have the most profound effect on plants. Some are narrowly restricted to the serpentine, while many others are excluded. See Kruckeberg Country, Hike 31, and its accompanying "Art's Notes" to get a fuller appreciation of serpentine's influences on plants. ■ A. R. K.

Near 5600 feet, dry meadows become marshy meadows, and then meadows drop away to reveal an expanse of glittering serpentine. The best reward is saved for last: One final climb leads to the boundary of the Alpine Lakes Wilderness at Navaho Pass, 6040 feet, an autumn-gold stand of western larch, and the magnificent, encompassing view of the Stuart Range.

BEAN BASIN. The flowers at Bean Basin are definitely worth the effort, but there is a difficult crossing of Bean Creek during the snowmelt period, which also is the best flower season.

The trail starts on an abandoned logging road. Half a mile from the Beverly Creek trailhead to Bean Creek, turn right on trail No. 1391.1. The

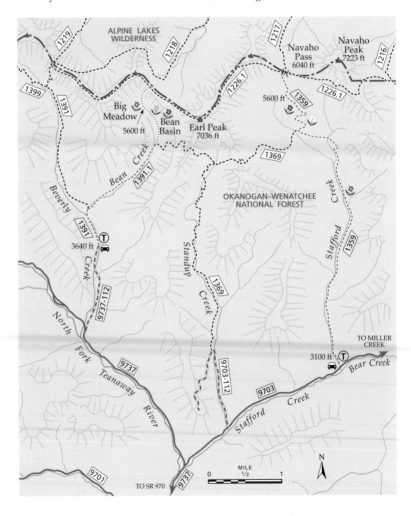

The Stuart Range from Navaho Pass

trail climbs in open forest ¼ mile to the difficult creek crossing and an abundance of buckwheat species.

The trail splits at 2 miles, 5000 feet. Go left for the Big Meadow, at 5200 feet. The trail ends in a tall-grass marsh with monkeyflower and willow-herb, which gives way to a dry rock-garden hillside of skyrocket, brake, and heather leading to a view of Mount Stuart. ■ I. S. & A. R. K.

Art's Notes

The Stafford Creek trail catches the attention of the wildflower watcher's eye most vividly when one reaches a broad, sloping serpentine barren near the south side of the ridge top. Find here most of the same Teanaway Country serpentine rarities, like the purple *Douglasia* and the pyrola-leaved buckwheat. Day hikers absolutely must go on to the ridge for the grandest view of the Stuart Range and its lofty eminence, Mount Stuart. Here you stand among stark skeletons and living whitebark pine (five-needled *Pinus albicaulis*), timberline's lofty sentinel.

If you are base camping in the upper Stafford basin, take a side trip off to the east, to the summit of Navaho Peak, an easy mile or two through thickets of whitebark pine and rich alpine flora. It is an especially spectacular side trip on a moonlit night!

31 KRUCKEBERG COUNTRY: IRON PEAK AND LONGS PASS

Iron Peak round trip ▪	**6½ miles**
Difficulty ▪	Moderate
High point ▪	6510 feet
Elevation gain ▪	2590 feet
Longs Pass round trip ▪	**5 miles**
Difficulty ▪	Moderate
High point ▪	6230 feet
Elevation gain ▪	2100 feet
Best flowers ▪	July to late August
Hikable ▪	July to November

Getting there ▪ For the Iron Peak trailhead, drive SR 970 east from Cle Elum. In 6.6 miles turn north on North Fork Teanaway Road (Forest Service Road No. 9737). The end of pavement is reached in 13 miles; continue on the unpaved road another 8.7 miles to Iron Creek trail No. 1399, on the right, elevation 3920 feet. Parking is limited. For the Longs Pass trail, follow the road to its end, 13 miles beyond the end of the pavement, elevation 4243 feet. A Northwest Forest Pass is required.

Map ▪ Green Trails No. 209 Mount Stuart

Information ▪ Cle Elum Ranger Station, phone (509) 674-4411

In early summer, hikers on Kruckeberg Country trails may be so entranced by the flowers that they may never note all the wonderful views, for the open forest screes display a distracting assortment of buckwheats and desert parsleys and orange-and-yellow paintbrushes. Under the leadership of Dr. Art Kruckeberg, the University of Washington botany professor who practically invented serpentine flora, the plant community on Iron Peak has been dedicated by the Forest Service as the Eldorado Creek Research Area.

IRON PEAK. When the parking lots for other Teanaway trails are full, the Iron Peak parking area is often empty. If only people knew! Flower-wise, view-wise, and energy-wise, this is the best of the best, with views that start at the car. In early summer, the same is true of the flowers.

The trail switchbacks upward across a rib between Eldorado Creek and another small creek, within sound of the water but never in reach. Then the trail crosses the meadow headwaters of Eldorado Creek to a rocky saddle, 6100 feet, at 2½ miles. Naturally, the best is "just around the corner," in this case a steep ½ mile and 450 feet higher. A relatively easy scramble goes around buttresses and past flower rockeries to the summit of Iron Peak, 6510 feet. Beyond the rare flowers, the views are of the whole Teanaway region, topped by Mount Stuart.

Unless you are a flower expert, bring the biggest flower book you can find, for there are uncommon flowers here that do not appear in most books. Little benches in the side of the ridge hold snow late and feed wet-meadow plants. The serpentine barrens support only a scattering of life but include species that grow nowhere except in serpentine soils, bringing botanists from afar to admire the rarities, some found only in this vicinity. The crazy rocks of the crest are notable for violet cushions of douglasia.

Alpine spring beauty

LONGS PASS. Longs Pass is popular with climbers on their way to Mount Stuart and hikers headed for Ingalls Lake. Where does that leave us flower watchers? With the best seat in the house. There are no big flower meadows here, but a special treat can be found in the serpentine soil.

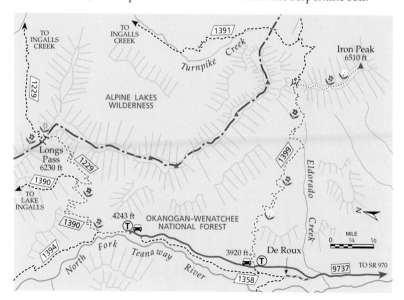

Mount Stuart seen from Iron Peak

Starting out on the Esmerelda trail, the flowers begin with cliff penstemon on the rocks above the trail. In ¼ mile the trail splits. Straight ahead goes to Esmeralda Basin (Hike 29); go right, switchbacking upward. Scarlet gilia, paintbrush, and partridgefoot are tucked in here and there.

At 2 miles, 5400 feet, the trail splits again. The Lake Ingalls trail goes left; go right on trail No. 1229, switchbacking onward and upward over the orange-colored serpentine talus. At 2½ miles the way crosses a bench and reaches Longs Pass, 6230 feet, and a face-to-face view of 9415-foot Mount Stuart.

By the time the pass is reached, trees have mostly given up the struggle to live in the serpentine soils, lacking as it does certain essential minerals, vitamins, and water. Only plants that can adapt are found, such as the brilliantly blossomed douglasia.

And nearby is a bonus hike, one well worth taking—to that wildflower mecca, Red Top Lookout:

Take SR 970 and US 97 from Cle Elum going toward Leavenworth via the Swauk Creek valley. Just beyond Mineral Springs Campground and the lodge/restaurant of the same name, take road No. 9723 leading west from US 97 going up toward Teanaway Ridge. About halfway up, take road No. 9702, marked for Red Top. At the end of the road, take the marked trail from the ample parking lot to the lookout, about ¼ mile. The trail, at first in old-growth Douglas fir and grand fir, breaks out into open scree slopes where wildflowers reign in profusion. Bitterroot *(Lewisia rediviva)* glorifies the scree here, along with penstemons, buckwheats, and assorted low perennials. The lookout has been staffed in the summer in the recent past. Glorious views can be had from the summit into the Mount Stuart country and the Upper Teanaway River area. ▪ I. S. & A. R. K.

Art's Notes

The Iron Peak ascent and the ridge traverse to the summit of Iron Peak is a perfect place to witness the meaning and significance of serpentine (and peridotite) rock to the flora. First, the geologic story: A worldwide family of rocks, the ultramafics, intrudes other geologic formations, especially where restless plates of the Earth's crust meet. Here, upper Earth's mantle of molten rock, beneath the crust, emerges. These rocks are rich in iron and magnesium, along with nickel, chromium, and cobalt. Unaltered, the rocks of igneous iron–magnesium silicates are known as peridotite or dunite. Both occur in Washington State. Should they be altered by heat, water, and pressure, however, they are "serpentinized," yet retain their high levels of iron, magnesium, and nickel. The soils weathering from these rocks lack the needed nutrients for normal plant growth; they are low in calcium, nitrogen, phosphorus, and potassium.

These adverse conditions should inhibit any plant cover at all. But Nature meets the challenge: Some plants adapt to these intimidating excesses . . . and deficiencies. Thus is born a serpentine flora, often with plant species found nowhere else—*endemics*. Endemics are often species of local and unique habitats, restricted to narrow stretches of land. Wenatchee Mountain serpentine endemics are a bouquet of rarities: the rare grass *Poa curtifolia*, the brilliant reddish-purple primrose kin, Douglasia nivalis var. dentata, holly fern (*Polystichum lemmonii*), the showy yellow paintbrush, *Castilleja elmeri*, and the gray-leaved desert parsley, *Lomatium cuspidatum*. Narrow restriction to a local geologic formation is known worldwide and its best examples are the serpentine outcrops of the world, found in temperate and tropical regions. Rich in serpentine endemics are the floras of California and Oregon; they are prominent in the Mediterranean basin; and top honors go to serpentine endemism in New Caledonia and Cuba. "Kruckeberg Country" in the Wenatchee Mountains modestly shares honors with the rest of the world's serpentine floras.

32 ┆ TRONSEN RIDGE

Round trip ■	**5 miles**
Difficulty ■	Moderate
Best flowers ■	June
Hikable ■	Late May through October
High point ■	4870 feet
Elevation gain ■	900 feet

Getting there ■ From Seattle, take I-90 east over Snoqualmie Pass and get off at exit 85. Follow US 97 to Blewett Pass. Continue 5 miles beyond Blewett Pass to Five Mile Road No. 7224 and turn right. Drive 3½ miles on the gravel road to a signboard and primitive campsite, elevation about 4210 feet. There are no facilities. This road is narrow, steep, and deeply rutted, with a couple of sections that are badly eroded and may not be suitable for passenger cars.

Map ■ Green Trails No. 210 Liberty

Information ■ Leavenworth Ranger District, phone (509) 548-6977

Getting to the northern trailhead is the most challenging aspect of this hike. A pickup truck or four-wheel-drive vehicle is recommended. If you don't have a high-clearance vehicle, you can also get to this trail from the southern trailhead via Forest Service Road No. 9712. However, this approach is apt to be snowed in until early June, and the flower show begins earlier.

Butterfly on a Canada thistle

Therefore, the hike is described from the northern trailhead.

Timing is everything. The flower show begins as the snow melts, and as the snow melts, trails in this region are also popular with motorcyclists. However, the northern section of the trail is closed to motorcycles between October 1 and June 15. You can make the hike as short or as long as you like.

The Tronsen Ridge trail runs the length of Tronsen Ridge (about 7 miles) and also provides a link to Red Hill trail No. 1223. Starting

Bitterroot

from the north, you'll still get the best views and the most dramatic scenery at 2½ miles. Elevation gain is not a problem; this is a "ridge-run" through open terrain, ideal for wandering at will with no destination. Views and flowers begin as soon as you step out of the car, so be sure to bring a map and flower guide. In late May, I saw balsamroot, glacier lilies, and lupine, but more flowers will bloom in June. Overall, there are more than fifty-five varieties of wildflowers to be found here. Later in the season, look for *Lewisia tweedyi* and Lyall's mariposa lily.

From the north, the trail climbs through mostly open terrain with a few

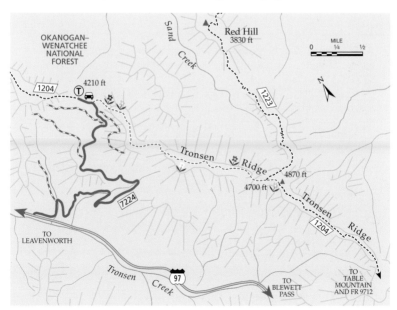

scattered evergreens, pines, and grassy slopes carpeted with glacier lilies, balsamroot, and spring beauties. In addition to early flowers, the views are amazing: Mission Ridge and Devils Gulch are to the east, and to the west are Mount Stuart and the Stuart Range. On a clear day you can see Mount Rainier, and you may be able to see Mount Baker.

At 2¼ miles the trail comes to the well-signed Red Hill trail junction (4700 feet). The Tronsen Ridge trail continues another ¼ mile to the high point of the trail, at 4870 feet. The high point is a poetic arrangement of rocky outcroppings, evergreens, white snags daubed with colorful lichen, floral displays, and a sea of peaks and ridges extending in every direction. Carry plenty of water—the trail is hot and dry later in the season. ■ K. S.

Art's Notes

I have traveled this trail by both approaches. Coming at it from Haney Meadows, atop Table Mountain, gives one a good feel for the grandeur of Table Mountain and the upper Tronsen Creek area. The gravel road from Swauk Pass, off US 97, takes one along a series of sidehill switchbacks before emerging on the Table Mountain summit. Watch for wildflowers along the rocky basalt talus en route to the top: buckwheats, fiddleneck phacelias, columbine, and other rock denizens. On Table Mountain and on the slopes of the Tronsen trail, watch for the deciduous conifer western larch (*Larix occidentalis*), grandly golden in the fall. The undulating terrain of Table Mountain is a rich mix of open flowery meadows joining shrubby sagebrush (*Artemisia tridentata*) and everywhere bordered by mixed conifer forest—stands of Douglas fir, ponderosa pine, lodgepole pine, and the larch.

The Tronsen Creek encounter with *Lewisia tweedyi* is the capstone of the trip. Refer to Chiwaukum Creek, Hike 24, for an account of this glorious perennial.

If you can stay a while on Table Mountain, find a good campground near Haney Meadows, created for horsebackers. With a longer stay on Table Mountain, visit Mount Lillian via an easy trail beginning east of Haney Meadows, on road No. 9712. Mount Lillian, a massive sandstone pinnacle, overlooks the Wenatchee River country and the town of Cashmere. The site supports a diverse array of showy perennials in a natural rock garden. You may even find the rare *Valeriana columbiana* and the showy *Clematis columbiana*.

Yet another spectacular spot on Table Mountain is its highest promontory, Mission Peak, still farther east from Haney Meadows; it is reached by a side road off road No. 9712. Here find another basalt rock garden in early July; the bitterroot *Lewisia rediviva* will enchant.

Opposite: *Phlox and balsamroot in the Umtanum Creek valley (Hike 33)*

SOUTHEAST
WASHINGTON

33 UMTANUM RIDGE

Round trip	■	**6 miles**
Difficulty	■	Strenuous
Best flowers	■	April through June
Hikable	■	April through October
High point	■	3370 feet
Elevation gain	■	2000 feet

Getting there ■ From the west, take I-90 east and take exit 110 for I-82 east. Leave I-82 at exit 3 (Thrall Road). At a stop sign, turn right on SR 821. At the next stop sign, turn left and follow SR 821 into the Yakima Canyon (signed "Yakima Canyon"). Continue 8 miles to the Umtanum Recreation Area (between mileposts 16 and 17), elevation 1340 feet, with parking lot and rest rooms. A Washington Department of Fish and Wildlife Vehicle Use Permit is required.
Maps ■ USGS Wymer and The Cottonwoods
Information ■ L. T. Murray Wildlife Area, phone (509) 575-2740 or (509) 925-6746

May is the best time to see flowers on the east side of the Cascades. The L. T. Murray Wildlife Recreation Area is nestled in the Yakima River Canyon, a geologic blend of basalt cliffs and desert hills that rise above the river between Yakima and Ellensburg. The L. T. Murray Wildlife Area is on the west side of the river. It is administered by the state Department of Fish and Wildlife. In addition to prolific wildflower displays that change week by week in spring, this region is also a good place to observe wildlife.

Several trails are suitable for hikers, some easier than others. Most trails here are unsigned but obvious and easy to follow. Experienced hikers can also hike cross-country to one or several high points along Umtanum Ridge.

Begin at the parking lot on the Umtanum Creek trail and immediately cross the Yakima River on a suspension bridge. Just a bit beyond, the trail crosses railroad tracks and soon comes to an unsigned junction. Hikers must decide here: hike the path along the creek or climb to the ridge. The easier hike is Umtanum Creek; it parallels the northwest branch of Umtanum Creek. Golden currant and Oregon grape were blooming in May along the creek. The Umtanum Creek trail continues about 2 miles up the valley and passes beaver dams and gnarled fruit trees that designate the sites of ancient homesteads.

For the greatest variety of flowers I recommend Umtanum Ridge. To get to Umtanum Ridge, turn left at the unsigned junction onto a trail that climbs beside a canyon (right). This canyon holds an intermittent stream. In ½ mile the trail levels out at the floor of the canyon and a Y junction

The Yakima River and the Umtanum Creek footbridge

marked with a large rock cairn near a grove of willows and aspens. This junction can be confusing for a first-time visitor, as several unofficial trails take off from here. One option is to double back to the northeast and make a sharp left turn along an old road. The road climbs to a viewpoint 700 feet above the Yakima River with views of peaks of the Stuart Range. This is a shorter and easier hike than the 2000-foot climb to Umtanum Ridge.

Hikers can continue on to Umtanum Ridge by choosing one of several unsigned trails that head uphill from the junction at the big cairn. It is easy to find your way in this open terrain, but try to stay on the trails or game

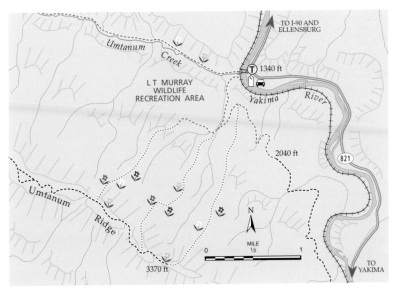

trails rather than hiking cross-country as it is hard on fragile plants. Several bumps along the ridge suffice as high points and all have views.

The wildflower habitat changes every few feet on the climb to the crest. Climb through areas of shootingstars, arrowleaf balsamroot, and bladderwort. About midway through May, small yellow composites carpet the hills and are interspersed with bluebells *(Mertensia)*. Near the ridge crest you may see hedgehog cactus but in May it was not yet in bloom. In May, lupine and showy large-headed clover were blooming. There was also a variety of violets, including sagebrush violets. All along the ridge crest are impressive views of Mount Rainier, Mount Adams, the Stuart Range, and the Kittitas and Yakima Valleys. ■ K. S.

Art's Notes

Delight in the historical route down the grand canyon of the Yakima River. Its highway, now SR 821, was the only main road to Yakima from Ellensburg and Seattle, a branch of old US 10, the Sunset Highway. The first transcontinental railway from Seattle to Chicago, the Northern Pacific, still takes this canyon route (now the Burlington Northern–Santa Fe Railway). Once in the winding canyon, you can be awed by the massive exposures of Columbia Plateau lava, layer upon layer of basalt, some "frozen" in hexagonal columns.

En route to the Umtanum Recreation Area, there are convenient pullouts to witness spring wildflowers: purple penstemons and yellow daisies clinging to the sheer walls. Or find a riverside park to inspect the riparian flora along the river.

Cacti in Washington State? Indeed, we can boast of at least three different kinds. The one occurring here, the hedgehog cactus *(Pediocactus simpsonii)* is a baseball-size orb of spines: When in bloom, the spiny ball is topped with several showy pink to purple flowers—most photogenic. I've seen it elsewhere, notably at the Rattlesnake summit along old US 10, between Ellensburg and Vantage; look for it in and near Gingko Petrified Forest State Park. It is not common now, especially as it has been dug ruthlessly by cactus fanciers. It is now on the Sensitive List for state rarities by the Washington Natural Heritage Program. So don't dig it, just feast your eyes on it. Another Washington cactus grows, of all places, at Sequim and in the San Juan Islands, in dry, rocky spots overlooking the Strait of Juan de Fuca. It is one of the pricklypear or cholla cacti, *Opuntia fragilis*. Yet another opuntia, *O. polyacantha*, is widespread in sagebrush country. It is said to have made the portage by Lewis and Clark around the Great Falls of Montana a prickly hazard afoot. Curious about the origin of Um(p)tanum? It is a First Peoples' word for "contentment," referring to the early snowmelt here that brought deer down to the creek in good numbers.

34 BLACK CANYON

Round trip	▪	**4 to 6 miles**
Difficulty	▪	Moderate
Best flowers	▪	April through June
Hikable	▪	Late April through October
High point	▪	3900 feet
Elevation gain	▪	900 to 1500 feet

Getting there ▪ From Seattle, take I-90 east, turn right onto I-82 at exit 110, and get off I-82 at exit 26 (Selah). Follow signs to Selah on SR 823, and at a T-junction in Selah turn right onto North Wenas Road. Continue 1.6 miles past a reservoir (left) to a gravel road (right) with a large yellow sign reading "Public Notice," elevation 2000 feet, 18 miles from Selah. At the yellow sign, a map on the signboard indicates which roads are open to the public; they are marked with green dots. Park at the sign or drive 0.5 mile to a metal gate. The gate is closed but not locked. If the gate is closed, be sure to close it when you return. You may be able to drive beyond the gate with a high-clearance vehicle another mile or so (1.3 miles from the highway), to a berm and room to park at the end of the road, elevation 2400 feet. There are no facilities at the trailhead. A Washington Department of Fish and Wildlife Vehicle Use Permit is required.

Map ▪ USGS Wenas Lake

Information ▪ L. T. Murray Wildlife Area, phone (509) 575-2740 or (509) 952-6746

Even in late summer Black Canyon is a lovely hike, despite the lack of blooming flowers, with tall grasses and black outcroppings of rock set against a deep blue sky. Find a breeze and watch the tall grasses ripple like waves across the tawny hills.

From the "Public Notice" sign, turn right and drive or hike ½ mile to a metal gate. When I was there in August, I found aspens, golden currant, flowers gone to seed, and assorted shrubs beside the road.

From the gate, the terrain on the right side of the road consists of grassy slopes with black basalt talus

Hedgehog cactus

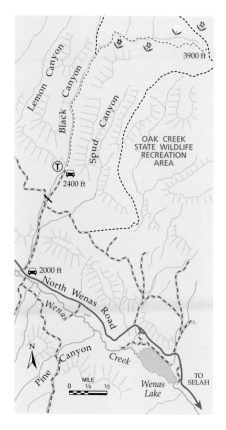

slopes and outcroppings. On the left are aspens, a few ponderosa pines, numerous shrubs, and grasses, indicating a hint of a stream in mid-August. In spring, this is a favorite haunt of bird watchers. You may see bluebirds, mourning doves, grouse, and western kingbirds. This is also rattlesnake country—one crossed the trail directly in front of me as I walked the road. Be alert; if it is windy, it may be hard to hear them rattle their warning.

It is about a mile from the gate to an ancient cabin (left) that can be hard to spot as it is partially obscured by aspens and alders. Alders are growing up through the floor of the cabin, adding a poignant touch to an untold story. This is a good turnaround as it is level, grassy, and partially in the shade provided by the tall aspens. On a hot day the shade is welcome. It is about 900 feet of elevation gain to this point.

About ½ mile from the cabin the road splits. The right fork is a steep, 2-mile climb to the crest of the ridge. According to the map at the signboard, you can also make a long loop back to the car by turning left at the fork and descending the other side of Black Canyon.

The ridge crest is about 4½ miles from North Wenas Road and the parking area. To reach the highest point of the ridge (3900 feet), at the split, turn right and continue another mile to a 3900-foot viewpoint. This is another good turnaround, with views to the south over the Wenas Valley and north to the Stuart Range.

By August, many flowers have gone to seed but blazing stars, asters, yarrow, penstemon, and rabbitbrush are in bloom. Golden currant is fruiting and by late September the aspens will turn golden. Wildflower enthusiasts may be able to identify flowers that bloom earlier in the season by studying their desiccated leaves and seedpods. I recognized balsamroot, wild onions, and roses. Early in the season look for buckwheat and bitterroot. Watch for wildlife, too—elk and deer are not at all uncommon. ■ K. S.

Balsamroot, phlox, and bitterbrush

Art's Notes

"All flesh is grass," so sayeth the Bible's book of Isaiah. The deep meaning of this truism is nowhere more apparent than in the dry interior east of the Cascades. Native grasses indeed epitomize the ponderosa pine and sagebrush-bunchgrass country we call the high desert or shrub–steppe ecosystem. The most important of all dry country grasses is blue-bunch wheatgrass, *Agropyron spicatum*. It is a perennial bunchgrass, "bunch" because it forms a compact clump of blue-gray leafy stems. In flower, its stems are up to 2 feet tall, bearing a tight spike of grass flowers. The discrete clumps form an impressive "sea of grass," especially in sagebrush country. Look for other grass species: In ponderosa pine country, dense swards of the leafy perennial pine grass *(Calamagrostis rubescens)* hold sway under the old-growth pines. Wild rye, *Elymus glaucus*, a 4–5-foot-tall bunchgrass, is frequent in more mesic (moister) places. Grass does become flesh here, for native elk and deer thrive on the nutritious grass forage. Then Euroman introduced cattle and sheep that ate the native grasses to death. In overgrazed lands, a pestilential alien has taken over: The annual cheatgrass *(Bromus tectorum)* has inundated the land where the native bunchgrasses once grew.

35 DUSTY LAKE

Round trip	■	**3 miles**
Difficulty	■	Easy
Best flowers	■	May through June
Hikable	■	Year-round
High point	■	1200 feet
Elevation gain	■	400 feet

Getting there ■ From Seattle, go east on I-90 over Snoqualmie Pass to exit 149 (George) and turn left at the overpass stop sign, heading north on SR 281 toward Quincy. After 5.6 miles turn left onto White Trail Road (sometimes shown as 5 NW on maps) and continue 3 miles. At a curve in the road, turn left onto a road signed "Fishing." The road becomes gravel and at 0.4 mile enters the Quincy Wildlife Area. The gate is closed from October through January; park by the gate when it is closed. Continue 1.7 miles to the Burke Lake and Dusty Lake trailhead, 1200 feet. A Washington Department of Fish and Wildlife Vehicle Use Permit is required.

Map ■ USGS Babcock Ridge

Information ■ Quincy Wildlife Area, phone (509) 754-4624 or (509) 764-6641

Spring is a capricious season for hikers from the west side of the Cascades. Hungry for warm days and flowers, they are often driven east by bad weather. It's a good thing there are sweet gems like Dusty Lake to visit, situated in the same geological neighborhood as Ancient Lakes. Though the hike is short and the drive is long, it is worth it. You may feel as if you've gotten away with something when you drive through a late spring storm at Snoqualmie Pass into open terrain where clumps of phlox cast a purple glow against rolling hills and the golden fire of balsamroot warms the heart.

You will get a view of Dusty Lake from the parking area. It is a large lake with two small islands. This is just one of several lakes to explore, most of them small, each one different, all linked by trails. Go

Bluebell

slow and savor. In spring or summer it is easy to spend a day here, perhaps even a weekend. Every nook and cranny of this seemingly desolate area is teeming with life and color. In July, look for wild onions, mariposa lily, yellow blazing star, fireweed, buckwheat, and, near streams, Russian olive trees. These trees scent the air with the smell of vanilla when they blossom, earlier in the season. Wildlife is abundant; some of the small lakes are home to beaver and turtles, and the cliffs are home for a variety of birds.

Before you head down to Dusty Lake from the parking area, walk an obvious path to the cliffs (right) for a better view of the lake and valley floor beyond. In July, you may find mariposa lilies scattered through profusions of sage.

The trail descends from the north side of the parking area to the first of numerous little streams that empty into Dusty Lake and continues to the lake at 832 feet elevation. Paths go in every direction—a path on the right goes around the lake on talus and a path to the left climbs to a ridge above. Here, bird watchers may find red-winged blackbirds, yellow-headed blackbirds, swallows, raptors, and a variety of waterfowl. Rocks and cliffs border the lake and keep you from walking all the way around it.

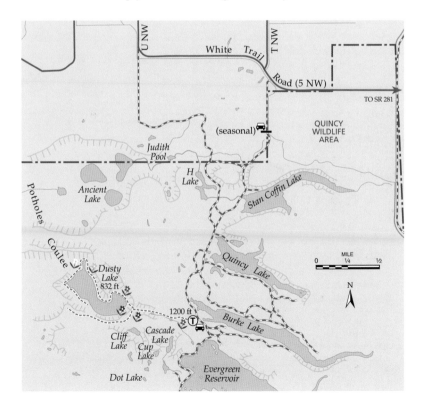

An unidentified DYC, left, *and linear-leaved daisy,* right

In May, wildflower enthusiasts can look for purple sage, daisies, balsamroot, larkspur, wild onion, wild roses, alumroot, elderberry, buckwheat, and serviceberry.

Be sure to treat your water, as water comes from agricultural areas. Watch for rattlesnakes. ◾ K. S.

Art's Notes

Spring on the dry side of the Cascades is a blaze of transient color as glorious yellow dominates. Many members of the sunflower family *(Asteraceae)* turn to yellow for attracting pollinators. Like birders with their cute acronym for small, brown, unidentified birds (LBJs = Little Brown Jobbies), we wildflower seekers have one, too: DYCs, for just another Darn Yellow Composite. Yellow and more yellow: fleabanes, Oregon sunshine, balsamroots, and sunflowers . . . the parade of yellow is endless. The most common and showiest of them is the balsamroot or desert sunflower; several of them grace the high desert of shrub–steppe and yellow pine country. All are variants in the genus *Balsamorhiza*. Their big sunflowerlike "heads" nestle close to the ground, surrounded by large spear-shaped leaves. All parts of balsamroots were used by First Peoples: roots and sunflowerlike seeds for food and leaves for smoking. For some tribes, the blooming time signaled the urge to return up a tributary river of the Columbia for spring and summer foraging.

So be captivated—and often bewildered—at the profusion of DYCs. And remember, "composite" tells you that the "flower" is a compact cluster of florets: showy ray florets and a dense, central pincushion of disk florets.

36 ANCIENT LAKES

Round trip	■	8 miles
Difficulty	■	Easy
Best flowers	■	April through June
Hikable	■	Year-round
High point	■	1100 feet
Elevation gain	■	100 feet

Getting there ■ From Seattle, go east on I-90 over Snoqualmie Pass to exit 149 (George). Turn left at the overpass stop sign and then head left (north) on SR 281 toward Quincy. After 5.6 miles turn left onto White Trail Road (sometimes shown as 5 NW on maps) and follow it for 4 miles to where it turns north on U NW. In 3.8 miles go left (west) onto Road 9 NW and continue 5.9 miles (pavement ends at 2 miles). Continue to the end of the road, with parking for up to eight vehicles at the gate, 1000 feet. Avoid the last road (right); it is a private driveway. No toilets or facilities. A Washington Department of Fish and Wildlife Vehicle Use Permit is required.

Maps ■ USGS Babcock Ridge and West Bar

Information ■ Quincy Wildlife Area, phone (509) 754-4624 or (509) 764-6641

Ancient Lakes are aptly named—they even feel old. As a matter of fact, they are very old leftover bodies of water from the glacial Lake Missoula floods that shaped the land ages ago. It is almost a sacrilege to hurry here. To tarry is better. There are three Ancient Lakes: two are side by side; the third lake is above and is more hidden. The sprawling terrain invites you to ramble, camp, fish, explore, look for wildflowers, and listen to coyotes sing under the chilly stars. Lower Ancient Lake is practically next door to Dusty Lake (Hike 35), another geological leftover.

In May, the air is fragrant with sage and wildflowers. The flowers get an early start on the east side of

Yellow paintbrush

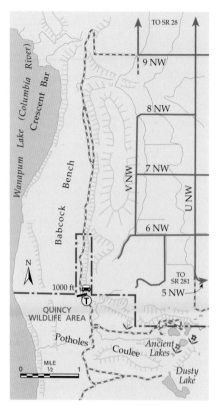

the Cascades—some begin to emerge as early as April. Enticing paths go hither and yon, some leading to the shores of small lakes nestled behind cliffs of columnar basalt, others leading to lonesome views. Now imagine these lakes under hundreds of feet of water, as they were long ago when the glacial Lake Missoula floods covered most of the state.

In spring find flowers, some gaudy, others dainty, in meadows around the lower lake. In late May, I saw yellow paintbrush, orange globemallow, narrow-leafed phacelia, Indian currant, daisies, balsamroot, yarrow, and bastard toad-flax (a type of sandalwood). At dusk, small birds dart in and out of the cliffs, and where waterfalls once roared, small rivulets trickle down like lace from above. Though the wildlife area is surrounded by farms you will feel you are miles from anywhere, perhaps even in another day and age when ancient beasts roamed the land and Man believed the world was flat.

Getting to the lower lake is easy. It's the leaving that is hard. From the gate, walk ½ mile on the gravel road to an unsigned junction; turn left and continue about 3 miles. The road rises slightly as it approaches Ancient Lake, and you'll see a small, marshy lake off to your right. Lower Ancient Lake is the larger, deeper lake (left) near a grove of cottonwoods. If you are camping, the grassy area between the lakes provides an ideal camp. A path goes around the lake on the left, passes under the cliffs, and climbs above a waterfall to a rocky shelf with more unsigned trails. Don't worry about getting lost—the worst fate that will befall you if you get turned around is ending up in someone's backyard.

If Ancient Lakes are crowded, you can walk back to the road and hike another 3 easy miles to Dusty Lake. Experienced hikers with routefinding skills can look for a boot-beaten path climbing from lower Ancient Lake, hike cross-country, and descend on steep talus slopes to Dusty Lake, rather than hike the road. ■ K. S.

Ancient Lakes

Art's Notes

The Columbia Gorge is a national treasure, both for its fascinating geology and its bountiful flora. Geologists tell us that this grand gap in the Cascade Range has persisted for eons of time, way back to the beginnings of modern plant and animal life. The awesome events that gave the Gorge its present massive canyon topography began just after the last Ice Age (ca. 12,000 B.P.). As the great continental ice sheet began to melt, it created a succession of temporary lakes (glacial Lake Missoula in western Montana). Many times these ice-melt ponds dammed by ice broke to release a gargantuan flood of meltwater down the Columbia River. These gigantic surges of meltwater scoured the river's channel, making its most titanic mark on the Gorge and surrounding lava plateau country. More than fifty times did these walls of water flood the gorge and beyond the river's channel, cutting through and eroding the lava and soils laid down well before the last Ice Age.

Dramatic signs of the effects of the glacial Lake Missoula floods are also well upriver beyond the Gorge to western Montana. One of the most spectacular vistas of what is now called the Bretz floods is at Dry Falls State Park. And therein lies a tangled controversy. J Harlen Bretz, a glacial geologist, advanced the thesis that the deeply scoured Columbia River canyon and the vast eroded "scablands" and coulees east of the river were the results of the repeated outpouring of glacial meltwater from glacial Lake Missoula. Bretz's theory, first lampooned by eastern geologists, was finally accepted shortly before his death. Several books tell the story of this grand flood catastrophe: J. E. Allen and M. Burns, *Cataclysms on the Columbia*, David D. Alt's *Glacial Lake Missoula and Its Humongous Floods*, and Marge and Ted Mueller's *Fire, Faults and Floods–A Road and Trail Guide Exploring the Origins of the Columbia River Basin*.

37 ┇ BLYTHE LAKE AND COULEE

Round trip	■	1 to 5 miles
Difficulty	■	Easy to moderate
Best flowers	■	May
Hikable	■	April through October
High point	■	1250 feet
Elevation gain	■	350 feet

Getting there ■ From the west, take I-90 east to Vantage, cross the Columbia River, and take exit 137 for SR 26 (Othello). Continue on SR 26 about 25.5 miles and turn left onto SR 262. The road continues north and bends east to become O'Sullivan Dam Road. At milepost 14 look for the Mar Don Resort (right). Directly across from the resort find a gravel road signed for public fishing and a small sign for Blythe, Corral, and Chukar Lakes. Drive this road (pass Corral Lake) and in 1.3 miles enter the Columbia National Wildlife Refuge. The road ends in 1.7 miles at Blythe Lake, elevation 900 feet (no facilities). A Washington Department of Fish and Wildlife Vehicle Use Permit is required.

Maps ■ DNR Priest Rapids, USGS O'Sullivan Dam

Information ■ Columbia National Wildlife Refuge, phone (509) 466-2668

In April, the mountain passes are still subject to snow, but spring begins early on the other side of the Cascades. When winter lingers in the west, hikers impatient for spring flowers often head east and don't need to venture far from their car to see them. April and May are the best months to experience the flowers and visit destinations such as the Columbia National Wildlife Refuge. Later in the summer, conditions are hot and dry and are not as conducive to hiking.

Spring in the Columbia Basin is short and intense. The air is sweet with the smell of sage and flowers are popping up everywhere. In May, the hills are still fresh and green and dotted with soft, colorful cushions of spreading phlox and balsamroot.

Blythe Lake is a gem in May and is just one of several lakes located in the refuge. The refuge is ideal for hikers of all abilities, especially for those with a variety of interests (such as geology, natural history, photography, and birding). You can wander as little or as far as you like. The terrain is open, with columns of basalt towering over sagebrush–steppes and wetlands.

Blythe Lake is ideal for birding enthusiasts; sandhill cranes can be seen during spring migrations. In spring, birds and small mammals are busy, and every shrub seems to hold a red-winged blackbird.

Hikers with an interest in geology will enjoy prowling the basalt columns and buttes to get an appreciation of how the Columbia Lava Plateau

Columnar basalt encrusted with lichens

and its buttes and coulees were formed by sweeping geologic events.

In May, the flowers you are most likely to see are larkspur, phlox, penstemon, and balsamroot. Depending on conditions, you may also see white-stemmed evening primrose, though these are not as common as the other flowers mentioned.

The hike begins at the end of the gated road, from the parking area. The road is level as it lazily meanders through floral displays and sagebrush; it comes to an end in ½ mile. Find an unmarked path climbing to the right toward a bluff. A short climb leads to the top of the bluff for views down to Blythe Lake and rolling hills beyond. From the bluff, there are other options, including returning the way you came. Trails around the bluff lead to views of Chukar Lake and Crab Creek.

Experienced hikers can easily descend cross-country to Blythe Lake and return to the trailhead on a path that parallels the lakeshore. You can also walk to the other side of the lake and explore beyond. Though trails are not

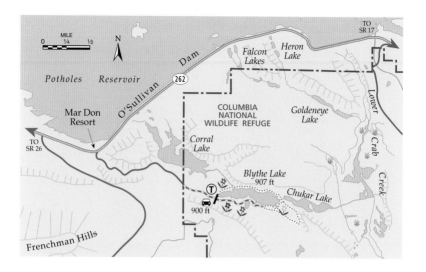

signed, the terrain is open and it would be difficult to lose your way.

I made a loop by hiking to the end of the road and climbing to the bluff. From the bluff I descended to Blythe Lake and followed the lakeshore path back to the car. I hiked about 2 miles through a varied terrain, ranging from lichen-splashed basalt to the peaceful lakeshore, with promontories ideal for observing wildlife.

Be on the lookout for ticks and rattlesnakes. ■ K. S.

Art's Notes

Here on the dry east side of the Cascades, the hiker encounters a landscape vastly different from any on the wet side of the mountains. Here and elsewhere on the vast expanse of the Columbia Lava Plateau, plants adapted to cold winters and hot dry summers prevail. Before Euroman came, oceans of sagebrush *(Artemisia tridentata)*, bitterbrush *(Purshia tridentata)*, and bluebunch wheatgrass dominated eastern Washington, on into Idaho and eastern Oregon. Only in the brief spell of spring (April and May) does the sere gray of sagebrush country come alive with color. Then, witness among the shrubby sage and bitterbrush a galaxy of colorful herbs: phlox, penstemons, balsamroot, evening primrose, *Brodiaea*, purple sage, buckwheats, and a host of other charmers. You may also find, in the shallow slopes of lava talus, swathes of the showy pink gem, bitterroot, named *Lewisia rediviva* for Meriwether Lewis. This is the place and season to whip out your copy of Ron Taylor's *Desert Wildflowers* or *Sagebrush Country* so as to fully immerse yourself in the sagebrush "ocean."

38 ┆ SADDLE MOUNTAINS

Round trip ■ 3 miles
Difficulty ■ Easy
Best flowers ■ April through June
Hikable ■ Year-round
High point ■ 2692 feet
Elevation gain ■ 718 feet

Getting there ■ Drive I-90 east to Vantage, cross the Columbia River, and take exit 137 signed to SR 26 and SR 243. Turn right and after 0.9 mile take another right onto SR 243. After 14.3 miles turn left onto SR 24 Southwest, toward Mattawa. Continue 13.8 miles and turn left on SR 24. At milepost 60, turn left onto a single-lane, paved road signed "Wahluke National Wildlife Refuge," which is guarded by a cattle grate. The road becomes gravel and climbs steeply for 4.2 miles, to a split. Turn right and continue 1.2 miles, to the end of the road and turnaround among the foundations of a Cold War radar station, elevation 1974 feet. There are no facilities. A Washington Department of Fish and Wildlife Vehicle Use Permit is required.
Maps ■ USGS Corfu and Wahatis Peak
Information ■ Wahluke Slope Wildlife Area, phone (509) 765-6641

Spring comes early to the Saddle Mountains, and easiest to access is the eastern part of the 50-mile-long range, bisected by the Columbia River. This is isolated, lonesome country, where you can hike cross-country along the

Buckwheat

crest of the broad ridge with easy ups and downs as far as time and energy allow. Enjoy sprawling views to the Columbia River and beyond. Even in a cold spring, by late April flowers are beginning to emerge from the ground. From the road, you can hike to and explore rocky outcroppings and towers of basalt, splashed with vivid lichens. Game trails go everywhere, and the country is so open it is almost impossible to get lost. You will occasionally run into private land, so respect any posted signs you may encounter. You can walk the road or ramble cross-country—with care.

From the end of the road and radar station, turn right to explore the rolling hills and outcroppings. Gentle ups and downs lead to a flat spot filled with undisturbed bunchgrass, a rarity in this region. High points lead to views of farmlands to the east. On clear days there are views of Mount Rainier and Mount Adams. North are views of more farmlands and Crab Creek. And, of course, you will be looking down on the Columbia River and across to the ghostly buildings of Hanford.

The Saddle Mountain range rises about 2000 feet above the surrounding desert. There are sand dunes on the western slopes, created by strong winds, and the Beverly Sand Dunes Recreational Area is popular with off-road vehicles. Other activities that attract people to the Saddle Mountains are bird watching, hang gliding, horseback riding, hunting, and rock-hounding. Rockhounds come from afar to find petrified wood; no permit is required for noncommercial collectors to gather petrified wood on BLM-administered land.

There are no trails here in the usual sense of the word. Wander where you will cross-country (carefully) and on roads and game trails, and you will find odd and/or amazing objects—antlers, badger holes, coyote dens, and tiny flowers emerging from a long winter sleep. ■ K. S.

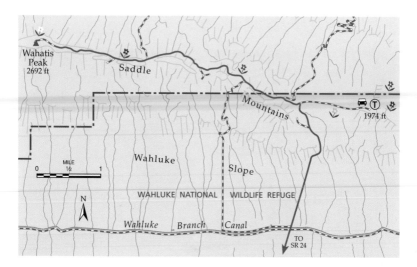

White lupine and balsamroot

Art's Notes

Should you find fossils of ancient plant life here, contemplate a bit on their origins. Most all plant fossils in eastern Washington are petrified wood. And wood is not from prehistoric wildflowers, but from woody plants—trees and shrubs. The "bodies" of wildflowers, annual or perennial, rarely get preserved in the fossil record. Leaves, twigs, and trunks of trees give the paleobotanist a biased glimpse of the past. The fossilized fragments can often be linked to their modern descendents. Fragments of fossilized wood are formed via petrification—turned to stone. The original wood became impregnated with a mineral, mostly silica.

Nearly all the Columbia Plateau country was formed over the long stretches of "deep time," the 60 million years of the Tertiary. This pre–Ice Age epoch started here as a semitropical lowland environment. Its plant life was far different from the present sere sagebrush–bunchgrass vegetation. Most of the fossils of that balmy era were close relatives of the present-day warm temperate floras in eastern Asia: maples, alders, katsura trees, sweet gums, magnolias, and dawn redwood prevailed in those ancient times. A choice place to recapture the essence of this ancient plant life is at Gingko Petrified Forest State Park, just west of Vantage. The most active fossil dig in Washington is in the northeastern part of the state, at Republic, where rich deposits of early Tertiary plants and animals have been found. Check out their fossil museum.

39 WHITE BLUFFS

Round trip	■	**4 to 6 miles**
Difficulty	■	Easy
Best flowers	■	April through June
Hikable	■	Year-round
High point	■	714 feet
Elevation gain	■	300 feet

Getting there ■ From Seattle, take I-90 east to Vantage, cross the Columbia River, and take exit 137 signed to SR 26 and SR 243. Turn right, and after 0.9 mile take another right onto SR 243. After 14.3 miles, turn left onto SR 24 Southwest, toward Mattawa, and continue 13.8 miles, turning left on SR 24. Just beyond milepost 63, turn right onto a dirt road marked "Wahluke National Wildlife Refuge," which is guarded by a solar-powered gate. Drive through, continue 4 miles to an intersection, and turn right, then head downhill 1.3 miles to a parking area by a grove of cottonwoods, elevation 400 feet. No overnight camping is permitted, and there are no facilities or trail signs. The area is closed from 2 hours after dusk until 2 hours before sunrise. A Washington Department of Fish and Wildlife Access Stewardship Permit is required.

Maps ■ USGS Coyote Rapids and Locke Island

Information ■ Wahluke Slope Wildlife Area, phone (509) 765-6641

As in many regions in the Columbia Basin, this one is more of a ramble than a true hike with a beginning, middle, and end. Maybe we are more goal-oriented on the western side of the Cascades; if you must set a "goal" for this ramble, aim for the White Bluffs above Hanford Reach, approximately 3 miles from the start point. My first visit was in late April, a bit early for most of the flowers, but signs of spring were already in the air and there was warmth in the sun.

Before you start your hike, you can continue on foot or in your vehicle to the end of the road, not far from the cottonwood grove, for a taste of history. Here you may encounter a few fishermen during fishing season, and there is a historical cabin that was once a blacksmith's shop. The remnants of other buildings and historical sites can be seen on the other side of the Columbia River, including the original town of White Bluffs, although it is off-limits to the public and is part of the U.S. Department of Energy Hanford Site.

Don't let the word "Hanford" scare you away. This is a fabulous area to explore, with wildlife refuges, points of historical interest, and trails that provide plenty of material for wildflower enthusiasts.

True, it is a long drive if you're from the Puget Sound region, but a weekend

Sagebrush flowers: buckwheat and phlox

is plenty of time to take a good bite of this gorgeous chunk of land, river, and sky. I find it odd that so few people walk here in the spring; having been here twice, I have encountered only one other hiker. When I asked him how often he hiked here, his reply was, "Whenever I need to."

From the parking area, look for a faint path through tall grasses that heads uphill to bluffs overlooking the river. Watch for rattlesnakes in the grasses. Once you are on the bluffs, keep left. Once you are above the Columbia River, you will find something of a trail that weaves along the crest of the bluffs, but exercise caution as some of the bluffs are slowly crumbling into the river—don't get too close to the edge.

I saw many flowers on another visit in May, including evening primrose

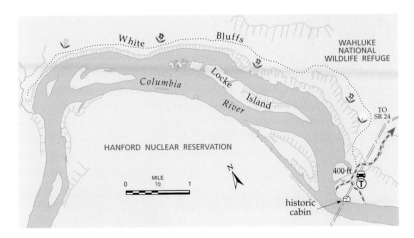

mixed in with sagebrush. Balsamroot and other flowers added color to the subdued hues of the shrub–steppe environment. Your goal, if you need one, is the sand dunes of the White Bluffs that appear much farther away than they are. The bluffs are a product of wind and erosion. The white bluffs are made white by caliche, a limelike deposit. The bluffs served as a landmark for Native Americans for thousands of years.

Hanford Reach is the last free-flowing stretch of the Columbia River and a spawning ground for wild Chinook. The views are expansive as you gaze across the river to the Wizard of Oz–type buildings in the distance that are Hanford. In April the weather can be capricious and can change within an hour. Take raingear. By late April, purple clumps of locoweed are painting the tawny hills, and you may find an entire hillside covered with yellow bells.

This is a climate of fire and ice. Winter is cold and bitter and summer can be an inferno. Spring is the best time to hike in this region, but hike carefully—shrub–steppe habitat may give the impression of durability, but it is very fragile. Do your best to stay on trails and roads to minimize disturbance to vegetation and wildlife. Members of the Washington Native Plant Society recommend that hikers clean boots, pants, and vehicles before and after hiking to halt the spread of invasive weeds, such as cheatgrass. Once invasive plants take hold, they prevent native plants from growing. ■ K. S.

Art's Notes

There must be a better common name for the many locoweeds native in our state. Should any native plant be stigmatized as a weed? And "loco" ("crazy" in Spanish) only applies in certain cases. When members of this huge genus, *Astragalus,* grow over a certain soil type, the plant can poison livestock, causing "loco" behavior (blind staggers). The soil culprit is the element selenium, which can replace sulfur in proteins. It is doubtful if any *Astragalus* species grow on seleniferous soils in our region. Better common names for these showy legumes are milkvetch and rattlepod. There are more than 100 species of *Astragalus* native to the Northwest, mostly east of the Cascades and commonest in the Columbia Plateau country. Ron Taylor's *Sagebrush Country* wildflower guide lists several milkvetches. Common is the dense carpet of *Astragalus purshii,* with reddish purple flowers. Most species also have showy inflated pods that, when dry, may rustle in the wind . . . thus the other common name, rattlepod. *Astragalus,* named for the anklebone of our lower extremities, refers to the anklebone shape of some milkvetch pods.

Opposite: *Bear grass along the Sunrise Peak trail (Hike 46); Mount Adams in the distance*

MOUNT RAINIER
& SOUTH

40 : RAINIER VIEW TRAIL

Round trip ■	**3 miles**
Difficulty ■	Easy
Best flowers ■	June through September
Hikable ■	Late June through October
High point ■	6000 feet
Elevation gain ■	300 feet

Getting there ■ From Enumclaw, go east on SR 410 for 30 miles and turn left onto gravel Forest Service Road No. 7174 (Corral Pass Road) and continue 6 miles to a road junction. Turn right into the parking area, elevation 5651 feet. This road is narrow, rough, and steep. There is a rest room and an information kiosk. (For Noble Knob, turn left at the junction and park.) A Northwest Forest Pass is required.

Map ■ Green Trails No. 271 Bumping Lake

Information ■ White River Ranger District, phone (360) 825-6585

Everyone in the family will enjoy the Rainier View trail once the snow has melted. The trail begins next to the rest room in the parking lot and starts out fairly level as it travels through forest, passes a boggy meadow, and gradually breaks out into the open.

The trail climbs to a rocky ridge, and in about 1 mile Mount Rainier comes into view. If The Mountain is hidden behind a layer of clouds, the variety of flowers will hold your interest. There are several viewpoints and vistas as the trail follows along and near the ridge crest. From the ridge crest, a climber's path continues toward Castle Mountain (right), but hikers should

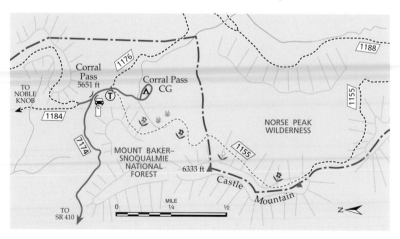

Mount Rainier from the Noble Knob trail

stop well before at one of the obvious viewpoints. In addition to views of Mount Rainier there are views of Mount Adams, Mount Baker, Mount Stuart, the Snoqualmie peaks, and many others.

In early July the snow is just about gone. I saw forty different varieties of wildflowers. In the meadow I saw false hellebore, marsh marigolds, and shootingstars. Other flowers I noted were magenta Indian paintbrush, Sitka valerian, arnica (not yet in flower), an abundance of Jacob's ladder, two varieties of asters, lupine, wild strawberries, pasque flowers, and saxifrage (alpine and spotted). A few glacier lilies were still blooming in the boggy meadow. Along the ridge I saw stonecrop and cliff penstemon.

For another hike at Corral Pass, you can hike part—or all—of the Noble Knob trail (No. 1184). This is a moderate hike of 7 miles round trip with 800

Shootingstars

feet in elevation gain. In early July there weren't as many flowers as there were on the Rainier View trail, but it is still a pleasant hike. June is a better time for hiking Noble Knob. The large meadow at the base of Noble Knob seemed to be about finished with its floral display for the season. ■ K. S.

Art's Notes

It may come as a surprise to learn that shootingstars are members of the primrose family *(Primulaceae)*. Their kin, besides gaggles of primroses world-wide (species of *Primula*), include cyclamens, soldanellas, and the native star flower *(Trientalis)*. The several native shootingstars are species of *Dodecatheon*, a name of Greek or Roman mythological connotation. *Dodeca* is Latin for "twelve," and *theon* is for "god"; it is a fanciful allusion to the plant being protected by twelve gods. It was the eighteenth-century Swedish naturalist Carolus Linnaeus who gave these cometlike flowers their mysterious name. The eight species range from near sea level (*Dodecatheon pulchellum*, often seen in the Fort Lewis–Tacoma prairies) to the subalpine *D. jeffreyi*. Unmistakable is its flower, little streamlined rockets, with the five petals thrust backwards (reflexed) to expose the yellow pollen sacs—the rocket's "engine." Its flowers are usually pendant (upside-down), trusting to pollinating visitors like hummingbirds and bumblebees. When you reach the ridge above the trailhead, enjoy the grand view of Mount Rainier, then at your feet find choice rockery plants, especially the prostrate *Penstemon davidsonii*.

41 ┊ SHEEP LAKE AND SOURDOUGH GAP VIA PACIFIC CREST TRAIL

Round trip	■	6 miles
Difficulty	■	Moderate
Best flowers	■	July through August
Hikable	■	July through October
High point	■	6400 feet
Elevation gain	■	1100 feet in, 200 feet out

Getting there ■ From Enumclaw, drive east on SR 410 to Chinook Pass (44 miles from Enumclaw), elevation 5400 feet. Just east of the wooden overpass, look for the Pacific Crest Trail 2000 (PCT) trailhead and parking area (left). The PCT parking area has stock access and portable toilets. A Northwest Forest Pass is required.

Maps ■ Green Trails Nos. 270 Mount Rainier East and 271 Bumping Lake

Information ■ Naches Ranger District, phone (509) 653-1400

The Pacific Crest Trail to Sheep Lake is better known to backpackers than to wildflower enthusiasts, but this stretch of the PCT is gentle, scenic, and only a short distance from Chinook Pass.

This trail provides a good introduction to the flowers of Mount Rainier. Late July through early August is generally the best time to experience the floral displays, but if you hike later in the season you will also find ripening blueberries and plenty of flowers still in bloom. The combination of berries, late summer flowers, meadows, and views of Mount Rainier make this a hike to remember. Sheep Lake is also an ideal destination for beginning backpackers or families with small children. Because the lake is not in Mount Rainier National Park, camping is allowed on a first-come, first-served basis, though solitude may be hard to come by.

If you have time, there is a great side trip from Chinook Pass on an abandoned but easy-to-follow trail to an overlook of Deadwood Lakes. Beyond the overlook the trail down to the lakes is more of a challenge as the trail is not maintained and can be brushy. The two lakes are surrounded by meadows and separated by a forested isthmus. For the side trip from Chinook Pass, head east on the PCT as it parallels the highway. In about ⅓ mile, an unsigned spur leads to Deadwood Lakes. If you are looking for this trail, it is not difficult to find. The lakes are just shy of the park boundary, about 1½ miles from Chinook Pass. In September, the meadows around Deadwood Lakes are blue with gentians and musky with the scent of elk. This abandoned trail also provides a bounty of berries that most hikers miss out on as they head to other destinations.

Sheep Lake is 2½ miles from Chinook Pass and the nearby Naches Loop (Hike 42), but there are differences in flora to ponder. You may well wonder,

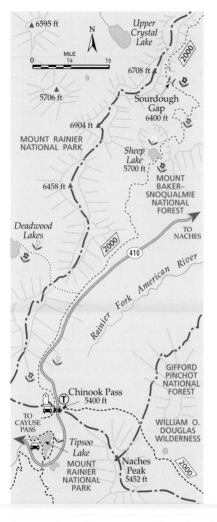

as I do, why Indian paintbrush on the Naches Loop is magenta and Indian paintbrush near Sheep Lake is orange.

In late August you may also see asters, pearly everlasting, cow parsnip, harebells, buckwheat, pasque flower, yarrow, bistort, agoseris, and fireweed. Many were still in bloom when I hiked here, except for false hellebore, whose leaves were like yellowing old lace.

At about 1½ miles, the trail rounds a corner and enters forest, leaving the highway behind. The trail climbs a gentle grade to the green, shallow waters and shores of Sheep Lake, at 5700 feet, 2½ miles from Chinook Pass. Since Sheep Lake is apt to be crowded, campers can look for more isolated camps on benches a few hundred feet away from the lake. In August, the meadows around the lake were dotted with the white blooms of narrow-leafed cotton grass, a sedge. Cotton grass bears a slight resemblance to pasque flowers when they are in seed but these are smaller blooms.

The PCT crosses the outlet stream of the lake on a bridge and starts climbing away from the lake through meadows and rock gardens to the rockier terrain of Sourdough Gap, 6400 feet. In late August, the meadows between the lake and Sourdough Gap are lush with yellowing hellebore and lavender asters still in bloom. You will also begin to notice scattered pine trees mixed in with fir and hemlock.

About 500 feet below the gap, you can get a glimpse of Mount Rainier between two peaks (to the west). For a better view of Mount Rainier and Crystal Lake, look for a boot-beaten path (left) that climbs about 300 feet to a rocky ridge crest. Crystal Lake is straight below, and Mount Rainier fills the sky above. Look down to the zigzags of the PCT as it contours the rocky bowl to pretty Placer Lake and beyond. ■ K. S.

Tipsoo Lake and Mount Rainier

Art's Notes

Color variations are legion in the Indian paintbrush clan, *Castilleja*. Some are dependably constant, as is the red *Castilleja miniata*, the most common paintbrush at midaltitudes. Other species can be white, orange, yellow to magenta; and when color forms coexist, hybrids can appear, usually with intermediate colors. Such rampant variations, not only in color but also in other features, give botanists nightmares. Just what is a "good" species in this continuum of forms? Even conservative botanists (called "lumpers") have recognized nearly fifty species in the Northwest. The genus name commemorates an eighteenth-century Spanish botanist, Domingo Castillejo.

The harebell seen along the trail is the common *Campanula rotundifolia*. Large bell-shaped (campanulate!) blue flowers adorn its leafy stems. You could call it "bluebell"; but that common name has been attached to several other unrelated herbs, like mertensia and the European introduction *Endymion non-scriptus*. Like our native twinflower and bunchberry, the common harebell, or lady's thimble, spans the north temperate continents— circumboreal, no less. It can also grow at low elevations; I have seen it on the Mima Mounds and adjacent prairies east of Olympia, happy there at nearly sea level.

42 NACHES PEAK LOOP

Round trip ■	**4½ miles**
Difficulty ■	Easy
Best flowers ■	July through August
Hikable ■	Mid-July through October
High point ■	5800 feet
Elevation gain ■	600 feet

Getting there ■ From Enumclaw, drive east on SR 410 to Chinook Pass (44 miles from Enumclaw), elevation 5400 feet. Just east of the wooden overpass, look for the Pacific Crest Trail 2000 trailhead and parking area (left), with stock access and portable toilets. Parking is also available at Tipsoo Lake and picnic area, ½ mile west of Chinook Pass. A Northwest Forest Pass is required.

Maps ■ Green Trails Nos. 270 Mount Rainier East and 271 Bumping Lake

Information ■ Mount Rainier National Park, phone (360) 569-2211

Chinook Pass is one of several access points to the Pacific Crest Trail. You can hike either north or south on the PCT, but for a variety of scenery the Naches Loop is recommended. Hiking clockwise is also recommended—

Indian paintbrush

the window of opportunity to hike this trail without running into snow is limited, and in late July or early August you may still find lingering snow on the east slopes of Naches Peak. If in doubt, take an ice ax, or begin the loop counterclockwise and turn back if you hit significant snow. In late July, come for the flowers. In September, come for the fall colors and berries. Or come anytime Chinook Pass is open.

From the parking area, turn left (south) and hike about ⅛ mile on the PCT as it passes Yakima Peak (right) and crosses SR 410 on a wooden overpass. Avoid side trails and follow the main trail as it contours around the east side of Naches Peak and enters the William O. Douglas Wilderness.

From some vantages Naches Peak

looks deceptively gentle, but it is more challenging than it looks. Don't be fooled by the easy slopes; it is a tough scramble. Save the peak for climbers, and stay on the trail as it contours above a valley, crossing several small streams and a waterfall. Flowers peak here from late July to early August, though there were plenty of flowers still in bloom when I was there in late August, including magenta paintbrush, asters, lupine, cow parsnip, bistort, partridgefoot, pink monkeyflowers, and leatherleaf saxifrage. The trail skirts a tarn in 1 mile—Naches Peak rises above meadows filled with western pasque flower, gone to seed. In late afternoon this is especially scenic as the fluffy white seedpods of these flowers are backlit by the sun.

From the tarn, the trail climbs to a high point and re-enters Mount Rainier National Park. At about 2 miles, the trail comes to an overlook of Dewey Lakes and a view of the Goat Rocks in the distance. Just past the viewpoint, the PCT descends (left) to Dewey Lakes and designated campsites. To continue the loop, stay right as the Naches Loop trail climbs a small rise to another tarn and to meadows on the west side of Naches Peak. The meadows are gradually replaced with evergreens and mountain ash. By September, the leaves of mountain ash are yellow and the berries are aglow. Mount Adams comes into view and, to the west, the dark towers of Governors Ridge stand out against the snow and ice of Mount Rainier.

The easy flow of the trail is interrupted as it comes out at Tipsoo Lake on SR 410, ½ mile from Chinook Pass. From here you can follow SR 410 back to Chinook Pass, but most hikers prefer to cross the highway and take

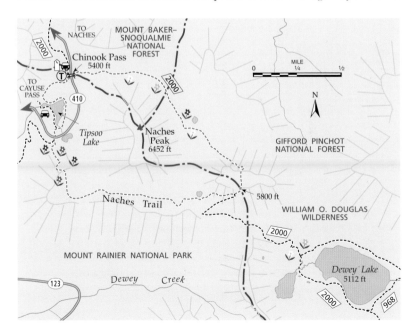

Flower garden on the side of Naches Peak

the trail. To do so, cross the highway and follow tread around the shore of upper Tipsoo Lake (in either direction) to an unsigned junction near a picnic area. Turn right and follow the trail back to the wooden overpass at Chinook Pass to close the loop. ■ K. S.

Art's Notes

A lovely ground cover seen here and elsewhere in the high country is the partridgefoot or Alaska spirea, *Luetkea pectinata*. Its masses of yellowish white flowers are on perky 3-inch stalks above a sward of delicately dissected foliage. Each leaf does resemble a partridge's foot, with four to five "toes." It is related to *Spiraea* and other members of the rose family *(Rosaceae)*, but partridgefoot is an herbaceous perennial. You must have guessed that it is named for a Russian, Count F. D. Luetke, a famous explorer.

Let us say that you have visited two or three hiking sites east of Mount Rainier already. A careful recording of all the wildflowers seen will yield an ecological truism. The chances of adding many more kinds to your field notes diminish with territory covered. In other words, you have witnessed the leveling off of the "species-area curve": numbers of additional species encountered diminish as more area is traversed. It can happen anywhere along a trail, so long as you remain in the same habitat type. So go ahead—draw a "species-area curve," virtual or actual.

CHINOOK PASS

In fall, Chinook Pass offers a spectacular scene. Looking east down into the upper reaches of the American River, the dense old-growth forest puts on a dazzling show. Amid the dark green of firs and spruces, the golden flames of western larch spires punctuate the evergreen landscape. Western larch *(Larix occidentalis)* and its alpine kin, Lyall's larch *(L. lyallii)*, are our only deciduous conifers. Lyall's larch grows at timberline to the north of Chinook Pass and is accessible to hikers, in fall gold, in the upper Enchantments, north of Mount Stuart and at the summit of the Lake Ingalls trail. By fall, all the wildflowers have gone to seed and are not very showy—except western pasque flower *(Anemone occidentalis)*. Its large, creamy-white flowers in alpine spring turn into the most bizarre feather mop of plumed seeds. No wonder its other common name is towhead baby. One nature writer, Dan Mathews, says of it: "It looks like something Dr. Seuss would have dreamed up." Or, more traditionally, it answers to the epithet, "the old man of the mountains." All one such feathery mop needs is a pair of glassy eyes to look like the towhead of an old man. In fact, I saw just such a plant so decorated by an inspired hiker a few years ago.

The pass is also a choice place to see the unique conifer Alaska cedar *(Chamaecyparis nootkatensis)*. Its telltale funereally drooping branches greet the visitor on both sides of the pass. ■ A. R. K.

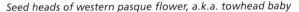

Seed heads of western pasque flower, a.k.a. towhead baby

43 BURROUGHS MOUNTAIN LOOP

Round trip ■	**6 miles**
Difficulty ■	Moderate
Best flowers ■	July through August
Hikable ■	Late June through October
High point ■	7400 feet
Elevation gain ■	1200 feet

Getting there ■ From Enumclaw, drive east on SR 410 to 4.5 miles past the Mount Rainier National Park archway and turn right onto the well-signed White River/Sunrise turnoff. Drive 1.2 miles to the park entrance fee station and in about 3.9 miles pass the turnoff for White River Campground. Continue 10.1 miles to Sunrise, elevation 6400 feet.
Map ■ Green Trails No. 270 Mount Rainier East
Information ■ Mount Rainier National Park, phone (360) 569-2211

Most visitors come to Sunrise to see Mount Rainier, but many hikers know that the other attraction at Sunrise is the wildflower display that begins in mid-June and extends through the summer. Several nature trails take off from the parking lot, but if you have time for only one hike, Burroughs Mountain is suggested. Burroughs Mountain is unusual because this region verges on a tundralike environment. Here, trees that look "young" are actually hundreds of years old. Their growing season is short and conditions are harsh. In addition to flowers, this trail offers views of Mount Rainier, glaciers, moraines, and the White River valley.

You can hike this trail one way or make a loop. Pick up a free trail map at the visitor center to help you plan a loop, though trail junctions are well signed. Tourists and beginning hikers can hike the trail partway and still get a good experience as the views of Mount Rainier and the flowers begin at the parking lot. If you are not familiar with the flowers of Mount Rainier, you can get a sneak preview at the visitor center. Signs near the entrance of the building identify flowers you are apt to see along the trails at Sunrise.

Buckwheat growing at 7000 feet in the shifting pumice of Mount Rainier

The Burroughs Mountain trail

Late July is ideal for this trail, and I hiked the loop counterclockwise. Near Sunrise and along the trail to First Burroughs Mountain, I saw Cusick's speedwell, magenta paintbrush, Sitka valerian, arnica, Jacob's ladder, phlox, Newberry fleeceflower, asters, pasque flower, lupine, mountain dandelion, mountain ash, false hellebore, and a variety of penstemon. On the return loop to Sunrise, marsh marigolds were blooming in the meadows near Shadow Lake with a smattering of bear grass on the slopes.

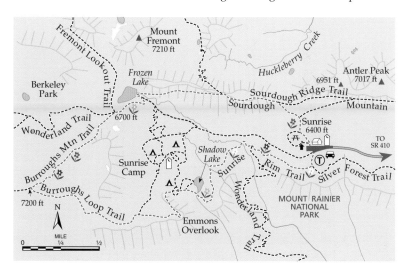

If hiking counterclockwise, start near the rest room on the wide trail that heads up to Sourdough Ridge. In a few paces you'll come to junctions for Mount Fremont, Dege Peak, Grand Park, and Burroughs Mountain. For Burroughs Mountain continue straight, and at the next junction (just below the crest of Sourdough Ridge) turn left toward Mount Rainier. The trail follows along and near the crest of Sourdough Ridge with views down to Grand Park; Mount Baker can be seen in the distance. At 1½ miles you'll come to Frozen Lake (off-limits to hikers) and another junction (6700 feet) for Mount Fremont. Continue along the ridge line toward Burroughs Mountain on the Burroughs Mountain trail and notice how the vegetation changes as the trail gains elevation. Be sure to stay on established trails as the plants able to survive in this environment are slow growing and fragile. Stop anywhere for the best-ever views of Mount Rainier—you may hear the clatter of rock fall. In late July, expect snow patches across portions of the trail. If it is icy, turn back—unless you have an ice ax and know how to use it.

Burroughs Mountain has three summits, but Second Burroughs (7400 feet) is a good turnaround. Be prepared to share this summit with plenty of other hikers and ground squirrels. Yes, it is tempting to feed the squirrels, but our food is not good for them—take photographs instead. Strong

Little Tahoma, Mount Rainier, and the Emmons Glacier

hikers can continue to Third Burroughs for closer views and a better chance of solitude.

For a 6-mile loop, backtrack to the trail junction near Frozen Lake and turn right onto the Sunrise Rim trail at 7200 feet (on the handout map it shows as the Burroughs Loop trail). In July, one large snow patch still covered a portion of the trail as it contoured beneath a steep rocky slope with the consistency of broken crockery. Look down to stagnant pea-green glacial ponds below the Emmons Glacier.

At the next junction (7200 feet), follow the trail signs back to Shadow Lake ⅓ mile from the parking lot and Sunrise. Camping is available at the White River Campground, and walk-in campsites are located about a mile from the parking lot, near Shadow Lake at Sunrise Camp. ■ K.S.

Art's Notes

Upon reaching the top of Burroughs Mountain, you have reached a genuine alpine landscape, the "land above the trees." The nearly flat surface here is strewn with boulders, which German ecologists call a *felsenmeer* ("sea of rocks"). The short growing season (four to six weeks) and harsh, cold winds, freezing temperatures, and shifting snow cover challenge plant life to the utmost. And the challenge is met with plants forming compact, low-growing cushions, no matter what the species. Dwarf lupine *(Lupinus lepidus* var. *lobbii)*, sandwort *(Arenaria)*, and phlox huddle at ground level. One spectacular alpine is the moss campion *(Silene acaulis)*. Before its lovely pinkish-purple flowers appear, it does look like a cushiony "bun" of moss. Moss campion, a carnation relative, is a global alpinist, occurring in Eurasia as well as North America.

Just before gaining the Burroughs summit's alpine scene, the trail goes through classic pygmy forest, universally known as Krummholz, a worldwide dwarfed forest type, at timberline. A common timberline tree in the Northwest, whitebark pine *(Pinus albicaulis),* is subject to the Krummholz effect, although at slightly below timberline they can reach 30 to 50 feet as multibranched pines (with five needles per cluster). It affords an elegant example of coevolution. The pine's cones do not open to shed seeds; they must be opened by corvid (crow family) birds, either Clark's nutcracker or the gray jay, both known to hikers as "camp robbers." Though these birds cache the seeds underground for later foraging, some caches escape their recovery. Thus, a new generation of pines is created. Bird and pine are "made for each other"; that is indeed the title of a marvelous book by Dr. Ron Lanner. Bird and pine have coevolved this mutual kinship, assuring each other's survival. Alas, the coevolutionary drama has a villain: Whitebark pine is under attack by a blister rust fungus in Glacier National Park. Here in Washington, signs of the pestilence have been noted.

PARADISE FLOWER TRAILS

Round trip ■	1 to 5 miles
Difficulty ■	Easy to moderate
Best flowers ■	July through August
Hikable ■	July through October
High point ■	7100 feet
Elevation gain ■	500 to 1700 feet

Getting there ■ From Seattle, go south on I-5 and get off at exit 127 (SR 512), continuing east on SR 512 to SR 7. Then go south on SR 7 to SR 706, in Elbe. Go east on SR 706 through Ashford to the Nisqually Entrance of Mount Rainier National Park. From the entrance station, continue to the Paradise parking area, elevation 5400 feet, 19 miles from the park entrance.

Maps ■ Green Trails No. 270S Mount Rainier East, park handout

Information ■ Mount Rainier National Park, phone (360) 569-2211

Late July and early August are the best times to experience the Paradise flower trails. These are popular trails, and you will encounter many hikers and tourists when flowers are at their peak. You may also encounter climbers coming or going from Mount Rainier.

Bear grass

You can get by without a map as most of these trails are short and trail junctions are signed with mileages. However, if you are a first-time visitor, it is easier to navigate these trails if you've got a map (you can pick up a free trail map inside the park). The trails begin from Paradise, near the Paradise Ranger Station and Guide House, a historic structure currently under rehabilitation.

When it comes to flowers, timing is everything; you can call Mount Rainier National Park ahead of time to see when the flowers are at their peak. Conditions change from year to year—sometimes these subalpine meadows will still be under snow until late summer. In July 2003 most

Avalanche lilies on Mount Rainier

of the avalanche lilies had already peaked, though I saw plenty on the seldom-hiked Moraine trail, which descends to the Nisqually Glacier. In the meadows around Paradise, magenta paintbrush was dominant, and I also saw lupine, rosy spirea, western pasque flower, cinquefoil, alpine asters, phlox, Cusick's speedwell, Jeffrey's shootingstars, false hellebore, broad-leafed arnica, Sitka valerian, bear grass, and more.

For some, the most challenging aspect of Paradise may be deciding which trail to hike. For an easy hike with great views of flowers and Mount Rainier, pretty Myrtle Falls is only ½ mile from Paradise. To get there, climb uphill on the paved trail from the Paradise parking lot near the ranger station and turn right at a junction for the Skyline trail; just follow the signs to Myrtle Falls. For a better view of the falls, turn right and descend a short path to a viewing platform. The view of Mount Rainier above Myrtle Falls is stunning.

Another short hike is the Nisqually Vista trail, a 1¼-mile paved loop that begins near the Jackson Visitor Center. Alta Vista is another short hike leading to great views at 5940 feet (1 mile round trip) and Glacier Vista at 6336 feet (about 2 miles round trip). All of these junctions and trails are on the Green Trails map.

More experienced hikers can hike the Skyline trail, a 5-mile loop that encompasses the best of the scenery. Hikers should wear sturdy boots, as

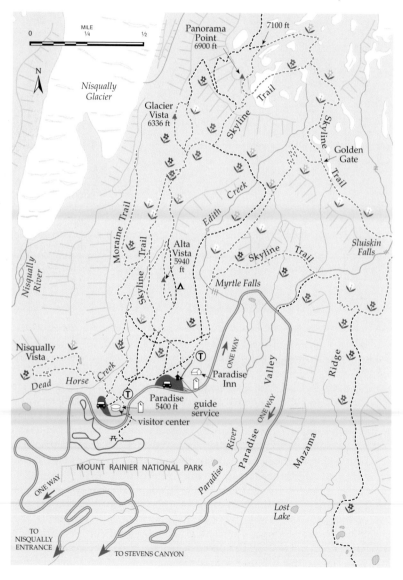

Mount Rainier flower fields

some sections of the loop hold snow through the summer. Hiking clock-wise, the trail starts from Paradise, climbs to the left of Alta Vista, then to a junction for Glacier Vista (an optional short loop), and proceeds to Pan-orama Point at 6900 feet. You can continue to a high point at 7100 feet. From here the trail descends to a junction for the Golden Gate trail. Follow this trail back to Paradise for a shorter loop, or follow the Skyline trail as it descends to the Stevens–Van Trump Memorial (6400 feet) and a junction for the Paradise Glacier trail. Stay on the Skyline by turning right here and right at the next junction; the trail drops into the Paradise valley, traverses flower meadows, crosses above Myrtle Falls, and returns to Paradise. Strong hikers can study the map for other possibilities.

My favorite is the ½-mile Moraine trail, a short hike that starts out from the Skyline trail near Paradise. Follow the signs to Dead Horse Creek and turn left at the Moraine trail junction for a glimpse of the Nisqually Gla-cier. Experienced hikers can continue farther with caution: The trail climbs the crest of a moraine to a high point overlooking the glacier. This trail is also your best bet for solitude. ■ K. S.

A rare double-flowered mutant of western anemone found in Paradise valley

Art's Notes

There is something special about our Cascade volcanoes, and Paradise on Mount Rainier reveals the contrast with magnificence. First is the elevation difference. Our volcanoes rise well above the normal (accordant) summits in the surrounding nonvolcanic Cascades. At Paradise Ranger Station (5400 feet), you are still in that renowned landscape of isolated tree groves (the "timbered atolls" of Steve Arno) and intervening stretches of flowerful mountain meadows. This is the ecologist's parkland subzone of the mountain hemlock zone, just below. Here, "atolls" of mountain hemlock and Pacific silver fir occur in a "sea" of meadowy herbaceous diversity. Upwards, always on volcanoes, timberline is met where the last trees become gnarled bushes, called Krummholz ("crooked wood" in German). Still above, where "wood is a luxury" (*fide* Ola Edwards), one enters the alpine zone, where plant life still makes out. Only on our volcanoes can you revel in the true alpine—land above the trees. Yet above, permanent snow and ice put an end to plant life. For some reason, snowfall seems to be heaviest on our volcanoes. In 1955–56, Paradise recorded 1000 inches (93 feet) of snow, the highest record in the U.S. And snowy Mount Baker holds the world's record for snow depths in the late 1990s. Two wildflower books can give the hiker sure identity of the glory of the high country: Ron Taylor and George Douglas's *Mountain Wildflowers* and, for the more determined flower watcher, latch onto David Biek's *The Flora of Mount Rainier National Park*.

45 McCOY CREEK FLOWER WALKS

Tongue Mountain round trip	■	**3½ miles**
Difficulty	■	Moderate
High point	■	4750 feet
Elevation gain	■	1300 feet
Juniper Peak round trip	■	**8 miles**
Difficulty	■	Moderate
High point	■	5611 feet
Elevation gain	■	2000 feet
Dark Meadow round trip	■	**8 miles**
Difficulty	■	Moderate
High point	■	4800 feet
Elevation gain	■	1000 feet in, 500 feet out
Best flowers	■	Early July to mid-August
Hikable	■	July through October

Getting there ■ For the Tongue Mountain and Juniper Peak trailheads, drive US 12 to Randle, turn south on SR 131, and cross the Cowlitz River. Drive 1 mile, turn left on road No. 23, and 9 miles from Randle turn right on road No. 28. At 10 miles, road No. 28 branches right; leave the pavement and go straight ahead on road No. 29. In 14 miles turn left on road No. 2904 and at 18 miles from Randle, reach Lambert Saddle, elevation 3640 feet. For Dark Meadow, follow road No. 29 to its end, some 15 miles beyond the road No. 23 intersection.
Map ■ Green Trails No. 333 McCoy Peak
Information ■ Randle Ranger District, phone (360) 497-1100

Flowers of forest and meadows and dramatic views. While flowers are secondary on Tongue Mountain, the trail ends on top of a near-vertical 3300-foot cliff with high views. Juniper Peak has a good showing of forest and meadow flowers and ends at a 360-degree view of volcanoes and forest.

For pure flowers, Dark Meadow is the best.

Tongue Mountain. At Lambert Saddle, elevation 3640 feet, take the northbound trail (left). This trail, like most in the Randle District, is motorized and rutted. The ruts are annoying but negotiable on foot. Unless born extremely unlucky, you will encounter more hikers than ORVers.

From the parking lot, the trail starts steeply. On the Fourth of July weekend, Canadian dogwood lined the trail mixed with strawberry blooms and

Sunrise on Mount Adams from Juniper Ridge

white anemones. Trilliums were finished but vanilla leaf was coming into flower; large Solomon's seal and Hooker's fairybells were starting to bloom. Single coralroot orchids gave promise of more forest flowers to come.

In a short but steep mile is a junction, elevation 4000 feet. The motorcycle trail goes straight ahead. Take the right fork signed "Tongue Mountain Hiker Only Trail," climbing even steeper for almost another ½ mile.

The Tongue Mountain trail breaks out of forest at about 4700 feet to a rich display of wildflowers. Look for penstemons, alumroot, and Indian paintbrushes lining the precipitous ridge overlooking the Cispus River to the east and Juniper Peak to the southwest. Tread cautiously here, for the ridge borders a sheer drop to the river. Just below the ridge you will hike through thickets of buckbrush, *Ceanothus velutinus* var. *laevigatus*; it can be laden with creamy white flowers in midsummer.

The final ¼ mile switchbacks up in a rock garden with bouquets of orange paintbrush, blue lupine, bright rose cliff penstemon, yellow wallflower, and strawberry.

In grade school it is every child's ambition to spit a mile. They will have to be satisfied with half that. The adults will be delighted just to hang onto their hats and look down on the twists and turns of the Cispus River, 3300 feet below their feet.

JUNIPER PEAK. Forest flowers and ridge-top meadow flowers and a 360-degree view of the four major volcanoes and some little cinder cones. A classic hike with dramatic views up the Cispus River to Mount Adams, out to Mount Rainier and Mount St. Helens, and over endless forested hills and valleys—all while walking a long ridge, sometimes on open hillsides covered with huckleberries, sometimes in young forest just getting established after the great Cispus fires of 1902 and 1918. The route provides a variety of trips: an easy afternoon stroll to a 4808-foot saddle (the trail this far generally is free of snow in early or mid-June); a day hike to Juniper Peak; an overnight backpack; or a long approach to the Boundary Trail.

Juniper Ridge is a dividing line between east and west. We have found mariposa lilies mixed in with what we think of as western Washington flowers.

Drive to Lambert Saddle and start out on the trail headed south (righthand side of the parking area). This trail also starts steeply on a motorized trail. The first 2 miles have the same forest flowers as the Tongue Mountain trail—Canadian dogwood, strawberries, trilliums, and white anemones—mixed with occasional views. After about 2¼ miles the trees give way to meadow flowers and at 2½

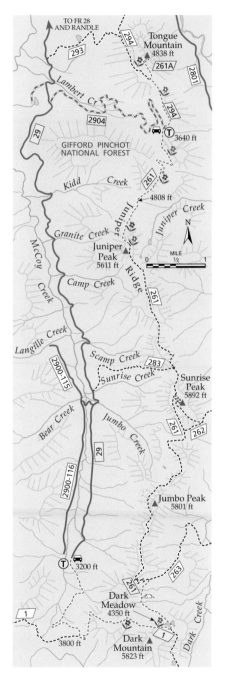

Sego, or mariposa lily

miles the trail reaches a 5400-foot saddle on the shoulder of Juniper Peak. This is a good turnaround point, with a great view of Mount Adams and Mount Rainier.

From here the trail continues on a narrow ridge with a mixture of flowers and trees added to the promised view of the four major volcanoes plus volcanic peaks of Tongue Mountain and McCoy Peak. One summer we looked down on a bull elk grazing below; another time in the fall there was a bear in the same place gobbling up the blueberries.

DARK MEADOW. The flower field of the Dark Meadow beckons. Add, in season, buckets of blueberries and a head-on view of Mount Adams.

From the end of road No. 29, walk the rough abandoned road a long 2 miles to where Boundary Trail No. 1 crosses the road, elevation 3800 feet. Take the trail on the left, climbing steeply over a 4800-foot high point covered with huckleberries, lupine, and paintbrush, and then drop 500 feet into Dark Meadow.

In late July, arnica, lupine, paintbrush, and bear grass were clamoring for attention. Take a sleeping bag and hike another ¼ mile and go left on the Juniper Ridge trail No. 261 to one of the tributaries of Dark Creek. Find a smooth spot and snuggle in between the lupine and bear grass.

We once spent 3 nights here camping among the flowers and had the fun of watching two mountain goats on the side of 5823-foot Dark Mountain. ■ I. S. & A. R. K.

Art's Notes

Dark Divide has been linked with Sasquatch (a.k.a. Bigfoot), which makes being in this country ever so mysterious, even sinister. Though Dark may suggest mystery, it was named for a pioneer miner, D. Dark. Yet the Bigfoot connection persists. Of all the remote places in the South Cascades, Dark Divide has been prime hunting ground for true believers in Bigfoot. Naturalist Robert Pyle's engaging book, *Where Bigfoot Walks*, explores in depth both the Bigfoot legend and the rich natural history of Dark Divide.

46 : SUNRISE PEAK AND JUMBO'S SHOULDER

Sunrise Peak round trip	■	**5 miles**
Difficulty	■	Moderate
High point	■	5892 feet
Elevation gain	■	1600 feet
Jumbo's Shoulder round trip	■	**7 miles**
Difficulty	■	Moderate
High point	■	5500 feet
Elevation gain	■	1600 feet in, 400 feet out
Best flowers	■	Early July to mid-August
Hikable	■	July through October

Getting there ■ Drive US 12 to Randle, turn south on SR 131, and cross the Cowlitz River. Drive 1 mile, turn left on road No. 23, and pass the junction with road No. 21 in 19 miles. Stay right on road No. 23 another 4.6 miles and go right on road No. 2324. At 4.2 miles from road No. 23, at an unmarked junction, go sharply right. In another mile go left on road No. 2324-063. At 5.6 miles from road No. 23 find Sunrise Peak trail No. 262, elevation 4400 feet.

Map ■ Green Trails No. 333 McCoy Peak

Information ■ Randle Ranger District, phone (360) 497-1100

Meadows filled with wildflowers; miles of them. But also glorious views north and south to Mount St. Helens, Mount Hood, Mount Adams, and Mount Rainier. About those meadows: flowery meadows to a high point on an open ridge, and more flowery meadows to the site of a 1930s fire lookout. All this, plus blueberries, too!

SUNRISE PEAK. Sunrise Peak is where you'll find the site of the old fire lookout. The trail crosses a clear-cut and climbs steeply in forest, and then, at ½ mile, the first decision: flowers first, or views? Mount Adams and Mount Rainier vie in

Tiger lily and Mount Adams from Sunrise Peak

competition with the first of the meadows dotted with myriad wildflowers. (And which wildflowers? You'll want to go see for yourself.)

The trail follows a ridge for a brief distance and then traverses a flower-covered slope to a junction at 5000 feet, 1 mile from the road. Go right on trail No. 262A, climbing steeply up the south side of the peak, crossing to the west side, and returning to the south side. Switchbacks bring you near the top, where you can use the old lookout's iron handrail for assistance. The last 30 feet are an easy scramble to the summit, 5892 feet, 2½ miles.

Jumbo's Shoulder. For Jumbo's Shoulder, back at the junction go straight ahead, losing 300 feet, and at 1½ miles join Juniper Ridge trail No. 261. Go

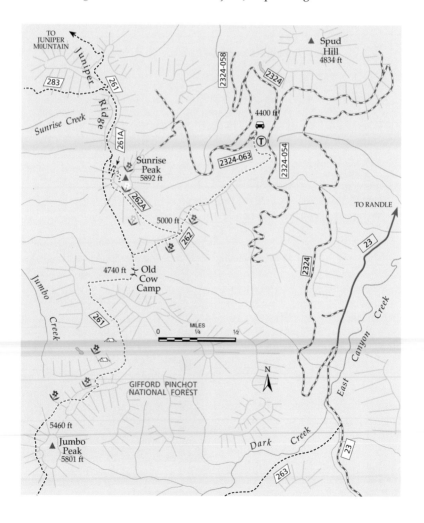

Juniper Ridge from Jumbo's Shoulder

left into the saddle of Old Cow Camp. The tread climbs 200 feet, rounds a ridge, contours the headwaters of Jumbo Creek, and ascends to a large basin with campsites. The trail levels off and climbs a snowbank, which may last through July, to Jumbo's Shoulder, 5460 feet, 3¼ miles from the road. ■ I. S.

Art's Notes

Bear grass, also called Indian basket grass, is no grass at all, but a member of the lily family. Confirm this kinship by a close look at the tiny white flowers—a genuine flower with white petals. Its botanical name, *Xerophyllum tenax,* aptly describes the foliage—tough, tenacious, and drought-resistant, grasslike leaves. First Peoples made hats, baskets, and capes from the tough *(tenax),* dry *(xero)* leaves *(phyllum).* Still a mystery is the unpredictable annual flowering: some years none; other years every rosette is crowned with the single flower stalk.

47 CONRAD MEADOWS

Tenday Creek Trail round trip	■	**3 miles**
Difficulty	■	Moderate
High point	■	4200 feet
Elevation gain	■	150 feet

Headwaters Loop round trip	■	**16 miles**
Difficulty	■	Moderate
High point	■	5450 feet
Elevation gain	■	1500 feet

Best flowers	■	May to early July
Hikable	■	Mid-July to mid-October

Getting there ■ Drive US 12 east from White Pass or west from Yakima to Rimrock Reservoir. Just east of Hause Creek Campground turn south on South Fork Tieton Road, heading west along Rimrock Reservoir. At 4.5 miles turn left on road No. 1000, signed "Conrad Meadows," and drive 14 miles to a gate at the edge of private property. Park near here, elevation 3900 feet. A Northwest Forest Pass is required.

Maps ■ Green Trails Nos. 303 White Pass and 335 Walupt Lake, USFS Goat Rocks Wilderness

Information ■ Naches Ranger District, phone (509) 653-1400

Bog orchid

A favorite of Harvey Manning. On a 2-hour walk up the Tenday Creek trail, he noted lupine, strawberry, Jacob's ladder, groundsel, desert parsley, sunflower, yarrow, cinquefoil, clover, penstemon, camas, thistle, larkspur, speedwell, spring beauty, vetch, phlox, violet, bistort, pussytoes, paintbrush, wandering daisy, forget-me-not, meadow parsley, elephant's head, white bog orchid, buttercup, monkeyflower, and false hellebore. The flowering begins in May, runs through its repertoire until July, and then the cows take over.

We drove to Conrad Meadows the last of May. It had been a heavy snowfall year and as the road climbed higher we began to encounter snow patches and I realized we were too early to photograph the flowers—so be sure to call for current conditions before you go. All we found were a few dandelions, spring beauties, Johnny jump-ups, and false hellebore, which were just sprouting up.

Much of the meadows were covered with an inch or two of water. The Tenday Creek trail where Harvey saw so many flowers was an impossibly gooey, muddy mess. We may have zeroed out on flowers, but *wow*, there were nearly a hundred elk grazing in the meadows. What a sight! What a thrill! The late season had kept the elk down low when normally they would have moved up to the high country.

Conrad Meadows is unique. It is a virtually level, 1½-mile-long series of meadows—the largest valley-bottom, midmontane meadow in the Cascades. They are partly on private land, which is open to pasture, and partly logged. Its unique features need protection from turning flower fields into cow chow.

TENDAY CREEK TRAIL. To reach the Tenday Creek trail, follow the gated road a short distance to South Fork trail No. 1120, left. Cross Short Creek and Long

Elk grazing in Conrad Meadows

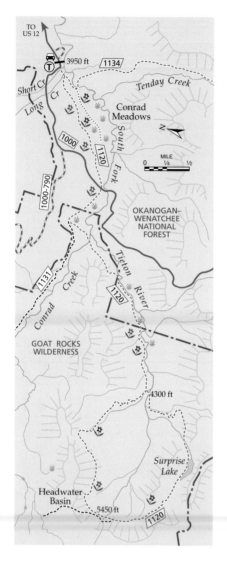

Creek (find a log or wade) to a fork. Go left on trail No. 1134 a long ¼ mile. The trail drops to a ford of Tenday Creek. Don't cross. For a flower walk along an informal route, proceed upstream near the bank on an intermittent elk trail–cow path. When you've had your fill of flowers, turn around and head back.

HEADWATERS LOOP. Flowers can probably be found along the Tenday Creek trail all summer, but if you have missed the big show, hoist a pack and follow the flowers up the mountain on the Headwaters Loop trail No. 1120, with a side trip to the Headwater Basin and a look at the Devils Horns.

The South Fork Tieton River is often within gentle sight and sound on this hike, with meadow and marsh a frame for much of its flowing countenance. In places, cow paths crisscross the main trail; be watchful that you don't lose the trail.

Follow the gated road a short distance to South Fork trail No. 1120, left. Cross Short Creek and Long Creek (find a log or wade) to a fork; go right. At 1½ miles, cross road No. 1000; in another ¼ mile cross into the Goat Rocks Wilderness; and in less than ¼ mile, reach a junction with trail No. 1131. Go left, continuing on trail No. 1120, close enough now to touch South Fork Tieton River. The trail and river meander meadows and forest companionably, parting ways occasionally only to meet up again.

At elevation 4300 feet is an intersection. Choose your route upward around the loop: To the left will bring you to Surprise Lake sooner, a lovely scoop of water known to those who fish and ride horses, with more elevation gain to the 5450-foot high point. Better camping is above; perhaps go

Conrad Meadows

right at the junction and save the lake for the descent. After the loop, the way out is the way you came in. ■ I. S.

Art's Notes

At Harvey Manning's suggestion, the Washington Native Plant Society visited Conrad Meadows in June 1986. Their floral survey of this rich and expansive meadow yielded a total of around 125 native annuals and herbaceous perennials. We select here some choice wildflowers from each of the several habitat types: in the open lodgepole pine woods bordering the meadow, look for camas, paintbrush, larkspur, golden yarrow (a.k.a. Oregon sunshine), penstemons, and phlox. In sandy and rocky borders above the meadow, we find wild buckwheat (*Eriogonum* species), scarlet bugler (*Gilia aggregata*), penstemon, fiddleneck (*Phacelia hastata*), and the rare *Frasera albicaulis*. The heart of Conrad Meadows is the wetland habitat, with such showy wildflowers as bog orchid, lousewort, cow parsnip, corn lily, and monkeyflower. In a nutshell, Conrad Meadows is a paradigm of ecological diversity, fabricated out of a variety of microhabitats—all stitched together with no really uncommon species, but, ecologically, a most uncommon Cascade landscape.

For those wildflower seekers who desire a more detailed account of this and other Washington flora trails, the Washington Native Plant Society keeps a full file of plant lists available to members and friends.

48 ADAMS CREEK MEADOW

Round trip ■	8 miles
Difficulty ■	Moderate
Best flowers ■	Mid-July through August
Hikable ■	Mid-July toh mid-October
High point ■	6880 feet
Elevation gain ■	2300 feet

Getting there ■ From the center of Randle (on US 120) drive the road signed "Mt. Adams" a scant 1 mile south to a split. Veer left on road No. 23, signed "Cispus Center, Mt. Adams, Trout Lake, Cispus Road." Stay on road No. 23, paved at first, then gravel, to 32 miles from Randle. Turn left on road No. 2329. In 2 miles pass the side road to Takhlakh Lake and at 6 miles (37.7 miles from Randle) find the parking area at the Killen Creek trailhead, elevation 4584 feet. A Northwest Forest Pass is required.

Maps ■ Green Trails Nos. 366 Mount Adams West and 334 Blue Lake, USFS Mt. Adams Wilderness

Information ■ Mount Adams Ranger Station, phone (509) 395-3400

Forest flowers, meadow flowers watered by a trickle of a stream, and brave and daring flowers fighting for survival on a storm-swept ridge. Views of ridge after ridge topped by Goat Rocks, Rainier, and the truncated cone of St. Helens. Closer are bare moraines and boulder-strewn lava flows, little ponds and waterfalls. Mount Adams towers over the flower-covered meadows,

Mount Adams rising above a small tarn

and the Adams Glacier, flowing a vertical mile from the summit, dominates the scene.

Killen Creek trail No. 113 (which never goes near Killen Creek) enters the Mount Adams Wilderness, ascends open pine forest brightly flowered by bear grass in early summer, and at 2½ miles, 5840 feet, opens out in a broad meadow brilliant early on with shootingstar, avalanche lily, and marsh marigold, later with paintbrush, heather, cinquefoil, and phlox. East Fork Adams Creek, found here, affords pleasant camping.

The trail ascends a lava flow to cross the Pacific Crest Trail 2000, 3 miles, 6084 feet. Continue upward from the PCT on High Camp trail No. 10 for a long mile to the broad Adams Creek Meadow, 6880 feet, called High Camp, Mountaineers Camp, Adams Glacier Camp, your choice. No campfires are allowed above the PCT. Between climbers and hikers, weekends can be crowded; best to find your own camp spot ½ mile either way. Use an existing site rather than creating a new one. ■ I. S.

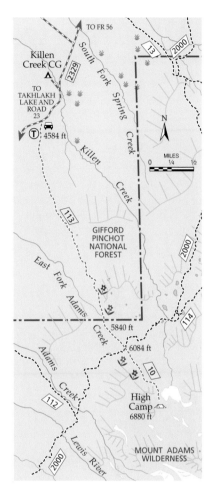

Art's Notes

By the time you reach the Pacific Crest Trail, swards of mountain heather appear. The common purple mountain heather *(Phyllodoce empetriformis)* is nearly everywhere in the Cascades at this elevation. The higher reaches offer still other heath kin: The pale yellow one, *P. glanduliflora*, is usually near and above timberline, yet where the two cohabit, bumblebees have crossed the two to make the hybrid *P. X intermedia*, with pale pink flowers. Unmistakable is another heather kin, the white-flowered cassiope *(Cassiope mertensiana)*; its tiny overlapping scale leaves form a four-angled leafy twig.

49 NORWAY PASS AND MOUNT MARGARET

Norway Pass round trip ■	**5 miles**
Difficulty ■	Easy
Hikable ■	July through September
High point ■	4508 feet
Elevation gain ■	900 feet

Mount Margaret round trip ■	**11 miles**
Difficulty ■	Moderate
Hikable ■	August through September
High point ■	5858 feet
Elevation gain ■	2300 feet

Best flowers ■	July through September

Getting there ■ Drive US 12 to Randle, turn south on SR 131, and cross the Cowlitz River. In 1 mile bear west on road No. 25 and follow it for 19.6 miles to road No. 99, turning right and entering Mount St. Helens National Volcanic Monument. In 9.3 miles, turn right again onto road No. 26, pass Meta Lake on the left, and in 0.9 mile from road No. 26 find the Norway Pass trailhead on the left, elevation 3680 feet. A Northwest Forest Pass is required.

Map ■ Green Trails Spirit Lake No. 332

Information ■ Mount St. Helens National Volcanic Monument Headquarters, phone (360) 449-7800

Discover how vegetation is returning to the barren slopes of Norway Pass, swept clean on May 18, 1980, by the eruption of Mount St. Helens.

On slopes facing the eruption, trees were flattened in neat rows. However, on the back side of Norway Pass there must have been a whirlwind, for the trees were piled on top of one another in all directions like jackstraws. On a hot, dry day in 1982, we made our way through the tangled mess—over and under countless logs—to peer into Spirit Lake. To our surprise, we found a small oasis of flowers in bloom on the side of Mount Margaret.

The flowers were explained by the deep winter snow that had covered the plants during the blast, protecting them from heat that reached up to 400 degrees, scorching all the plants elsewhere.

At first the only flowers to bloom were ones that survived under snowbanks, but the hillsides have become mostly green since then. Where did the plants come from? Dandelions and fireweed are the easiest to explain—their seeds can be carried on the wind for maybe 100 miles—but the huckleberries, willows, and alders are another story.

Mount St. Helens in 1982, from the side of Mount Margaret

For a number of years we made a yearly pilgrimage to check on the flowers. Each year new plants showed up. The climax came in 1999, when a huge patch on the side of Mount Margaret turned blue with lupine.

Avalanche lilies generally have one bloom to a stem, but occasionally you will find twins or even triplets. Once we found a fivesome, and that was a "wow-ee" day. Then, shortly after the St. Helens eruption, I was hiking alone on the newly restored Norway Pass trail and came upon a

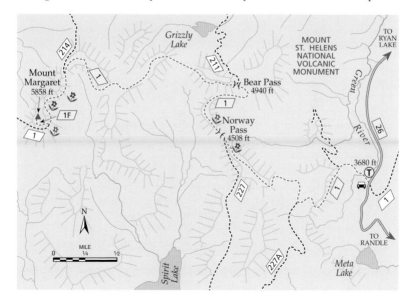

Rare four-blossom avalanche lily found at Norway Pass

seven-blossom lily. It was in too awkward a location to be photographed, so no one believed me.

We kept an eye on the spot. The next year the best we found was five blossoms on one stem; still no pictures. The following year, all we could find was a foursome.

NORWAY PASS. In 1984, a trail was reestablished to Norway Pass and to the top of Mount Margaret, so compared to our 1982 ordeal, the pass and mountain are now a relatively easy walk.

The trail switchbacks upward through blown-down timber that looks as if giants long ago lost interest in a game of pickup-sticks. Look down to log-filled Spirit Lake and outward to the greening of the devastation, and wonder at the destructive and regenerative powers of nature. It's an easy hike to the flowers of Norway Pass at 2½ miles, 4508 feet.

MOUNT MARGARET. From Norway Pass, the trail heads north and then west and then north again, reaching 4940-foot Bear Pass in about ½ mile. Over hill and dale, generally gaining in elevation, at about 5½ miles find a short spur trail to the right that climbs to within 20 feet of the summit of 5858-foot Mount Margaret. Views of Rainier, Adams, and Hood, and flowers at your feet. ■ I. S.

Art's Notes

Mount St. Helens had been called the Mount Fuji of North America. Its symmetrical cone epitomized the form of a stratovolcano. But with its eruption on May 18, 1980, came a cascade of environmental fallouts. Besides losing its Mount Fuji–like summit, acres of nearby forest were laid flat. Slumbering ground-cover plant life was buried in inches to feet of volcanic ash (tephra). But this was nothing new, for Mount St. Helens, the most restless of the Cascade volcanoes, had blown its top several times in the postglacial past. The most recent were witnessed by Indians and early settlers in the early nineteenth century. Repeated eruptions had kept the vegetation from reaching its full Cascade potential; it was still a pioneer landscape. In summer of 1979, a Washington Native Plant Society field party recorded much of the flora on the upper north slope. This checklist served well the many research projects on the effects of the eruption and its posteruption recovery.

The 1980 eruption gave ecologists a prime opportunity to study the effects on plant and animal life from "ground zero." Besides the devastation of forest—swathes of timber laid low—the effects on the understory vegetation varied dramatically. In the worst case, the pyroclastic flows above Spirit Lake, total extermination of plant life occurred. But in areas elsewhere on St. Helens and nearby terrain, volcanic ash covered plant life to varying depths. Buried herbs and low shrubs, though covered with ash, were not killed. Many native herbaceous perennials emerged through the ash in later years. The most spectacular was the recovery of corn lily (false hellebore, *Veratrum viride*). Though buried even to the depth of many inches, these stout herbs emerged from their large rootlike storage organs. Other responses also were remarkable. Ash-covered heather meadows in the Goat Rocks country actually benefited from a light whitish ash layer. It served as a heat-reflecting mulch to make for a more lush growth in later years.

Especially resilient in recovery were penstemons, mountain lupines, wild buckwheat, and other pioneer (early successional) native species. Also making a comeback are a number of weedy aliens like willow-herb, tansy ragwort, and a variety of thistles.

Unlike the more quiescent volcanoes, like Mount Rainier, Mount Adams, and Mount Baker, restless Mount St. Helens never had a span of eruption-free time to create a mature and fully diversified flora.

50 ❘ DOG MOUNTAIN

Round trip ■	**7½ miles**
Difficulty ■	Strenuous
Best flowers ■	April through June
Hikable ■	March to January
High point ■	2948 feet
Elevation gain ■	2900 feet

Getting there ■ From Seattle, take I-5 south, and from Portland go onto I-84 east to Cascade Locks (east of Portland). Cross the Bridge of the Gods to the Washington side of the Gorge ($1 toll bridge), turn right (east) on SR 14, and continue to the Dog Mountain trailhead, between mileposts 53 and 54, on the left (north) side of the road, elevation 184 feet. A Northwest Forest Pass is required.

Map ■ Green Trails No. 430 Hood River

Information ■ Columbia River Gorge National Scenic Area, phone (541) 386-2333

Trails in the Columbia River Gorge are favorites of wildflower enthusiasts. The flowers begin from the trailhead in early April and continue all the way to the summit of Dog Mountain as summer progresses. By June the summit is a yellow carpet of balsamroot, and in addition to floral displays there are views of Mount Hood and across the Columbia River to Starvation Ridge, Mount Defiance (identified by towers), and other high points in the Gorge. This trail is steep enough to provide a workout, and that attracts many hikers, as well. Unless you hike on a bitter day in November, you'll share this summit with other hikers, many with dogs.

Arnica

Watch for ticks, rattlesnakes, and poison oak on this and other trails in the Columbia Gorge. A sign and a photograph at the trailhead identify poison oak; it is prevalent along the trail, and there are several "look-alikes." To be safe, stay on established trails. Mileages are not ex-

The Columbia River Gorge from Dog Mountain

act; there are discrepancies between trailhead signs, signs at trail junctions, hiking guides, and maps. Allow for some flexibility.

Two routes to Dog Mountain begin from the trailhead: The Dog Mountain trail No. 147 is right (east) and the Augspurger Mountain trail No. 4407 is left (west). This makes an attractive loop, though you can hike either trail one way and back. For a loop, I recommend starting from the Augspurger trail and heading to the trail junction for Dog Mountain. Trail No. 4407 stays mostly in the forest until the junction for Dog Mountain (about 1½ miles). At the junction, turn right (east) and continue on open slopes to the summit. Conifers on the summit provide shade, but the top is mostly in the open and it can be very windy.

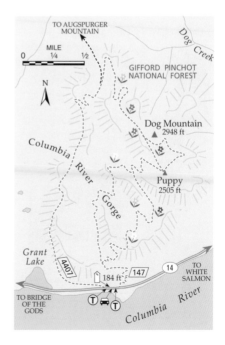

To finish the loop, hike the Dog Mountain trail to a junction below the Puppy Lookout site. It was called "Puppy" because you are only partway up Dog Mountain at this point. The lookout was constructed in 1931 and dismantled in 1967. Two trails descend from Puppy. You can take either one back to the trailhead. From the knoll, the tip of Mount Hood comes into view.

The Dog Mountain trail No. 147 is considered the "old trail" and is shorter, steeper, and more direct than the Augspurger trail. If you start your hike on the Dog Mountain trail, you will be heading east—at the first junction, turn right, onto the "new trail" built about 1980, or follow the "old" trail. The trails converge below the Puppy Lookout site, at about 3 miles (2505 feet).

In the forest, look for vanilla leaf, Solomon's seal, Indian pipe, arnica, wild ginger, and cow parsnip, though they were not blooming in August. Foamflower was still in bloom at higher elevations. At higher elevations, asters, yarrow, and pearly everlasting were still in bloom. There are large patches of thimbleberry and balsamroot near the summit.

Earlier in the season, look for prairie star, penstemon, spreading phlox, meadow rue, and goatsbeard to bloom on open slopes. You may spot endemics on the summit—smooth douglasia and long-beard hawkweed. You may also see chocolate lilies at lower elevations. ■ K. S.

Art's Notes

My most vivid memory of this trek was seeing the ghostly white phantom orchid (*Eburophyton austinae*) in profusion. It was gregariously scattered in open Douglas fir woods at the lower elevation. This seldom-seen orchid is encountered only sporadically and some years may not reappear in a known patch. Like the coralroot orchid (*Corallorhiza spp.*), it is a hyperparasite, unable to make its own food. Instead, it feeds on mycorrhizal fungi, in turn attached to a maker of carbohydrates, some conifer.

Just above the trailhead, look for clumps of a narrow-fronded sword fern. It was once thought to be merely a "sun form" of the common sword fern. But fern specialist David Wagner has convinced us that this is a distinct species, *Polystichum imbricans*.

Opposite: *Cliff penstemon*

WILDFLOWER PORTRAITS

The selection of native wildflowers for the following portraits has an element of parochial favoritism. Ira and I have favorites that appeal to us and that we think will appeal to the flower-watching hiker. First and foremost is their eye appeal: They are showy. Then, too, they are reasonably common, appearing widely in our woods and meadows. Then there is the challenge of picking the best of a given habitat—deep woods, meadows, or rocky places. We have given just homage to wildflowers of these contrasting habitats. ▪ A. R. K.

Editor's note: Wildflowers grow to best take advantage of soil, sun, and other characteristics inherent to their habitats. In this section, rather than following strict conventions of ordering the wildflower portraits by common or botanical names, we have opted to allow them to roam a little more freely to better display Ira Spring's lovely images—and perhaps, also, to get a bit more sun. ▪ C. C. T.

WILDFLOWER PORTRAITS CONTENTS

WILDFLOWERS OF THE FOREST

Dwelling under the cover of old-growth and late-successional forests is a galaxy of forest floor perennials. Much less is the wildflower diversity in young second-growth stands—just too dense and dark! The forest floor habitat ranges from sea level upward into stands of mountain hemlock and Pacific silver fir, to nearly 5000 feet in elevation.

Some wildflowers occupy the full altitudinal range, like bunchberry, thimbleberry, and fireweed. Where the ground is permanently moist and along streams, find an array of moisture-loving herbs: bog orchid, wild ginger, red and yellow monkeyflower, lady fern, maidenhair fern, and especially skunk cabbage (a.k.a. swamp lantern).

Bunchberry or Dwarf Dogwood ▪ Startling it is to learn that this ground-hugging shrublet is kin to our native tree, Pacific flowering dogwood, *Cornus nuttallii*. In both, their "flower" reveals a unique structure. The four white "petals" are leaflike bracts enclosing a tight cluster of tiny flowerlets. These in turn become a clusters of red berries, ergo bunchberry. It is a common forest floor inhabitant often forming broad leafy displays and many blooms.

Bunchberry or Dwarf Dogwood

Cornus canadensis (now, C. unalaschensis)

Calypso or Fairyslipper ■ This delicate princess of the forest is never very abundant. It may occur sporadically in one place in fair numbers or appear only as a single waif here and there in the deep duff along the trail. The solitary rose-purple slipperlike flower, barely 4 inches above the ground, can waft a delicate fragrance.

Calypso or Fairyslipper

Calypso bulbosa
Orchid Family

Corn Lily or False Hellebore ■ It does resemble a corn plant! Its
stately 3–5-foot-tall stalks with broad, parallel-veined clasping leaves yield

at its summit tassles of small greenish lily flowerlets. It likes the lusher sites in upper montane forest openings and high meadows. There is nothing like it in our high country. Like most of our perennial herbs, it dies down completely when winter sets in. A white-flowered corn lily is frequent on the dry side of the mountains, in spring-wet places; it is *Veratrum californicum*.

Corn Lily or False Hellebore

Veratrum viride
Lily Family

Devil's Club ■ Hardly a wildflower is this formidable, tall spinose
shrub. Yet it will tell the hiker that he or she has reached a wet habitat in

the woods. It does have a massive cluster of tiny white flowers atop the large tropical-like bristly leaves. Nearby, look for other wetlanders: skunk cabbage, bog orchid, and lady fern.

Devil's Club

Oplopanax horridus
Ginseng Family

Indian Pipe ■ Who would not be fascinated by this ghostly white plant in the deep forest? Its companion, called many-flowered Indian pipe, cannot compare with this single-flowered silvery stem. Unlike green plants, Indian pipes get their solar power by devious means: They parasitize the mushroom–conifer mutualism. Both mushroom fungi and conifers benefit from the intimate association of the two: The fungus offers the conifer both nutrients and water, while the conifer gives the fungus its organic, solar-generated food. This is the universal mycorrhizal association. Neat trick, wot!

Indian Pipe

Monotropa uniflora
Heath or Wintergreen Family

Coralroot Orchid ■ This, too, parasitizes the mushroom–conifer symbiosis. Its startling pink-flowered stalks catch the hiker's eye like no other woodland orchid. Like all of our flowering parasites, you come upon them by chance. Unlike bunchberry or bead lily, coralroot orchids are sporadic—but the encounter is unforgettable.

Coralroot Orchid

Corallorhiza mertensiana
Orchid Family

Indian paintbrush and Mount Shuksan

Indian Paintbrush ■ Widely called common Indian paintbrush, indeed it is most everywhere, from lowlands to the high parklands—in open woods, meadows, and trailside clearings. What is red is not the flowers!—rather the showy red floral leaflets (bracts) surround, hiding each flower. Another paintbrush surprise: most all are partial parasites, their roots penetrating some nearby host plant roots, a grass, a stonecrop, or other herb. See "Art's Notes" for Sauk Mountain, Hike 9, for more on this intriguing clan of herbs.

Indian Paintbrush (cinnabar red)

Castilleja miniata
Figwort Family

Indian paintbrush coated with frost

Western Pasque Flower ■ Our only high-mountain anemone consorts with a host of other herbs in sunny parkland meadows. Look for it

about the time that avalanche lilies are in their full glory. Its finely dissected leaves are at the base of a stalk bearing showy, creamy-white single blooms. Later, the flower turns into a fluffy brownish mop of plumed seeds. It is abundant at Chinook Pass and most parkland meadows in Mount Rainier National Park.

Western Pasque Flower

Anemone occidentalis
Buttercup Family

Pine Drops ■ This 2-foot wonder is never common. But when you encounter it, there's no mistaking this tall wand of reddish brown, goblet-shaped flowers. Like Indian pipe, pine drops parasitize the mushroom–

conifer symbiosis. Some years all one sees is a lone black stalk from the previous year.

Pine Drops

Pterospora andromedea
Heather Family

Pipsissewa or Prince's Pine ■ This evergreen shrublet frequents the forest floor. In bloom, its pink to rose bells resemble those of its kin, pink wintergreen, *Pyrola asarifolia*. The two common names are a bit of a mystery.

Pipsissewa or Prince's Pine

Chimaphila umbellata
Heather Family

Pink Pyrola or Pink Wintergreen ■ This, the showiest of our wintergreens, has basal heart-shaped leathery leaves. Its 8–10-inch-high flower stalk bears numerous deep pink saucer-shaped pendant flowers—a winsome charmer in bloom.

Pink Pyrola or Pink Wintergreen

Pyrola asarifolia
Wintergreen Family

Queen's Cup or Bead Lily ■ Some years, this common woodlander offers only two or three basal strap-shaped leaves. But when in bloom, this single stalk is tipped with a dazzling white lily. Later, its blue beadlike berry also is eye-catching.

Queen's Cup or Bead Lily

Clintonia uniflora
Lily Family

False Solomon's Seal ■ The lush, arching leafy stems end in a plume of tiny, lilylike white flowers. Later in summer, witness the reddish berries, often dotted or striped with purple. Its demure cousin, the starflower Solomon's seal, can be gregarious in open woods; look for its star-shaped white flowers followed by greenish berries striped in red.

False Solomon's Seal

Smilacina racemosa
Lily Family

Star-flowered Solomon's Seal

Smilacina stellata
Lily Family

Swamp Lantern or Skunk Cabbage ▪ How unsuitable is the more familiar name, skunk cabbage. It hardly emits a "mephitic" (skunky) odor and is far removed from the cabbage (mustard) family. The huge, platterlike leaves lie at the base of that miraculous yellow lantern, the yellow cloak (spathe) surrounding the erect cluster of tiny male and female flowerlets. So try *swamp lantern* for the older misnomer, skunk cabbage. The plant deserves it!

Swamp Lantern or Skunk Cabbage

Lysichiton americanum
Arum Family

Twinflower ▪ Ground-hugging shrublet, forming expansive carpets of evergreen foliage, topped with 4-inch erect stalks bearing two pendant lavender trumpets. See "Art's Notes" for the Ira Spring Memorial Trail, Hike 26, for more on twinflower.

Twinflower

Linnaea borealis
Honeysuckle Family

Vanilla Leaf ■ Drifts of this lovely perennial frequent the forest floor on both sides of the mountains. Like trilliums, each plantlet bears a three-parted leaf and a separate 10-inch stalk of tiny white flowers. When dried, the leaves give off a sweet, vanillalike odor. Pioneer women made sachets out of the leaves to freshen closets and clothes chests.

Vanilla Leaf

Achlys triphylla
Barberry Family

Western Wake-robin or Trillium ■ This wide-ranging lily relative is easy to identify: a single three-parted leaf with a separate 10-inch stalk bearing a single pure-white, three-parted large flower. It occurs on both sides of the Cascades and Olympics from sea level to the Pacific silver fir zone, about 3500 feet. The white flowers fade in time to pink, yet are just as showy.

Western Wake-robin or Trillium

Trillium ovatum
Lily Family

Wild Ginger ■ This vagabond, from a chiefly tropical clan, charms in at least two ways. The handsome, heart-shaped evergreen leaves, when crushed, reveal an odor sure to conjure up the smell of ginger. Hidden among the leaves is a remarkable bowl-shaped flower, adorned with three long "feelers" and chocolate in color. Be dazzled by this wonder.

Wild Ginger

Asarum caudatum
Birthwort Family

Yellow Violet ■ Two species grace the forest floor. The small evergreen violet hugs the forest duff while the other one delights in wetter sites in the woods. Ira tells of his youth by calling these two Johnny jump-ups. Violets or not, every one has "irregular" flowers, with two large and three smaller petals. More like Ira's idea of a violet is the common pink one, nay violet in color, *Viola adunca*, widespread in open woods and grasslands.

Yellow Violet

Viola glabella
Violet Family

WILDFLOWERS OF MONTANE MEADOWS

The land above the forest opens up to a dazzling array of habitats. The lowermost meadow landscape one encounters is the parkland, where forest is no longer continuous. Rather, the high country is now a blend: Islands of trees dot seas of mountain meadows, aptly called "timbered atolls." Still higher, parkland yields to timberline, with scattered, stunted, and twisted trees (Krummholz), to be succeeded above by the treeless alpine zone. These three higher habitats are where the hiker is beyond continuous forest. Views abound, and the open, sunny meadowland luxuriates in color. The selected plant portraits that follow just skim their surface, for the land above the forest is endowed with vast floral richness and variety.

Bear Grass or Indian Basket Grass ▪ When it is in bloom, fields of this white candelabra are stunning. Its 2-foot-tall flowering stalk bears a

tight cluster of tiny white lily flowerlets, surmounting a dense basal tuft of grasslike leaves. In years when it fails to bloom, it mimics clumps of real grass. As Indian basket grass, it tells of ancient uses. The tough leaves were woven into hats and baskets by First Peoples. Though occurring from nearly sea level to the subalpine, its best displays are in forested openings at the fringes of tree clumps in the parkland habitat.

**Bear Grass or
Indian Basket Grass**

Xerophyllum tenax
Lily Family

Mountain Bluebell ■ This is a graceful, tallish perennial with bunches of little, blue bell-shaped flowers. It likes moist openings in upper montane woods and parkland. Its several flowering stems in a tight clump may be up to 3 feet tall.

Mountain Bluebell

Mertensia paniculata
Borage or Forget-me-not Family

Columbine and Tiger Lily ■ Most often, our red columbine is found in springy places in the upper montane woods and meadows. The upside-down position of the flowers is ideal for the hovering nectar-seekers (and pollinators), hummingbirds and hawk moths. The five spurs on each flower are the sources of the nectar. The tiger lily has a more expansive choice of habitat: meadows, shrub thickets, and openings in the forest, from low elevations to the high parkland. Though buried by ash following Mount St. Helens' eruptive violence, tiger lilies shot up through the ash the very next year to over 6 feet.

Red Columbine

Aquilegia formosa
Buttercup Family

Tiger Lily

Lilium columbianum
Lily Family

Cotton Grass ■ Wooly plumes of flossy cotton atop 1–2-foot stems are the hallmarks of this bog and swamp inhabitant. Although it is widespread from northern Oregon to Alaska, it is not in every wet place. Look for it in the serpentine bogs bordering the Esmerelda Basin trail (Hike 29) in the Wenatchee Mountains.

Cotton Grass

Eriophorum angustifolium
Sedge Family

A meadow of cotton grass in the Gifford Pinchot National Forest

Cow Parsnip ■ This lanky 4–6-foot-tall herb almost seems out of place among the more demure small herbs of forest and parkland. Its large, coarse, hairy leaves are topped by a dense bouquet of small white flowers. It ranges from sea level to the parkland.

Cow Parsnip

Heracleum lanatum
Parsley Family

Tolmie's Penstemon ■ Look for this perky little penstemon near timberline. Its brilliant purple flowers in tight whorls are on one or more short, erect stalks. It is named for John Frasier Tolmie, early naturalist stationed at Fort Nisqually and the first European to explore Mount Rainier.

Tolmie's Penstemon

Penstemon procerus var. *tolmiei*
Figwort Family

Spreading Phlox ■ One often sees vast sheets of this ground-hugging mat, bedecked with copious showy pink, lavender, or white flowers. It prefers open rocky sites at middle to high elevations. It is most frequent on the eastern, drier sides of the Cascades.

Spreading Phlox

Phlox diffusa
Phlox Family

Elephant's Head Lousewort ■ This bog lover offers a truly unique flower. Each of the many blossoms on a 12-inch stalk is a startling match for an elephant's head, trunk and all. Its watery meadow habitat is in

high parkland country. Other louseworts have distinctively contorted flower parts; most are in the upper montane, but away from springy places. Lousewort—what a misnomer for such lovely wildflowers!

Elephant's Head Lousewort

Pedicularis groenlandica
Figwort Family

Harebell ■ This delicate perennial bears blue bell-shaped flowers on short stems, often nodding in the wind. Found on rocky ridges and dryish meadows.

Harebell

Campanula rotundifolia
Harebell or Campanula
Family

Montane Lupines ■ There must be a lupine for most every habitat in our state—low-elevation forest and prairie, montane forests, parkland meadows, and even yellow pine and sagebrush country. Lyall's lupine, shown here, is the dwarf of the clan, liking rocky ridges near timberline. The common forest lupines can be either the one of dry woods, *Lupinus latifolius,* or the more robust one of damper places, *Lupinus polyphyllus.* All lupines have five-fingered leaves and usually blue pea flowers.

Lyall's Lupine

Lupinus lepidus var. *lobbii*
Pea Family

Heathers ■ Bountiful drifts of mountain heathers are the hallmark of the high parkland country of both the Cascades and the Olympics. Dense, low thickets of the commonest red or pink heather, *Phyllodoce empetriformis*, festoon the borders of most high country trails. Often intermixed with the pink heather is the white moss heather *Cassiope mertensiana*. And on slightly higher, more exposed habitats, look for the yellow-flowered *Phyllodoce glanduliflora*. See "Art's Notes" for Railroad Grade, Hike 8, for more on heathers.

White Moss Heather

Cassiope mertensiana
Heath or Heather Family

Pink Mountain Heather

Phyllodoce empetriformis
Heath or Heather Family

Avalanche and Glacier Lilies ■ Just as the snow is melting in the upper montane, fields of yellow or white lilies carpet the wet ground. In some places they can form unending pure "monocultures," as at Paradise on Mount Rainier or on Hurricane Ridge. Unmistakable is their graceful form: two basal strap-shaped leaves and a 6–10-inch flower stalk bearing one to three nodding yellow or white lily flowers.

Avalanche Lily (white)

Erythronium montanum
Lily Family

Glacier Lily (yellow)

Erythronium grandiflorum
Lily Family

Tall Mountain Shootingstar ■ There must be a shootingstar for most every habitat and elevation in our state: sagebrush country, prairies, ponderosa pine woods, and where this one grows—wet places in the high country.

The 12–18-inch flower stalks arise from strap-shaped basal leaves to bear several flowers—unlike any other in our flora. Each flower is shaped like a streamlined rocket, the purple petals reflexed (turned backward) to expose brilliant yellow pollen sacs (anthers). Watch a bumblebee buzz the flowers, a novel way of exacting the insect's tithe of pollen.

Tall Mountain Shootingstar

Dodecatheon jeffreyi
Primrose Family

Sitka Valerian or Mountain Heliotrope ■ This gregariously growing white-flowered herb comes into its own in the lush meadows of the high country. From its opposite compound (divided) leaves arise a 12–

18-inch flower stalk bearing many small, white tubular flowers. Its other common name, mountain heliotrope, is attached to a high ridge, Heliotrope Ridge, on the north side of Mount Baker.

Sitka Valerian or Mountain Heliotrope

Valeriana sitchensis
Valerian Family

Monkeyflowers, Pink and Yellow ■ Tubular flowers with the face of a monkey? A bit fanciful, but let your imagination run wild. The dozens of monkeyflower species have the same floral form: long tubes with mouths contorted slightly into a face. Both the pink and white ones inhabit streamsides and other wet places in the high country. A third one, also yellow, seems to be everywhere in soggy sites; it is the common *Mimulus guttatus.*

Pink Monkeyflower

Mimulus lewisii
Figwort Family

Yellow Monkeyflower

Mimulus tillingii
Figwort Family

WILDFLOWERS OF PONDEROSA PINE AND SAGEBRUSH COUNTRY

The vegetation east of the Cascades is a whole new world. The regal old-growth ponderosa pine forests form a kind of lower timberline, east beyond which the vast sagebrush–bunchgrass country takes over. Wildflowers here abound but are of short springtime duration. The pine woods and semidesert shrub–steppe palettes boast a host of sunflower relatives—phloxes, biscuit roots, penstemons, bitterroots, milkvetches, and many others. Ron Taylor's *Desert Wildflowers* guidebook works famously for this part of the state.

Balsamroot on an eastern Washington slope

Balsamroot or Desert Sunflower  ■ No other wildflower celebrates spring on the dry sides of the Cascades as does this gregarious sunflower. Nearly everywhere in ponderosa pine country or in the sagebrush "ocean" one sees vast fields of this showy, 2-foot-tall herb. When in late April or early May balsamroots begin to bloom up the valleys of the tributary rivers to the Columbia, First Peoples knew it was time to return into the spring foraging grounds, up the Yakima, Wenatchee, Entiat, Methow, and Okanogan Rivers. One of the best desert sunflower shows of all must be on the low hills above the Methow River, between Twisp and Mazama.

Balsamroot or Desert Sunflower

Balsamorhiza saggitata
Sunflower or Aster Family

Bitterroot ■ Long before its botanical name commemorated Meriwether Lewis, bitterroot was a staple food of First Peoples. They, Shoshones and Nez Perce, showed the explorers how to prepare it. Yet even the cooked root was bitter and was nauseating to Lewis. This transient charmer prefers shallow rocky soils (lithosols) in full sun. The fleshy tubular leaves wither to give way to the exquisitely ornamental large flowers, at ground level. A choice place to witness fields of bitterroot in June is around the rocky summit of Red Top (see Kruckeberg Country, Hike 31), just below the lookout, on Teanaway Ridge.

Bitterroot

Lewisia rediviva
Purslane Family

Camas ■ Bulbs of camas were a most essential food plant for Salish and Sahaptin First Peoples. They steamed them in deep pits; the cooked bulbs could be eaten directly or sun-dried and stored for later use or for barter. Our two species of camas are widespread in spring-wet places on either side of the Cascades. In coastal areas, camas can even be found at sea level in the San Juan Islands and in the oak savannah and prairie country of the southern Puget Sound basin. Vast camas prairies can still be found mostly east of the Cascades. It was steamed camas bulbs that helped the Lewis and Clark expedition survive the winter of 1805 on the Clearwater River of Idaho. Nez Perce peoples provided the expedition with this starchy food. Then and now, native-foods gourmets must distinguish between the edible blue-flowered camas and its toxic companion, the yellow-flowered death camas *(Zygadenus paniculatus)*.

Common Camas

Camassia quamash
Lily Family

Skyrocket or Scarlet Gilia ■ This member of the phlox family has the distinction of bearing copious showy red trumpets, unlike most other gilias. In midsummer, find it bewitching hummingbirds in dry, sunny openings in ponderosa pine country and open rocky slopes. The tallish flower stalks arise from a rosette of finely dissected leaves. Often, in skyrocket colonies, one finds both the rosette stage and the "bolted" flowering stalks.

Skyrocket or Scarlet Gilia

Gilia aggregata
Phlox Family

Yellow Bells ■ This charmer must be one of Nature's supreme creations. There are other fritillaries, but this one heads the roster! Dainty, not over 6 inches tall, the single-pendant yellow bell brightens the forest floor in ponderosa pine country on into sagebrush–steppe. Its species name, *pudica,* means "bashful, shy, retiring." But only from a distance. Up close, it is a bold, golden gem.

Yellow Bells

Fritillaria pudica
Lily Family

USEFUL REFERENCES AND OTHER RESOURCES

Wildflower Guides

Parish, R. et al., eds. *Plants of Southern Interior British Columbia.* Redmond, WA. Lone Pine Publishing, 1996. Same format as the Pojar and MacKinnon book; it works well for eastern Washington.

Pojar, J. and A. MacKinnon. *Plants of the Pacific Northwest Coast: Washington, Oregon, British Columbia & Alaska.* Redmond, WA: Lone Pine Publishing, 1994. One of the best field guides for the Cascades, Olympics, and lowland Puget country; the notes on First Peoples' uses of plants, by Nancy Turner, are a fine feature.

Taylor, R. *Desert Wildflowers of North America.* Missoula, MT: Mountain Press Publishing Company, 1998.

——. *Sagebrush Country.* 2d ed. Missoula, MT: Mountain Press Publishing Company, 1992. Invaluable guide for plants of the "dry interior," east of the Cascades.

Taylor, R. and G. Douglas. *Mountain Plants of the Pacific Northwest: A Field Guide to Washington, Western British Columbia, and Southeastern Alaska.* Missoula, MT: Mountain Press Publishing Company, 1995. Another excellent field guide; has keys to plant families.

Field Manuals for Identification of Plants

These are for the serious seeker of identifications. All use "keys" for identifying Northwest plants. The first two are a bit easier to use.

Annable, C. R. and P. M. Peterson. "Plants of the Kettle Range." Seattle, WA: Occasional Papers of Washington Native Plant Society, 1988.

Biek, D. *Flora of Mount Rainier National Park.* Corvalis, OR: Oregon State University Press, 2000. This manual works well for most all of the Cascades and Olympics flora; most recent of manuals and very thorough.

Buckingham, N. *Flora of the Olympic Peninsula.* Seattle: Northwest Interpretive Association and Washington Native Plant Society, 1995.

Gilkey, H. M. and L. I. Dennis. *Handbook of Northwest Plants.* Corvalis, OR: Oregon State University Press, 2001. A simplified, condensed version of the Hitchcock; covers only the Cascades and westward.

Hitchcock, C. L. and A. Cronquist. *Flora of the Pacific Northwest.* Seattle and London: University of Washington Press, 1973. The unabridged "bible" for serious students of our flora; covers the entire Pacific Northwest, from Montana to the coast and from British Columbia to the Oregon–California border; worth the effort of learning to use.

Lichen, P. K. *Brittle Stars and Mudbugs: An Uncommon Field Guide to Northwest Shorelines and Wetlands.* Seattle: Sasquatch Books, 2003.

Ecology and Natural History

Allen, J. E. and M. Burns. *Cataclysms on the Columbia.* Portland, OR: Timber Press, 1986.

Alt, D. *Glacial Lake Missoula.* Missoula, MT: Mountain Press Publishing Company, 2001.

Darvill, F. *Hiking the North Cascades.* Mechanicsburg, PA: Stackpole Books, 1998.

Franklin, J. and C. T. Dryness. *Vegetation of Oregon and Washington.* Corvalis, OR: Oregon State University Press, 1969. Best descriptions of all life zones and their plant communities—from coastal forest to alpine and on to sagebrush country.

Hitchman, R. *Place Names of Washington.* Tacoma, WA: Washington State Historical Society, 1985.

Kozloff, E. *Plants and Animals of the Pacific Northwest: An Illustrated Guide to the Natural History of Western Oregon, Washington, and British Columbia.* Seattle and London: University of Washington Press, 1976.

Kruckeberg, A. R. *Natural History of Puget Sound Country.* Seattle and London: University of Washington Press, 1993. Integrates geology, climate, flora, and fauna in the Puget Basin, from sea level to alpine country.

Mathews, D. *Cascade–Olympic Natural History.* Portland, OR: Portland Audubon Society, 1988. Combines natural history of the region with superb accounts of ecology and human history of the region.

Phillips, H. W. *Plants of the Lewis and Clark Expedition.* Missoula, MT: Mountain Press Publishing Company, 2003. Commemorates the 200th anniversary of the botanical discoveries of the first exploring expedition.

Ethnobotany: Plant Uses by First Peoples

Gunther, E. *Ethnobotany of Western Washington.* Seattle and London: University of Washington Press, 1973. A classic account, the first of its kind for our region.

Hunn, E. S. (with James Selam and Family). *Nchi-Wana, "The Big River": Mid-Columbia Indians and Their Land.* Seattle and London: University of Washington Press, 1990. Superb telling of Yakama Nation peoples' uses of natural resources.

Pyle, R. M. Where Bigfoot Walks: Crossing the Dark Divide. New York: Houghton Mifflin, 1997.

Turner, N. *Food Plants of Coastal First Peoples.* Victoria: Royal British Columbia Museum, 1995. Turner is our region's doyenne of ethno-botany.

——. *Plant Technology of First Peoples in British Columbia*. Victoria: Royal British Columbia Museum, 1998. Another Turner gem.

Geology: The Essential Link Between Habitat and Plant Life
Alt, D. D. and D. W. Hyndman. *Northwest Exposures*. Missoula, MT: Mountain Press Publishing Company, 1995. Another recent account of our region's geology told via the geologic time scale.

——. *Roadside Geology of Washington*. Missoula, MT: Mountain Press Publishing Company, 1984.

Lanner, R. M. *Made for Each Other: A Symbiosis of Birds and Pines*. Oxford: Oxford University Press, 1996.

Mueller, M. and T. Mueller. *Fire, Faults, and Floods: A Road and Trail Guide Exploring the Origins of the Columbia River Basin*. Moscow, ID: University of Idaho Press, 2001. The most recent account of the geology of our region.

Orr, E. L. and W. N. Orr. *Geology of the Pacific Northwest*. New York: The McGraw Hill Companies, 1996.

OTHER RESOURCES

Native Plant Gardens
Seattle: Kruckeberg Botanic Garden, Shoreline, WA. (206) 546-1281.

Seattle: Washington Park Arboretum, University of Washington, Box 358010, Seattle, WA 98195-8010. (206) 543-8800. *depts.washington.edu/wpa/*.

Tacoma: Point Defiance Park, Northwest Native Garden, 5400 North Pearl Street, Tacoma, WA 98407. (253) 591-5337.

National Forests
Colville National Forest, 765 South Main Street, Colville, WA 99114. (509) 684-7000.

Gifford Pinchot National Forest, 10600 Northeast 51 Circle, Vancouver, WA 98682.

Mount Baker–Snoqualmie National Forest, 21905 64th Avenue West, Mountlake Terrace, WA 98043. (425) 775-9720.

Okanogan–Wenatchee National Forest, 215 Melody Lane, Wenatchee, WA 98801. (509) 664-9200. *www.fs.fed.us/r6/wenatchee*.

Olympic National Forest, 1835 Black Lake Boulevard Southwest, Olympia, WA 98512. (360) 956-2300.

National Parks
Mount Rainier National Park, Tahoma Woods, Star Route, Ashford, WA 98304. (360) 569-2211.

North Cascades National Park, 2105 Highway 20, Sedro-Woolley, WA 98284. (360) 856-5700.

Olympic National Park, 3002 Mount Angeles Road, Port Angeles, WA 98362. (360) 452-0330.

Outdoor and Natural History Organizations

Kettle Range Conservation Group, P. O. Box 150, Republic, WA 99166. (509) 775-2667. *www.kettlerange.org*. Supports conservation in eastern Washington.

The Mountaineers, 300 Third Avenue West, Seattle, WA. (206) 284-6310. Good mix of hiking, mountaineering, and natural history.

North Cascades Institute, 2105 Highway 20, Sedro-Woolley, WA 98284. (360) 856-5700 ext. 213. Get their annual catalog of many outdoor and natural history events, including wildflower hikes, et cetera.

Seattle Audubon Society, 8050 16th Avenue Northeast, Seattle, WA 98115. (206) 523-4483. Birds and other natural history in "Earthcare Northwest," their official newsletter.

Washington Native Plant Society, 6310 Northeast 74th Street, Suite 215E, Seattle, WA 98115. (206) 527-3210. *wnps@wnps.org; www.wnps.org*. Fosters programs, field trips, and a newsletter—"Douglasia"—celebrating Washington's native plants. Their website features native plant lists for many Washington trails, catalogued by county.

Washington Trails Association, 1305 Fourth Avenue, Suite 512, Seattle, WA 98101-2401. (206) 625-1367. Supports on-site trail maintenance; "Washington Trails" magazine provides current trail information.

Public Agencies

Bureau of Land Management, Spokane District, 1103 North Fancher, Spokane, WA 99212. (509) 536-1200.

Washington State Department of Natural Resources, Land and Water Conservation Division, P. O. Box 47046, Olympia, WA 98504.

Washington State Parks, 7150 Clearwater Lane KY-11, Olympia, WA 98504. (800) 233-0321.

GENERAL INDEX

PLANT INDEX

ABOUT THE AUTHORS

ARTHUR RICE KRUCKEBERG was born (Los Angeles 1920) into a plant-loving family. Getting his B.A. degree at Occidental College, doing graduate work at Stanford, and earning his Ph.D. in botany at Berkeley's University of California campus all had a strong botanical flavor. In 1950, he began his fifty-year tryst with the flora of Washington and the Pacific Northwest. As professor of Botany at the University of Washington, Art's primary research focus has been to learn how geology—land forms and soils—has shaped the plant world. The Wenatchee Mountains of central Washington provided an ideal setting for the study of this geology–plant linkage.

Art founded the Washington Native Plant Society in 1976 and has written books meant for the general reader.

Photo: ©Mary Randlett/MSCUA

Three books epitomize Art's desire to share his knowledge of the natural world with others: *Gardening with Native Plants of the Pacific Northwest* (University of Washington Press, 1982, 2d ed. 1997), *Natural History of the Puget Sound Country* (University of Washington Press, 1993), and *Geology and Plant Life* (University of Washington Press, 2002). Art's love of plants comes to life in his 4-acre garden in Shoreline; he and his wife, Mareen, have created a rich collection of native and exotic plants, now preserved as the Kruckeberg Botanic Garden Foundation.

Ira Spring (1923–2003) inspired three generations of outdoor enthusiasts with his crisp, breathtaking photographic images. As photographer and author or coauthor he put his creative stamp on more than forty books, on subjects ranging from national parks and mountain climbing to the cultures of Japan and Norway, including many in The Mountaineers Books' *100 Hikes in* ™ series. His autobiography, *An Ice Ax, a Camera, and a Jar of Peanut Butter,* descibes his amazing career. He was one of the Northwest's most active trail lobbyists, was cofounder of the Washington Trails Association, and was presented in 1992 with the Theodore Roosevelt Conservation Award for his volunteer efforts toward trail funding and preservation.

KAREN SYKES is an avid hiker, photographer, and freelance writer. She is author of *Hidden Hikes in Western Washington* (The Mountaineers Books) and also writes a weekly hiking column for the *Seattle Post-Intelligencer* in the "Getaways" section. She has been active in The Mountaineers for many years and continues to lead hikes for the club. She is also a poet. Her book of poems, *Exposed to the Elements*, was published by Litmus Press (Salt Lake City) under her previous name, Karen Waring.

CRAIG ROMANO is an outdoor writer and mountain guide for whom hiking is a way of life. The Pacific Northwest, New England, Canada, and Europe are his favorite haunts. Craig's works have been published in *Backpacker, AMC Outdoors, Canoe and Kayak, Northwest Travel, Northwest Runner*, and elsewhere. He also contributes outdoor recreation content for Canada's Weather Network, and when not writing, he leads hikes in the Pyrenees Mountains.

THE MOUNTAINEERS, founded in 1906, is a nonprofit outdoor activity and conservation club, whose mission is "to explore, study, preserve, and enjoy the natural beauty of the outdoors . . . ." Based in Seattle, Washington, the club is now the third-largest such organization in the United States, with seven branches throughout Washington State.

The Mountaineers sponsors both classes and year-round outdoor activities in the Pacific Northwest, which include hiking, mountain climbing, ski-touring, snowshoeing, bicycling, camping, kayaking, nature study, sailing, and adventure travel. The club's conservation division supports environmental causes through educational activities, sponsoring legislation, and presenting informational programs.

All club activities are led by skilled, experienced instructors, who are dedicated to promoting safe and responsible enjoyment and preservation of the outdoors.

If you would like to participate in these organized outdoor activities or the club's programs, consider a membership in The Mountaineers. For information and an application, write or call The Mountaineers, Club Headquarters, 300 Third Avenue West, Seattle, WA 98119; (206) 284-6310. You can also visit the club's website at www.mountaineers.org or contact The Mountaineers via email at clubmail@mountaineers.org.

THE MOUNTAINEERS BOOKS, an active, nonprofit publishing program of the club, produces guidebooks, instructional texts, historical works, natural history guides, and works on environmental conservation. All books produced by The Mountaineers Books fulfill the club's mission.

Send or call for our catalog of more than 500 outdoor titles:

The Mountaineers Books
1001 SW Klickitat Way, Suite 201
Seattle, WA 98134
(800) 553-4453
mbooks@mountaineersbooks.org
www.mountaineersbooks.org

The Mountaineers Books is proud to be a corporate sponsor of The Leave No Trace Center for Outdoor Ethics, whose mission is to promote and inspire responsible outdoor recreation through education, research, and partnerships. The Leave No Trace program is focused specifically on human-powered (nonmotorized) recreation.

Leave No Trace strives to educate visitors about the nature of their recreational impacts, as well as offer techniques to prevent and minimize such impacts. Leave No Trace is best understood as an educational and ethical program, not as a set of rules and regulations.

For more information, visit *www.LNT.org,* or call (800) 332-4100.

OTHER TITLES YOU MIGHT ENJOY FROM THE MOUNTAINEERS BOOKS

Field Guide to the Cascades and Olympics,
Stephen R. Whitney and Rob Sandelin
The "what's that?" guide to Northwest plants and animals—now expanded, updated, and in full color!

Best Old-Growth Forest Hikes: Washington & Oregon Cascades,
John & Diane Cissel
Discover 100 paths to enchantment among the ancient old-growth forests of the Northwest

Nature in the City: Seattle,
Kathryn True & Maria Dolan
The best places to experience wildlife and wild surroundings in the city

Photography Outdoors: A Field Guide for Travel and Adventure Photographers,
Mark Gardner & Art Wolfe
Learn to capture outdoor images of whimsy and magnificence

ALSO FROM THE AUTHORS . . .

Best Winter Walks & Hikes: Puget Sound, *Harvey Manning and Ira Spring*

Hidden Hikes in Western Washington, *Karen Sykes*

Available at fine bookstores and outdoor stores, by phone at 800-553-4453 or on the web at *www.mountaineersbooks.org*

THE MOUNTAINEERS BOOKS